The Battle of Tsushima

The Battle of Tsushima

by

Phil Carradice

AN IMPRINT OF PEN & SWORD BOOKS LTD.
YORKSHIRE - PHILADELPHIA

First published in Great Britain in 2020 by
Pen & Sword History
An imprint of
Pen & Sword Books Ltd
Yorkshire – Philadelphia

Copyright © Phil Carradice 2020

ISBN 978 1 52674 334 3

The right of Phil Carradice to be identified as Author of this work has been asserted by him in accordance with the Copyright, Designs and Patents Act 1988.

A CIP catalogue record for this book is
available from the British Library.

All rights reserved. No part of this book may be reproduced or transmitted in any form or by any means, electronic or mechanical including photocopying, recording or by any information storage and retrieval system, without permission from the Publisher in writing.

Typeset in 11.5/14 Ehrhardt by Vman Infotech Pvt. Ltd.

Printed and bound in the UK by TJ International Ltd, Padstow, Cornwall.

Pen & Sword Books Limited incorporates the imprints of Atlas, Archaeology, Aviation, Discovery, Family History, Fiction, History, Maritime, Military, Military Classics, Politics, Select, Transport, True Crime, Air World, Frontline Publishing, Leo Cooper, Remember When, Seaforth Publishing, The Praetorian Press, Wharncliffe Local History, Wharncliffe Transport, Wharncliffe True Crime and White Owl.

For a complete list of Pen & Sword titles please contact

PEN & SWORD BOOKS LIMITED
47 Church Street, Barnsley, South Yorkshire, S70 2AS, England
E-mail: enquiries@pen-and-sword.co.uk
Website: www.pen-and-sword.co.uk

Or
PEN AND SWORD BOOKS
1950 Lawrence Rd, Havertown, PA 19083, USA
E-mail: Uspen-and-sword@casematepublishers.com
Website: www.penandswordbooks.com

Contents

Acknowledgements   vii
Introduction   xi
Prelude / Overture   xv

Chapter 1	A Samurai Attack	1
Chapter 2	War, Terrible War	15
Chapter 3	Rozhestvensky	35
Chapter 4	Early Disaster	51
Chapter 5	On Into the Wastes	67
Chapter 6	Felkersam's Fleet	83
Chapter 7	A Stagnant Pause	97
Chapter 8	Togo Waits, Mad Dog Moves	111
Chapter 9	Towards the Donkey's Ears	123
Chapter 10	Battle at Last	131
Chapter 11	Last Acts	147
Chapter 12	Aftermath	159

Conclusion   175
Notes   179
Bibliography   183

Acknowledgements

Thanks to so many people for their help and interest during the writing of this book, too numerous to mention but they know who they are.

In particular I owe a debt of gratitude to my grandfather, Robert Turnbull Carradice, who sailed these waters in the years after the First World War and talked to me for hours about Tsushima, the island and its battle.

And my father who, early one Christmas morning, presented me with a copy of Richard Hough's *The Fleet that had to Die* and awoke an interest that has never left me. The copy is now old and battered but I still have it.

As ever, Roger MacCallum, with his knowledge of technology, and the patience to keep helping a complete and confirmed Luddite. Thanks Rog, couldn't have done it without you.

Last, but certainly not least, my darling Trudy, whose presence I felt at my shoulder every inch of the way. The times that your memory and Willie Nelson ('Blue Eyes Crying in the Rain') kept me going were legion. Thank you, my love.

Cold death awaits us. There's no escape.
For he who, ruthless, sends us to death
Has no heart at all in his iron breast.
Victims are we by Fate's hand marked.

Alexei Novikoff-Priboy

Introduction

The Battle of Tsushima – the Battle of the Donkey's Ears as it is sometimes known – remains one of the most influential naval actions in history.

Its effects have been hugely significant, changing perceptions and altering the status of various nations across the world. And yet many people have never heard of the Battle of Tsushima, the violent and seminal encounter between the fleets of Russia and Japan that took place during one afternoon and evening in May 1905.

Out of the battle emerged the nascent Japanese Empire. The Japanese victory was so complete that many people believed the power of Russia had been destroyed forever. Japan suddenly became a major force, its aggressive and warlike ambitions taking the country to the brink of world domination in the 1940s.

It was inevitable, of course, that such a situation could not last. Metaphorically speaking, the Battle of Tsushima was a crossroads for Japan, and the path it took led, ultimately, to the disaster of Hiroshima and Nagasaki, to the deaths of millions, and to untold suffering in many parts of the world.

The battle also ushered in, significantly, the first real signs of economic and social change in Russia, a peasant country that would ultimately grow into the Soviet Union and become one of the most powerful nations on Earth. It spelled the beginning of the end for the Romanov dynasty and the founding of the world's first communist state.

The Battle of Tsushima was the first intense encounter between two large fleets of pre-Dreadnought ironclads where the effects of long-distance shelling and the use of wireless telegraphy were to play a significant part in the outcome. There had been ironclad clashes between Russia and Japan before Tsushima – notably the Battle of the Yellow Sea – but never before had the result been so disastrous for one side and so triumphant for the other. At the Battle of Tsushima, for the first time in history, one ironclad fleet was totally wiped out.

To modern readers and historians the battle still remains a largely unknown and unheralded affair. If it had taken place in the North Sea, between Britain, Germany or France, or any of the major European nations, it would almost certainly have been better documented. But it was fought thousands of miles away from the European mainland – at the time the political centre of the world – in the virtually unheard of Straits of Tsushima, and between two empires that did not figure largely in people's consciousness.

The battle itself was disastrous for Russia, but aside from its consequences, the 18,000-mile voyage of Admiral Rozhestvensky's 2nd Pacific Fleet, from the snow-bound Baltic to the steaming, mist-shrouded island of Tsushima, remains a feat of unrivalled skill. Ironclad battleships were not meant to go that far; not without regular overhauls and periods of rest. Yet Rozhestvensky did it.

The story of that voyage is one of courage and foolishness, of luck and good judgement. It is a tale with tragic dimensions, but, like all good tragedies, there are also moments of high comedy. They are what make the story of this epic voyage and its terrible conclusion so memorable.

We are lucky in that several first-hand accounts of the battle – primary source material of the most fascinating kind – still exist. Most of these are from the Russian survivors; men like Novikoff-Priboy and Vladimir Semenov who later became embroiled in the revolutionary movements that eventually toppled the czar.

Apart from commentaries and reports by people like Admiral Togo and Nikolai Klado, it is the words and feelings of ordinary sailors such as Semenov and Novikoff-Priboy that make the most impact. They, and others like them, experienced life on the ships of Rozhestvensky's fleet and witnessed death at first hand in the Battle of Tsushima.

The fact that such men felt inclined to put their memories down on paper is perhaps significant of the mood at the time, but for the historian it remains a blessing. The records are vibrant and dramatic, perfectly weighted accounts that catch the mood of the moment: 'Splinters whistled through the air, jingled against the sides and the superstructure. Then, quite close and abreast the foremost funnel rose a gigantic pillar of smoke, water and flame ... The next shell struck the side of the centre 6-in turret and there was a tremendous noise behind and below me on the port quarter. Smoke and tongues of flame leapt out of the officer's gangway.'[1]

Passages like that are not the words of journalists or professional writers. They come from men who were there; ordinary men who served on the ships alongside friends and colleagues, who fought, died and, in some cases, were lucky enough to survive.

When they set out on the voyage, such men had little thought of recording their impressions; apart perhaps from Vladimir Semenov who, to misquote Napoleon, carried his literary ideals in his knapsack. They were sailors, not writers.

After the disaster things changed and men were driven to record what they had seen and done. The words and descriptions are heart-felt and emotive, direct and unencumbered by literary devices. They put the modern reader in touch with a dramatic period of time and a moment in history that might otherwise have been totally forgotten.

If there is regret it lies simply in the fact that Admiral Rozhestvensky never expressed his emotions and memories of the battle, at least not in writing. And yet, in some ways that lack of comment says as much, if not more, than page after page of copious notes and explanations. An intuitive and interested student will know exactly where Rozhestvensky stood.

The story of the battle, its build up and its aftermath, remains fascinating. Arguably, nobody who is interested in the history of the modern world can afford to ignore it.

Prelude/Overture

When Tchaikovsky composed the 1812 Overture he was celebrating a magnificent if unexpected Russian victory over Napoleon Bonaparte. When Tolstoy sat down to write *War and Peace* that same war was a central theme to his novel, the thread on which the whole story hinged. Both the Overture and the book were – and remain – immense works of art that place the czar, his empire and the achievement of the Russian people in a glorious and heroic light.

Unfortunately, the same cannot be said for the largely forgotten Russo-Japanese War of 1904–05. By 1904 the situation had been reversed. No longer was Russia the victim or the underdog, her territory invaded by a powerful and rampant enemy. Now she was the aggressor, the contemptuous 'great power' that was intending to destroy the puny and unworthy Japanese forces, sweep them away and consign them to the rubbish tip of history.

Unfortunately for the Russians, things did not work out that way. Defeated and humiliated, her army and navy pummelled out of existence, there was no possible way that she could salvage anything glorious out of the war.

Try hard and the whole episode could possibly be regarded as a heroic failure. It was certainly misguided and doomed to disaster but nobody could ever bestow the appellation 'glorious' on any aspect of this badly managed, tragic and costly defeat. And that left the artistic element of society in something of a quandary.

Defeat on land was costly with both sides suffering huge casualties, but defeat at sea was both humiliating and world-changing. Disasters such as the Battle of Port Arthur and the Yellow Sea were catastrophic: the virtual extermination of Admiral Rozhestvensky's fleet at the Battle of Tsushima was unthinkable.

Inevitably, poets and authors, musicians and playwrights were at a disadvantage when it came to using the Russo-Japanese War and its battles as motivation for works of art. As a result, writing about the conflict was mainly factual, with most historian seeing the disaster leading directly, albeit it distantly, to the fall of the czar and his regime eleven years later.

If there was glory to be found then it rested on the powerful shoulders of Admiral Togo and his all-conquering battle fleet. There has never been such a resounding military or naval victory as Togo achieved at the Battle of Tsushima. It had a significance that went far beyond the war itself, impacting time and time again on the activities of the great nations of the world throughout the first half of the twentieth century.

So great was the Japanese success that even the traditional view of Russia and the Russian people as tragic heroes inhabiting a frozen landscape – a landscape that is equally as tragic and tormented as the personalities involved – has failed to impose itself on the conflict. That might not be a bad thing as the destruction of stereotypes can eventually lead to better understanding of people and problems. As Charles Solomon wrote (admittedly about the USSR, but his words can also apply to earlier Czarist Russia): 'The frustrations of daily life ... parallel those in the West. Civil servants are apparently as uncivil in Tallinn as they are in Los Angeles; bureaucracies are as unresponsive to human needs by the Volga as they are by the Potomac.'[1]

The wistful, snow-covered and poignant final scenes of David Lean's film *Dr Zhivago* might sum up the emotions and feelings of many when they think of the tragedy that was Russia at the beginning of the Twentieth Century. But those images have no place in the tale of the Battle of Tsushima; at least not as most people understand it.

Nobody has romanticised the battle or made Zhivago-like figures out of Rozhestvensky and the rest of the cast. There has, simply, been no room for poetics in the story. 'Forget it' seems to have been the initial Russian view and that idea soon spread to the rest of the world.

Even the Japanese, in the wake of the disastrous conclusion to the Second World War, now seem to have consigned the affair to the history books: 'The war and our victory at the Donkey's Ears are still remembered but it was such a long time ago. Now it is, for most people, just a page in the history text books – I don't know, perhaps the Second World War and its effects are still too close. After Tsushima we became immensely patriotic but now things have changed. That, I suppose, was inevitable.'[2]

Whatever the reasons for this neglect might be – perhaps deliberate, perhaps accidental – the sacrifice of so many men and ships remains almost beyond the realm of understanding. It is hard to know why this should have happened. Rozhestvensky and his incredible achievements, Togo and his superb tactics; they all seem to have been forgotten. Perhaps it is time to redress the balance a little.

If we can judge what went on in 1904 and 1905 simply as the incredible striving of men from both Russia and Japan to achieve an impossible dream then the battle and the lead up to it might finally achieve heroic status. For that, though, we have to look beyond the violence, the horror and the sheer magnitude of Russia's defeat.

In many respects the voyage of Admiral Rozhestvensky, a traumatic but inevitable journey to disaster in the Straits of Tsushima, is exactly the sort of sad and sorrowful event that many of us associate with the decline and fall of Czarist Russia. If we can view it as a misbegotten and doomed expedition, carried out with courage and fortitude, then the Admiral and his fleet will fit easily into the concept of tragic heroes. That is what makes the affair really interesting.

The old notion of three elements needed to make a good story – place, people and problem – are all present in this particular piece of history. But, as with any good story, it is the people who inhabit it that really make it work. Characters are here aplenty; fascinating characters that could not be invented. Those characters, not the significance of the eventual battle or the effects of Russia's defeat, are what make the story flow. Remember that as you read the tale of Rozhestvensky's epic voyage and consider him as a truly heroic but doomed figure.

Chapter 1

A Samurai Attack

The street was crowded, the noise and odour of several hundred sweating, jostling bodies rising and hanging above the city in a cloud that was almost touchable. Nicholas had never seen so many men, women and children before, at least not packed into just one tiny area.

This was meant to be the main thoroughfare of Otsu, he reminded himself, not some dark and haunting backwater. Main street or not, the place was narrow with sharp corners that jutted into the walkway like the bows of waiting warships. Houses that overhung the road in a phalanx of wooden cliffs threw out dark and impenetrable shadows, even at the height of day. Exciting and mysterious it might well be, but this was daytime and Nicholas reluctantly admitted to himself that he would not have liked to be here at night.

The thoroughfare was old; a curling, venomous snake hissing and sliding through the town. It was not like the Nevsky Prospect, he decided, the wide and glorious passageway that ran straight as an arrow across the width of St Petersburg. He could not imagine the dignitaries of Otsu parading and promenading along this roadway every Sunday evening as they did back in the imperial capital.

Russia, he concluded, this was definitely not. And yet it had an appeal. Despite the smells and the noise there was a sort of foreign or unknown enchantment to the place. He would not want to live here, to give up the comforts and delights of the Winter Palace and the other Royal residencies around St Petersburg, but it was good to visit, to broaden the mind as his father had so often told him he should do.

The scenery of Japan was wonderful, the towns and cities as compelling as a wild boar hunt out in the depths of a Siberian forest, with the hint of hidden danger lurking behind every tree or bush. He loved the countryside, but above all he liked the people; simple and friendly with no agendas lurking in the recesses of their brains. He thought back to the letter he had

2 The Battle of Tsushima

sent when his ship first docked in Japan. What had he said? 'I have been here only a few days and already I am in absolute heaven.'

So far his attitude had not changed except that, if it was possible, he was now even more in love with the country. Only yesterday he had got himself a dragon tattoo on his forearm. God knows how his father, Czar Alexander, would react to that. He touched the tattoo, still a little painful under his jacket sleeve, and decided that he didn't care. He loved this country and all it stood for, and that included the Japanese people.

Nicholas sighed happily as the rickshaw rolled slowly along, heavy and ponderous like a hearse. Momentarily his eye was drawn to the hunched back and shoulders of his driver as the man strained and grunted at the long pulling shaft. His muscles rippled like tiny wavelets on the Baltic shore. Nicholas shook his head. God knows how he and his fellow drivers did it, he wondered, manoeuvring carriages like this through the town every day and night of the year.

But it was a fleeting thought. The driver could not hold his attention for long. There were far too many other fascinating sights to see. His eager eyes darted to the open-fronted shops at the side of the roadway. They sold everything from richly embroidered kimonos and long, yellow-stemmed pipes to cups and bowls of delicate porcelain that were translucent as the morning mist in Crimea. There were straw hats and parasols, tiny pot-bellied Buddha statues and walking sticks like the one his cousin George had bought only that morning. Whatever you wanted, it seemed, was available here.

Every fourth or fifth shop had chairs or stalls along its front wall. Inside, exotic and fragrant food was being cooked and the townsfolk bustled in and out of the open doorways. Over everything hung the heavy, heady smell of some oriental fragrance that he could not place.

'Joss sticks,' called George from the second rickshaw.

They had come to a halt in the most crowded part of the street, waiting for the press of people to clear a little, and George's driver had brought his rickshaw alongside the lead vehicle. Now George was leaning back against the padded seat of his carriage, yawning and stretching, his giant arms reaching out like the wings of a buzzard.

'And opium,' he added.

Nicholas jerked around to stare at George. Older than him by a few years, his cousin was officially Prince George of Greece and Norway and Nicholas had always looked up to him. Well-travelled, experienced in the ways of the world, famous for his strength and size, he was the ideal companion for trips like this to exotic and mysterious Japan.

'Opium?' said Nicholas. 'You mean they sell the stuff here, openly, out in the streets?'

George grinned, 'Nikki, you must learn not to be so incredulous. I am here, as you know, to show you the world. I am not suggesting we buy opium, merely telling you about the smells.'

He paused, grinned and leaned over the side of his rickshaw. 'Girls, now, they're different. Tonight I have a special treat in mind.'

Nicholas grinned back at him as the rickshaw lurched into motion once more. It was slow going and the other rickshaws in the convoy had no trouble keeping pace. Even the guard of policemen – samurai he supposed – were trotting steadily alongside them, arms and legs moving in easy rhythm and their eyes fixed firmly ahead.

It was 11 May 1891 and the twenty-three-year-old Nicholas Alexandrovich Romanov was on the last stage of his grand tour around the eastern world. As the Tsarevich Nicholas, son of the mighty Czar Alexander III, he was heir to the imperial throne of Russia, and this trip was intended to help him understand the mysteries of the East. He was then to officially inaugurate the final stages of Czar Alexander's long dreamed of Trans-Siberian railway from central Russia to Vladivostok.

So far it had been a reasonably good tour, though he had hated the incessant hand shaking of visits to dignitaries and petty officials. Egypt, India, Siam; they were all the same. They were all necessary, he knew, but they bored the living daylights out of him. This final visit to Japan was less formal and undoubtedly the best part of it all.

Relaxed and happy, he lay back as the rickshaw rolled steadily on, thinking over the events of the day. They had left Kyoto early, visited Lake Biwa and spoken to the crowd. The reception, as always, had been nothing short of magnificent. They had shopped and tasted tea, as custom demanded, and now they were on their way to the governor's house here in Otsu for an informal but welcome meal.

'Another wait,' he heard George call from behind him and looked up as the rickshaw shuddered to a halt. 'A long one, I suspect.'

Nicholas watched his driver scrambling and pushing with his feet to halt their progress. His sandals slipped and bit at the surface of the greasy roadway. It had been a difficult manoeuvre but the driver made no sound, accepting the stop with a simple shake of the head.

Ahead of them was yet another gathering of locals. They were priests, he thought; they were dressed in white and yellow robes and stretched out in a procession of some sort, all chanting and ringing bells. There were dozens of them, crossing their path without a care in the world. They shuffled forward in a long line, left and right of the main roadway, before disappearing around one of the many corners. As George had predicted, it seemed as if this was going to be a long delay.

Time to stretch the legs, Nicholas decided, and he climbed to his feet. The rickshaw groaned as the weight distribution changed. Quickly but carefully he put one foot on the ground to steady himself and the vehicle.

'Nikki! Look out!' He heard George call as a shadow fell across his body. He looked up into the snarling face of one of the samurai guards and a sudden lurch of fear rolled like a boulder in his belly. Instinctively, he threw up his arm to protect himself.

Later he remembered the flash of sunlight on the guard's sword as it arced through the air, but at the time he could see only his attacker's face, lips drawn back in an ugly scowl. From the crowd along the pavements he heard a long, thin wail of anguish and then a jolt of pain smashed all rational thought out of his mind. The blow caught him on the forehead and blood spurted upwards. He screamed.

'Hold on,' he heard George call, 'I'm coming.'

Nicholas knew he had to get away before the samurai steadied himself for a second strike. 'The crowd', he thought; 'hide behind the crowd!' He began to run unsteadily, blood streaming down his face, into his eyes and mouth, then spraying out behind him like a crimson scarf.

'Help me!' he screamed, knowing he had to get to the sanctuary of the watchers.

But the crowd was scattering, too; rushing to find safety wherever they could. Desperately, Nicholas looked behind him. The samurai was still there, sword raised and charging towards him. He heard sobbing, suddenly realising it came from him, and threw up his arms to shield himself from the blow he knew had to come.

When nothing happened Nicholas opened his eyes and stared. The samurai was on the ground, George standing over him with his bamboo cane raised.

'Come on, you bastard!' George called at the fallen assailant, 'You've got your sword; I've only got my bloody walking stick.'

He glanced across at Nicholas, shrugged and smiled. It was only a momentary movement but it gave the samurai enough time to spring to his feet and run. The man barged his way past a group of spectators, sending them sprawling like skittles, and headed for the enveloping darkness of an adjacent alleyway.

'Stop him!' George shouted.

He took off in chase but before he had gone five yards two burly figures dived from the convoy of rickshaws and threw themselves at the would-be assassin. All three of them fell to the ground. There was a brief flailing of arms and then the samurai lay still, pinioned by the weight and strength of his captors.

'Well done, you men,' George bellowed.

Nicholas staggered out of the road and into a small kimono shop, blood still pumping from his forehead. He felt faint and the fear was like a knotted fist turning and grinding at his innards. He was sure he was going to die. He slumped down on the floor, stained and filthy from the feet of many customers, and tried to breathe as deeply and as normally as possible.

He was safe he kept telling himself, thanks to Cousin George and the two rickshaw drivers. But it did not stop the fear. Where there was one murderer there were bound to be more. And, worse than anything else, the man had been one of his own bodyguards. How could you trust people like that?

How long he sat there Nicholas never knew. He was aware of figures pushing past and, from the corner of his eye, saw guards and policemen hauling the samurai to his feet and dragging him away like the carcass of a dead cow. Then George was there, pushing a handkerchief against his wound and gazing with fear and compassion at the shaking prince.

'Come on. Let's get you to a doctor.'

Nicholas allowed himself to be led away. The next hour passed in a blur as his wound was treated. It was not, he was told, too serious, but how in the name of Heaven did they know that? They didn't feel the pain or remember the fear. 'Keep your damned platitudes to yourselves', he whispered; 'just stitch up the wound and let me get out of here'.

The doctor, a man by the name of Mikao Usui he was informed, was famous in Japan. He had founded Reiki, the Japanese technique for dealing with stress, but as he bent close to examine the wound all Nicholas could see and feel was the sharp touch of the man's long fingernails. Despite himself he shuddered.

'I am sorry,' the doctor whispered, 'did I hurt you?'

Nicholas looked up into the man's dark eyes. A shiver of distaste and horror flooded through his body. Who was this man and what was he trying to do? He smelled of unknown scents, something earthy and ancient, and without knowing why, Nicholas was immediately afraid of him.

'Assassin!' he shouted, pushing Usui away.

He was shaking now, huge uncontrollable sobs of anguish that flooded his body and mind. He leapt to his feet as George caught his arm. Slowly, carefully, he led Nicholas away. Behind them Dr Mikao Usui stood perplexed and unsure.

'Get me back to civilisation,' Nicholas whispered, 'back to the ship where it's safe.'

They staggered out to the rickshaws. Nicholas lay on the threadbare cushion of the first vehicle he found, feeling easier now but still wary. All he could think about was the snarling face of his attacker; one of his own guards, one of the samurai employed to keep him safe. As the rickshaw carried him away the sights, sounds and smells of Otsu came crowding in on him.

Suddenly there was nothing attractive or interesting about the streets. And the people, he realised now, how they stank of unwashed bodies and filth. Duplicitous, treacherous, not to be trusted; to think he had once liked this place and these people. Now, at last, he saw them for what they were. No one in the crowd had tried to help him; they had just run away to hide. They were cowards, all of them; cowards and traitors.

The rickshaws trundled on as Nicholas held the bandage to his head and cursed quietly under his breath. One day, he thought, I will get my revenge on every Japanese man and woman from this goddamned country. He suppressed his Christian compassion and fear; they were not worthy of it, these barbarians. He would be revenged. It was just a matter of time.

*　*　*

The attack on Nicholas Romanov by samurai guard Tsuda Sanzo did more than just leave the Russian prince with a 4-in scar across his face. It gave him a profound feeling of distrust, even hatred, for the Japanese people. Nothing would ever heal that particular wound.

The tragedy of Nicholas and Japan was very real. The relationship could, and should, have been far more propitious, but the coming together of the Russian prince, future ruler of one of the largest territorial empires in the world, and a rapidly growing and developing Asian state was effectively that of an unconquerable force meeting an unconquerable object. Once the battle lines were drawn neither of them would back down.

Nicholas was a man who was easily impressed, but also quickly driven to sudden and furious anger, and did not possess the maturity of most other men his age. He had been protected and cosseted all of his life, as his father, Alexander, belatedly realised. It was another of the reasons the czar had despatched his son on his tour of the Far East, to help him grow into his role and mature.

Like many young men, Nicholas was not really clear about his own feelings. Unfortunately, his position made such indecision not only unhelpful but sometimes downright dangerous. His character was such that he could swing suddenly and violently from one opinion to another, always in the knowledge that he was a Romanov and could not, therefore, ever be wrong. It was a potentially lethal combination.

When he encountered someone with strong opinions and the ability to express them – someone like his future wife, Alexandra – he was simply not equipped to tell good from bad or to separate common sense from flights of sheer fantasy. Invariably he went with the most powerful argument. And so it was with Japan. No one tried to modify his opinions. The one man who might have done so, his cousin George, had been dismissed from the royal entourage soon after the incident in Otsu.

George's crime was simply that he had written a letter, which was then published in the newspapers, stating that Nicholas had run away, screaming, from the attacker. It was not meant vindictively, nor was it ever intended for public scrutiny. It was as much a throwaway line as anything. But it was criticism that Czar Alexander would not tolerate.

Nicholas made no protest. He simply shrugged his shoulders and turned his back on his cousin and friend. It was not that he had a poor opinion of George, the man who had saved his life, but by this time his mind was on other things.

George could actually count himself as fortunate. He retired from the Romanov inner circle and did not, therefore, suffer like most of the other Russian rulers in the Bolshevik Revolution of 1917. He lived until the 1950s, dying at the ripe old age of eighty.

The fact that Nicholas could change his opinion so quickly was a disastrous personality flaw. He had begun by enjoying Japan, admiring the people, the culture and the architecture. Within the space of a few short minutes everything changed, admittedly under provocation, but the real problem was that having now been personally affronted and challenged by Tsuda Sanzo his fragile personality would not allow him to change his views again.

The Japanese government tried, of course. They were afraid the attack might mean war between themselves and Russia. Conflicts had been started over less and Japan was not ready for that particular situation; not yet anyway.

The Emperor Maiji travelled all night by train to visit Nicholas who was then lying in pain, but at least in safety, on board the cruiser *Pamiat Azova*. It was an unheard of act of respect and contrition by the emperor and, in a way, a great honour for the Tsarevich. Nicholas received him graciously but without affection or understanding. Over the next few days he also received as many as 10,000 telegrams of support from the Japanese people, undoubtedly urged on in their efforts by ministers of state.

Whether or not the telegrams and letters were spontaneous, there was genuine distress and concern in Japan: distress about what had occurred and concern about the safety of a man everyone had seemed to like. Japanese hospitality had been challenged by one of their own and people were offended by the actions of one lunatic attacker, as they considered him to be.

The strength of reaction varied across the country. One town in the Yamagata Prefecture forbade any future use of either the family name Tsuda or the given name Sanzo. In Kyoto, in front of the prefectural office, a young seamstress cut her throat with a razor in protest against the incident and as an act of public contrition. She was rushed to hospital but died within the hour.

The Japanese home minister and the foreign minister both resigned, having lost face and failed, as they saw it, in their duty towards their illustrious visitor. Emperor Maiji, when he arrived on board Nicholas's cruiser, offered a formal apology.

None of it had any effect, however. In hindsight it is difficult not to believe that this repressed and immature 'adolescent' was doing little more than sulking about his treatment. If it was sulking, the feeling did not diminish with time, as might be expected, but instead grew and festered inside the Tsarevich like a cancer.

Whatever the problem, the prince was not going to remain in danger. He immediately cancelled the rest of his tour and made preparations to leave for home. It was as if he could not bear the Japanese people or their country a moment longer.

His one concession was to the two rickshaw drivers who had bravely dashed forward and captured the would-be assassin. Mukailhata Jizaburo and Kitagouchi Ichitaro were summoned to the *Pamiat Azova*, given medals, a pension of 1000 yen a year, and also a one-off payment of 2500 yen, a massive sum of money at that time.

The two men became famous in Japan: until the Russo-Japanese War of 1904–05. Then they lost their pensions and were accused of being collaborators and spies for the Russians. They were subjected to harassment from the police and even from members of their own families.

And what became of Tsuda Sanzo? His motives for the attack were never made clear but he was sentenced to life imprisonment for his crime. The Japanese government had asked for the death penalty but capital punishment was only allowed for attempts on the life of the emperor and a few other dignitaries. There was no loophole within the Japanese legal system to allow such a punishment for someone attempting to kill a foreign visitor, no matter how important he might be. Tsuda Sanzo died in prison within twelve months, though the cause remains a mystery. Whether or not he was quietly murdered or simply fell prey to the debilitating conditions of prison life will never be known.

News of the attack on the Tsarevich was immediately communicated around the world. The *Times of London*, momentarily abandoning its anti-Russian stance, condemned the attack and warned the Japanese government of possible effects: 'Not to speak of its certain grievous effect on Japan's good name in the world.'[1]

Nicholas never forgave the Japanese: a decision that would rebound not only on him, but also on the Russian nation and on the Japanese people for some time to come.

Blocked by the British on the North-West Frontier of India, the Russian Empire was moving slowly but relentlessly eastwards, expanding its territories and developing links with various countries in Asia. The expansion was just one of the reasons that Czar Alexander III commissioned and built the Trans-Siberian Railway to Vladivostok on the north Pacific coast.

Japan certainly did not want Russia as an enemy, but the hatred that seemed to consume Nicholas quickly became a barrier to any friendship or alliance that might have developed between the two countries. Nicholas either failed to see it or pretended he didn't. An alliance, meanwhile, did seem to be growing between Japan and Great Britain. Many of the warships in the newly extended Japanese Navy were built in British shipyards and officers like Togo Heihachiro, already the backbone of the new fleet, were trained in British Naval Academies.

* * *

When Czar Alexander III died unexpectedly in October 1894 it was a shock to the whole Russian empire and to its people. Alexander was only forty-eight and had seemed to have many years of active life ahead of him.

Nobody had expected this sudden and premature end to his reign. The Tsarevich in particular was both shocked and appalled. More than anything he was terrified by the fact that, with the death of his father, he had now been thrust into a position for which he was unprepared and barely qualified.

Nicholas, at the age of twenty-six, had become ruler of perhaps the largest and most powerful autocratic nation in the world. His basic instinct was to reform a country and a society that badly needed it, but democracy and understanding were difficult concepts for a people kept in servility for years. Nicholas did not know how to begin such a process. Previous attempts at allowing freedom and offering reform had never been totally successful. Nicholas's grandfather had tried it and had been blown up by an assassin's bomb for his pains. Small wonder, perhaps, that Alexander III had been such a reactionary. In the end Nicholas followed his father's route.

There was no doubt that Russia, despite its setbacks in the Crimean War, was a powerful force, but it was also an empire riven by problems. Not least of these in the late 1890s was a ruler who did not really want to rule. Nicholas was a man who had so far garnered little respect and almost no admiration from other world leaders.

He may not have been the most astute or intelligent of men but he was certainly not a fool. From the outset he was clear that drastic measures were called for: 'He started looking for something capable of turning him into a respected ruler. War looked like the easiest option.'[2] It was a medieval response but then Russia was, in many respects, still a medieval country. Success abroad, Nicholas thought, might also help deflect the rancour of the many revolutionary groups that regularly pushed the regime to the limits of its collective patience with their demands for representation and reform.

From his first days on the imperial throne it was clear to almost everyone, the new czar included, that it would require a steady hand to steer the Romanov dynasty safely through the troubled waters that lay ahead. The naïve and wavering Nicholas was not the man to offer that hand.

The Russian Empire that Nicholas inherited was a draconian organisation. Despite having been technically abolished, serfdom still existed, with landowners holding the power of life and death over the peasants who tilled their fields and tended their crops. The czar, at the head of a multi-tiered society, was expected to be knowledgeable and, with the wisdom of God, in command of all things.

The governing classes of Russia made up less than one per cent of the population, but they retained a deep and inflexible prejudice against granting the people any of the rights that were slowly becoming available to their counterparts in the West, such as property ownership and suffrage.

The people of Russia remained largely a peasant population, even if more and more of them were beginning to abandon the countryside to work in the new industrial plants and factories. The majority remained oppressed; they were illiterate, uneducated and cowed. The 'dark masses' as they were known, not just for their leaden and sullen acceptance of the status quo, but also for the sheer weight of their numbers, were greatly feared by members of the aristocracy.

Any easing of the severe restrictions or repression heaped onto the masses would, the ruling classes felt, limit their own set of jealously guarded privileges. It meant that the concept of keeping the peasants in what was regarded as safe ignorance was common throughout the empire. But it also meant that the dark masses were ideal fodder for the growing revolutionary groups, usually made up of students, teachers, clerks and other minor dignitaries who possessed at least some degree of education.

Interestingly, many of the revolutionary agitators were women. It was a situation unparalleled in almost any other country, but these women, possibly even more downtrodden than most of their male counterparts, provided a solid backbone to the coming unrest.

* * *

It was hardly surprising that Alexander III had given little thought to his own premature death. It was not something that dictatorial rulers ever did, but as a consequence Alexander had not prepared his son well enough for the role he was to fill. These were difficult times in Russia:

> Nicholas's father's reign of uncompromising autocracy had also coincided with Russia's long-delayed industrial revolution, and the new Czar inherited not only a number of half-barbarous states in the Empire, but a huge and growing class of factory workers, all underpaid, all working together in large numbers and in close proximity, living in overcrowded conditions, and highly susceptible to subversion.[3]

How much the new Czar knew about this potential time bomb in his kingdom – at least in the early stages of his reign – is unclear. Nicholas had not pushed for more involvement in government, even though he knew that sooner or later the crown and all of its mighty power would come to him. But becoming the czar was tomorrow's problem: until it became today's.

He vehemently disliked the formalities of government. The receptions and state visits, the endless politicking that seemed to come so naturally for so many others bored him to death. His interests were religion and, after his marriage and the arrival of children, his family. Ruling the huge Russian Empire came way down on the list.

While the czar's chief advisors came from the ruling classes there was a middle class of civil servants in the country. The far-thinking Czar Peter I, a long-dead ancestor of Czar Nicholas, had created such a body in the early years of the eighteenth century, the aim being to create strong central government in all parts of the empire. Unfortunately, by the time Nicholas succeeded to the throne this group of administrators had become, to misquote Winston Churchill, neither civil nor servants.

The Russian civil service had grown into a corrupt and incompetent body. Anyone lucky enough to find himself with a post in this bureaucratic organisation was concerned, first and foremost, with his own position and prospects. Nepotism was rife and the civil service soon joined the aristocracy in keeping the working classes firmly in their place.

The autocratic nature of Russian society all but precluded anything other than limited reform within the country. The only way that genuine change could have been made possible would have been if Nicholas had been strong and totally committed to easing the burden on his subjects. He was not, having neither the courage nor the determination to oversee such change. He could see the problems but simply did not have the backbone to do anything about them.

Of course, he could always have refused the throne, but that would have been a complicated process and, anyway, whatever his shortcomings, Nicholas did at least have a firm and clear sense of duty. No matter what he might have wanted, God had intended him to become czar. He could do little else but accept the inevitable and try to make the best out of a bad job.

Nicholas married Alexandra Feodorovna (Alix of Hesse) on 26 November 1894, not long after the death of his father. The marriage would not normally have been allowed so close to the death of a czar but Nicholas, in love and unconcerned with protocol, wanted the marriage to take place sooner rather than later.

He had lost the support of his father and he needed the wisdom and comfort of Alexandra – stronger and more determined than him – to take its place. As far as he was concerned they could forget the spring date that had been set for the following year. He wanted to be married now, and so the wedding took place in St Petersburg that November. As a concession to the mourning period for Alexander III, there was no reception and no honeymoon. Nicholas did not care; he had realised his wish to marry his beautiful German bride. She quickly established herself as a diehard reactionary with a no-nonsense approach to government.

Alexandra's belief that the Russian people needed to be kept in check, preferably by the whip, did little to advance her husband's more liberal views and soon made her into a despised figure with the majority of the population. She never quite escaped the appellation of 'that German woman', and the scorn and dislike became even more pronounced after the czar declared war on Germany in 1914.

As he ascended the throne in the autumn of 1894, Nicholas Romanov was torn by insecurities and found himself thrust into a position he neither wanted nor enjoyed. There were many Russian nobles and grandees who understood his feelings and many more who questioned his suitability to rule at all. Even Nicholas doubted his own abilities.

The one thing the new czar did not doubt, however, was his hatred of Japan and the duplicity of the Japanese. Within the next fifteen years that hatred, and his inability to compromise, would have a stunning and fatal effect on the Russian aristocracy.

Chapter 2

War, Terrible War

The closing years of the nineteenth century were a period of uncertainty and unrest across most of the world. It was a time of rapid change and technological development, a time when old empires were dying as new regimes strove for recognition. Russia was no different from any other large nation desperate to extend its dominions; at the expense of other countries if necessary.

A long succession of czars had harboured territorial designs on the wide open wastelands that cut off Moscow and central Russia from the Pacific. Consequently, from 1613 when the first Romanov ascended to the Russian throne until the foundation of Vladivostok in 1860, Russia gradually accumulated and, where possible, cultivated territory in Siberia. By the time Czar Nicholas came to power in 1894 the Russian Empire stretched from Poland in the west to the Kamchatka Peninsula in the east.

When access to the Pacific Ocean was finally achieved one fact became apparent; the Russian Empire needed a warm water port. Vladivostok was operational only in the summer months; in winter it was iced in and useless. A port that was open all year around was vital if the Russian Navy, and indeed the whole empire, was to achieve its potential in the east. But it was also sure to bring Russia and Japan into conflict at some stage.

Japan had only been 'opened up' to the West fairly recently. It was still a remote and virtually unknown power, overshadowed to some extent by China, and its people looked down upon or snubbed by most Europeans. It was an innate and festering racism that nobody in Russia would have ever acknowledged.

The Japanese emperor and his government feared an extension of Russian influence in a region that was, in their minds if no one else's, something of a Japanese fiefdom. They feared the coming of the Trans-Siberian Railway, knowing that the Russians were already casting covetous eyes on Korea and Manchuria. Despite having a number of rich mineral deposits, dominance in the two countries offered little real financial benefit. These seemingly innocuous territories were really only needed by the Japanese as a buffer between themselves and imperialist powers like Russia.

Ownership or at least oversight of Korea was so vital to the interests of Japan that in 1894 the country went to war with China over its control. The conflict became known as the first Sino–Japanese War and the Japanese astounded the world by their understanding of modern, technological warfare. It was a short but brutal war that saw the Chinese armies routed on the Liaodong Peninsula and her navy virtually destroyed at the Battle of the Yalu River.

At the end of the war the resultant peace treaty ceded the Liaodong Peninsula and the island of Taiwan to Japan. The vitally important harbour at Port Arthur at the tip of the peninsula had already been besieged and captured during the war, but now Japan, realising the significance of the place as an all-year-round port and harbour, fortified the town. For the still-growing Japanese Empire there was more than just strategic value to Port Arthur: 'Taken by bloody banzai storm at prodigious cost, it was a symbol of the Japanese soldiers' bravery and the nation's new independence.'[1]

Czar Nicholas, with his hatred of Japan still burning, was never going to stand this for long and within two years diplomatic and political pressure from Russia, Germany and France forced the Japanese out of the Liaodong Peninsula and Port Arthur. As the Japanese forces moved out, the Russians moved in and by 1897 the peninsula and Port Arthur were firmly in the hands of Czar Nicholas.

Within weeks the Russian Pacific Fleet was based in Port Arthur, with a smaller detachment of armoured cruisers and torpedo boats under Admiral Uemura stationed at Vladivostok. In the meantime Germany built the fortress and harbour of Tsingtao and stationed their German East Asia Squadron in the new port.

Much has been made of the interweaving of the bloodline of the royal families of Europe, all of which appeared to be derived from one source: Britain's Queen Victoria. Apart from the minor royal houses of countries like Denmark and Sweden, the three 'big players' of the early twentieth century – Edward VII of Britain, Nicholas II of Russia and Kaiser Wilhelm II of Germany – were related; Nicholas and Wilhelm as cousins, Edward as their uncle.

After the death of Edward another cousin, George V, came to the British throne. This should have been a guarantee of stability and peace, but it was nothing of the sort. There is nothing in the royal or political handbook that says families have to like each other and with these men emotions were always somewhat fraught.

Nicholas did not like his cousin Kaiser Wilhelm of Germany and, at times, even suspected that the man was insane. But the strength, stature and political charisma of the kaiser and his empire, characteristics which the czar clearly lacked, cast what can only be described as a sort of enchantment over Nicholas. When Wilhelm suggested that he should become the 'Admiral of the Atlantic' while Nikki should become 'Admiral of the Pacific' it suited Nicholas to turn away from Europe and confine himself to Asiatic problems.

Over the next few years, at the behest of the czar and to the growing concern of the Japanese, Russia began to make significant inroads into Korea and Manchuria. With mining and forestry concessions along the Yalu River firmly in their grasp, Russian influence grew stronger by the day. When, in 1900 during the Boxer Rebellion, 170,000 Russian troops were sent to Manchuria – supposedly to protect a new railway that was being built to permit easy access to Port Arthur – alarm bells began to ring in many European capitals.

The czar promised the other great powers that he would withdraw his troops once the Boxer Rebellion was over, but two years after the uprising ended with defeat of the Boxers, Russian forces were still in the country. In fact, far from withdrawing, they had actually consolidated their positions. Hurried negotiations between Japan and Russia led to the Japanese proposal that Russia could control Manchuria as long as Japan was allowed sovereignty of northern Korea.

The dividing up of the two Asian states was not as easy as might be thought. Talks and proposals went on for over four months, governed by the knowledge that Japan was now officially allied to Great Britain. If war was to come Britain would surely throw in its might behind the Japanese. Despite this, the Russians soon made it clear that they were not prepared to compromise in any way: as well as Manchuria the Russian czar also had Korea in his sights.

Faced by such inflexibility, Japan began preparations for war. Staff at the Japanese Embassy in St Petersburg withdrew after burning their confidential papers in the garden of the residency, and in February 1904 Japan severed diplomatic relations with Russia.

There is no doubt that the Czar Nicholas's attitude played a part, but it was not just his hatred of Japan that was to blame for the state of affairs. Above all, Nicholas was a prevaricator, never really sure what position he should adopt in the game of 'high politics'. Part of his problem was that the draconian and despotic nature of the regime in Russia did not allow him the privilege of good quality advisors. Advice, such as it was, usually came from members of his family and was often suspect in the extreme.

Nicholas held the firm conviction that he was czar because of divine providence. He may well have been happier being a simple country gentleman, but whatever he did and however he did it, he was always intent on protecting the status and dignity of Russia. It was an attitude that led to constant delays in reaching an agreement with Japan, and one which, eventually, caused the Japanese government to lose patience.

* * *

Bolstered by a US$200 million loan from an American banker named Jacob Schiff, the Japanese were quietly confident about their prospects if the severing of diplomatic relations should ever lead to outright warfare. It was a significant amount of money and the motives behind Schiff's gift have never been made clear (perhaps it was to compensate for some of the czar's anti-Semitic pogroms that had recently taken place across the Russian Empire?)

Despite this the Russians were supremely confident. Their army and navy were both significantly larger than those of Japan and many of the generals and admirals in the St Petersburg government did not believe that the Japanese would ever be so foolish as to declare war on Russia. They developed an overwhelming and erroneous belief in Russia's military power and Nicholas, with his unswerving detestation of Japan and all she stood for was an important part of that false sense of security.

Outraged and out of patience, Japan formally declared war on Russia on 8 February 1904. However, just three hours before the declaration was passed to the Russian government the Japanese Navy got its retaliation in first as Admiral Togo's torpedo boats began attacking the Russian Pacific Fleet in the supposedly safe anchorage at Port Arthur.

The Japanese strategists were clear that before a successful war could be waged on land they had to first control the sea lanes. The Russian Pacific Fleet was an obvious threat and therefore had to be taken out. A sudden and surprise attack would, it was felt, disable the Russian ships and so neutralise the threat.

In Admiral Togo Heihachiro they had the ideal man to command the operation. He came from an ancient warrior family that could trace its roots back to the thirteenth century. Born in 1848 Togo was quick witted and intelligent although he sometimes displayed his impatience and inability to tolerate fools with what many regarded as a shocking disrespect for his elders.

He wanted to make a career in the navy and so, despite being over the age of admission, he was enrolled on the officer training ship *Worcester* which was then moored alongside the south bank of the Thames at Greenhithe. An independent and privately run training ship, the old wooden wall *Worcester* – like her equivalent, the *TS Conway* on the Mersey – took boys whose parents were able to pay the fees and turned them into officers for the British Merchant Marine and, occasionally, for the Royal Navy.

The key word in this description is 'boys'. Togo was already past the official entry age by at least ten years but the young man and his sponsoring government simply lied about how old he actually was. With the money safely in their bank account, the organising committee of the *Worcester* accepted their word. By turning a blind eye to the Japanese rule bending the training ship received a guaranteed income for at least two years and was more than happy to receive a dedicated and talented student. The training ship was later to hold up Togo as one of its star pupils.

In 1911 he even returned for a visit and received an almost royal reception. Togo, by then one of the most famous sailors in the world, even took time to write a glowing tribute to the ship and its regime in a letter addressed to all 'Worcester boys':

> I am one of the Old Boys of the Worcester who learnt to be sailors more than thirty years ago on this very ship, as you are doing now. Today I am so much pleased to meet you on board our beloved ship. Your cheerful and vigorous appearances make me firmly believe in your bright future.[2]

His English might not have improved very much but there was no denying the sincerity of Admiral Togo's words. He retained his affection for the *Worcester* until the end of his life, convinced that the schooling and the nautical training on the old ship had helped turn him into one of the most successful and important sailors of all time. At the very least it introduced him to the life and work of Lord Horatio Nelson, a man who quickly became a hero for the young Japanese naval man.

Togo had no great love for the British but his desire to serve in his country's navy was strong and so he gritted his teeth and got on with what he knew was the best nautical training available. His English was poor and, though he quickly developed in the art of seamanship, he made slow academic progress on the training ship. Gritty and determined, he stuck to his task and eventually graduated from the school. 'He was good at mathematics, and he surprised his local hosts with his keen interest in the Christian church ... he attended services regularly, even singing hymns with the help of a hymnal.'[3]

It may well have been a desire to improve his English rather than any religious fervour that kept Togo attending divine services and singing his hymns. Either way, the claim that he was baptised into the Roman Catholic Church while he was studying in England has no foundation.

Training completed, Togo expected a quick return to Japan. Instead he was ordered to head for Pembrokeshire to witness the final construction stages and launch of a new ironclad corvette, destined to be the first such vessel in the Japanese Navy. The corvette was being built at the private dockyard of Jacobs Pill, on the Pembroke River in West Wales.

Jacobs Pill was barely half a mile away from the Royal Naval Dockyard at Pembroke Dock, the only official naval dockyard ever to exist in Wales. Being so close to a British government facility, it is highly unlikely that Togo would not have inveigled his way into what was then the premier building yard of the Royal Navy. Visitors were always welcome in the dockyard and there Togo would have gazed in wonder and delight at the cruisers and pre-dreadnought battleships waiting on the stocks.

His principal purpose in West Wales, however, was to watch the launch of the new Japanese warship. This he duly did on 12 July 1877, along with Jushie Wooyeno Kagenori, the Minister Plenipotentiary to the Mikado. That evening there was a huge celebratory dinner at the town's finest hotel and then, a few weeks later, Togo sailed for home on the ship, the *Hi-Yei*. The journey was uneventful and within a few weeks Togo was in Japan again.[4]

Togo performed well in the 1894–95 war with China and was soon rising rapidly through the ranks. A strict but fair disciplinarian, he reached the position of Rear Admiral despite suffering from rheumatism – something of an occupational hazard in his chosen profession – but sustaining himself through belief in his own ability and by an amazingly high pain threshold.

The similarities between the Port Arthur attack and the Japanese bombing of the American Fleet at Pearl Harbour in 1941 cannot be ignored. Both came as a total surprise, even though an attack of some sort – on both occasions – had been expected. And while the attacks were denigrated by the victims, both of them were hugely successful. The attack on Pearl Harbour was delivered from the air; at Port Arthur the weapon of choice came from the sea in the shape of tiny destroyers and torpedo boats:

> Admiral Togo was relying on the new Whitehead torpedo, and at half past ten on the evening of 8 February, the low sleek little boats went in. "Show yourselves worthy of the confidence I place in you," Togo had told his destroyer and torpedo boat commanders; and they did.[5]

The Russian ships were lying peacefully at anchor in the outer roads of Port Arthur with many of their crews ashore in town. At that stage no war with Japan had been declared and the unsuspecting ships were lit from stem to stern. The twenty low and sleek Japanese torpedo boats approached to within a few hundred yards before they were spotted. By then it was too late. Two Russian battleships, the *Tsarevich* and the *Retvizan* were hit by nine of the new torpedoes and disabled, along with the heavy cruiser *Pallada*.

The following morning Togo, flying his flag in the newly launched battleship *Mikasa*, followed up the torpedo attack with a long range bombardment as the Russians attempted to leave Port Arthur for a counter attack. Shore installations were destroyed and four more Russian ships were badly damaged and put out of action as their commanders ordered a swift return to harbour.

The two engagements, known collectively as The Battle of Port Arthur, had crippled the Russian fleet and swung the balance of power firmly in Japan's direction. Furthermore, it had been achieved with the loss of only six Japanese lives.

Following his victory Admiral Togo was in no hurry to attack again. The depleted Russian fleet remained bottled up in Port Arthur, and Togo, cruising in the Yellow Sea, was not inclined to risk his ships against the powerful shore batteries that ringed the harbour. Control of the sea lanes was what mattered to Japan and as long as the Russians remained in Port Arthur, and in Vladivostok to the north, it rested with the Japanese.

Over the following eighteen months there were occasional skirmishes as the Russian fleet, urged on by the czar, occasionally ventured out of port. They were invariably forced back to base by swift attacks from Togo and all that these tentative excursions achieved was to further weaken the Pacific Fleet. Japanese mines also caused havoc, sinking ships like the cruiser *Boyarin* and the transport vessel *Yenisei*. Even the most objective of watchers back in St Petersburg or Moscow could see that the navy, always something of a talisman to the Russian people, was hopelessly unprepared for war.

* * *

Russian public opinion and criticism of the navy's performance grew louder and more intense as bulletin after bulletin from the East reported only death and disaster. Disbelief was quickly replaced by simmering anger and Nicholas realised that matters were rapidly coming to a head. He needed to do something before the grumbles of discontent became screams of outrage.

The autocratic regimes of successive czars had never been particularly popular. The nineteenth century in particular was the age of revolution, with revolts and uprisings occurring in France and Italy and monarchies across Europe fearing the growing strength of the working classes.

The year 1848 was a watershed. Students and revolutionaries manned the barricades in the streets of Paris, giving rise to Victor Hugo's classic *Les Miserables*. Even Britain, which had already undergone the trauma of its own civil war 200 years previously, seemed to be poised on the brink of revolution. In the end it all came to nothing. The revolts in Paris and elsewhere were eventually quashed, but the disturbances had frightened most of the well-established monarchies, many of which began to introduce elements of reform in their governments and in society in general.

Russia remained defiantly autocratic, and after the threat of 1848 had died away the Romanovs continued to incur the hatred of a growing number of revolutionary and reformist bodies. Their opposition did not diminish as the years went by and the threat of revolution and assassination were ever-present realities for the czars and their government.

Nicholas II was no more popular than his father although the 'sneak attack' of the Japanese had, strangely, worked in his favour. Crowds of students, normally the most critical and dangerous of groups, marched to the Winter Palace waving banners and chanting 'God save the czar'. It seemed as if Nicholas's hope that war would help make him the admired ruler of his imagination might just have come true. Of course, like much of his reign, the adulation of the people was a false dawn. It could not last.

The naval commander at Port Arthur, Admiral Oskar Viktorovich Stark, was one of over 100 men of that rank in the Russian Navy. In contrast, Britain, the most significant naval power in the world, had elevated only sixty-nine officers to the ranks of rear, vice or full admirals, all of whom were well employed and kept busy.

Like most of his contemporaries in the Russian Navy, Stark was lazy and inept. Even the mention of his name to the Russian sailors invariably brought out a hail of invective and foul language. Nicholas was clear that he would have to be replaced.

Admiral Togo, even though he done little more than sail up and down the Yellow Sea or lie waiting off Port Arthur, had clearly intimidated Stark. Fear of the Japanese Navy ran strongly through the port and town. Stark might bellow and complain but the unfortunate Russian admiral had no intention of setting sail to meet Togo in battle.

The Viceroy of the Far East, Admiral Evgeny Alexeev, thought for a while that he might take over command himself but he, like Stark, was unpopular with the sailors and the Russian public. He had a totally naïve and misplaced opinion of the Japanese, considering them no better than vermin. It was an underestimation that was to prove fatal for many Russian sailors in the months to come and it left Czar Nicholas in a dilemma.

He was confronted with the fact that there was only one choice if he was going to replace Stark and Alexeev: Admiral Stepan Osipovich Makarov. It was not that the czar distrusted or did not like Makarov; the opposite, in fact. Nicholas dreaded the thought that one of the most outstanding officers in his navy could well be sailing to his death.

Makarov was a popular and charismatic figure, standing apart from the court politics in St Petersburg. He was also good at his job. Pushing aside any fears or regrets, Czar Nicholas summoned Makarov to the Winter Palace in late February 1904 where he received his sovereign's blessing and orders to take command of the Russian Pacific Fleet. That same day Makarov boarded the Trans-Siberian express for the Far East. He was accompanied by Grand Duke Kyril, an ambitious and self-serving naval officer who was yet another cousin of the czar, and by the leading Russian painter and war artist of the time, Vasily Vereshchagin.

Makarov and his colleagues arrived at Port Arthur in March 1904. Once he arrived he immediately began to put things in order. The defences on the hills around the bay were strengthened, new trenches were dug along the crests, and the damaged battleships, still listing and half sunk in the harbour, were finally repaired. For the first time since the war had begun in February, things seemed to be going Russia's way.

Unfortunately, nobody, not even Admiral Makarov, had yet realised that Port Arthur was not so much a sanctuary as a trap. It was a bit like the neck of a bottle, and once the Russian Fleet was in the harbour there was no way it was going to get out again easily. The entry and departure channels were narrow and the bay wasn't large enough to allow capital ships to manoeuvre.

Togo's battleships were equipped with newly designed shimosa shells and explosive charges that set fire to almost anything they hit. Added to the efficient and accurate Japanese gunnery, these new shells only multiplied the disadvantages for Makarov. Fear of the unknown kept the Russians bottled up in port and Togo could afford to lie off Port Arthur for as long as he wanted, waiting for the Russians to make the first move.

Togo remained imperiously unimpressed by Makarov's moves. Not even the repairs to the half-sunk Pacific Fleet worried him unduly and he continued to cruise the waters outside the anchorage, encouraging and taunting the Russians to come out.

At one stage it seemed as if they might accept the challenge and Togo was ordered to block the entrance to Port Arthur, thereby sealing the Russian Fleet inside. The chosen method was by sinking old ships filled with cement in the approach channels. The idea was sound but the sunken ships failed to block the channels. They merely settled on the bottom and were totally ineffective.

The exercise was pointless anyway. Even with Makarov now in charge the Russians had little intention of venturing out from Port Arthur where they were safe from destruction. Makarov, like Togo, adopted a 'wait and see' approach. Only the intervention of Czar Nicholas could force them to abandon their position.

Not understanding Togo's tactics in remaining outside the harbour rather than launching a full-scale attack on Port Arthur, it would have been natural for the czar to think that the Japanese had lost their nerve and had, in fact, shot their bolt. Perhaps it was time for direct action. He immediately began to bombard Makarov with despatches and orders.

Strengthening the defences of Port Arthur was one thing but Makarov, at the behest of the czar, now prepared for a more offensive operation. He was reluctant to risk his fleet, but if Togo wanted a fight he would oblige him. On 12 April 1904, under cover of darkness, two Russian battleships, the *Petropavlovsk* and the *Pobeda*, slipped out of the anchorage at Port Arthur. Accompanied by support vessels, they were searching for Togo, intent on bringing the Japanese to battle.

The following morning, as Makarov stood impassively on the bridge of the *Petropavlovsk*, the Japanese fleet was spotted on the horizon. The artist Vereshchagin rushed below deck to pick up his sketchbook, eagerly anticipating the conflict to come. Before he could make it back to the bridge to begin drawing there was a sudden explosion and Grand Duke Kyril turned towards Makarov, wondering if they had been hit by a torpedo from some lurking submarine or torpedo boat.

Kyril got no reply. The admiral was still standing erect, but he had been decapitated. Shrapnel or a piece of flying metal had taken off his head as cleanly as if it had been done with the blade of a samurai sword. The damage had been caused not by a torpedo but by one of several Japanese mines laid only the night before.

> The *Petropavlovsk* was cloaked in a dark cloud, her bow diving into the sea, her stern high in the air and propellers still whirling. Under the rays of bright springtime sun, in mocking proximity to the friendly shore, the battleship sank in a matter of minutes. Among the numerous bodies never recovered was that of Admiral Makarov.[6]

Almost before the *Petropavlovsk* sank a second explosion ripped through the morning air. The *Pobeda* had also struck a mine. Luckily she was not as seriously damaged as the flagship but she still had to be towed back to Port Arthur for repair and was out of action for some time.

Russian disaster at sea was soon replicated by significant failures on land. While the Russians were still reeling from the death of their most beloved admiral, Japanese forces landed at Incheon in Korea. Moving with incredible swiftness, they occupied Seoul and then moved on the take the rest of the country. Russian strategy was a defensive one, delaying and holding off until reinforcements could arrive. Once again, the Japanese forestalled them.

In May 1904 the Japanese crossed the Yalu River and stormed Russian positions in Manchuria. The attack was followed by several landings on the Manchurian coast and, slowly but surely, Russian troops were forced back towards Port Arthur. It was intense and bloody fighting, both sides taking huge casualties. In a campaign where tactics were limited to charging and counter charging the enemy, Japan's ascendency was hard won.

It was not all one-way traffic, however, and Japanese losses, particularly when attacking well-fortified positions, were astronomically high. Traditional frontal attacks against troops in fixed and carefully prepared defensive lines were a recipe for disaster. The tactic had been more appropriate for the campaigns of Wellington and Napoleon one hundred years before. Now far more destructive modern weapons were at hand.

It was a lesson that the Japanese generals eventually learned, but it was not one that came easily. It was certainly not passed on to the commanders of the British and French armies on the Western Front in the forthcoming Great War where the same mistake of making useless and costly charges against well dug-in opposition was repeated time and time again.

Despite their initial successes, May 1904 was not a good month for the Japanese who, in addition to mounting casualties on land, now endured another major setback. This time it took place at sea. The Russians had taken a leaf out of the Japanese book and, like their enemies, began to lay out 'offensive minefields' along the approaches to ports. Mines were still a relatively new weapon; they were hard to spot and highly effective against slow moving pre-dreadnought battleships.

Within hours of each other the patrolling Japanese battleships *Hatsuse* and *Yashima* both struck mines and sank with serious casualties; over 400 on the *Hatsuse* alone. The cruiser *Yoshino* was also sunk on same day, again after colliding with mines. In just one day Admiral Togo had lost almost a third of his fighting force. Perhaps, Czar Nicholas thought, there was hope of victory after all.

Meanwhile the land war continued. The Japanese siege of Port Arthur had begun once the Russian troops came streaming back into the city after the Japanese landings in Manchuria. By the end of May Japanese troops had arrived in front of Port Arthur and the town and harbour were cut off from the outside world.

A series of unsuccessful frontal attacks against the fortifications on the hills surrounding the harbour and town led once more to high Japanese casualties. It was clear that the land war was going to continue as a bloodbath with significant casualties on both sides. The total number of Japanese dead and wounded ended up somewhere in the region of 50,000. The Russians fared a little better, mainly by operating defensively and waiting for the Japanese to attack, incurring losses of 32,000 dead, wounded or missing.

After a procession of seemingly unstoppable victories, the failed assaults during the siege of Port Arthur were a blow to the solar plexus for the Japanese commanders. To suddenly find themselves being outfought was an unfamiliar experience. Psychologically, the Japanese character was resilient enough to recover from such setbacks and they fought on with intense ferocity and bravery. It was the Europeans' first sight of the dedication and selfless courage of the little-regarded Asian peoples, but not their last, and it would come back to haunt them many times in the years ahead.

Only very slowly did the Japanese begin to understand that banzai-style charges where men were used as human battering rams had no real place in modern technological warfare. Such tactics might work once or even twice, but against fixed positions where defenders were protected and had the weapons to pour unrestricted fire onto charging infantry there could be only one victor.

Finally, using batteries of 11-in howitzers to 'soften up' the defences, the Japanese military forces managed to capture Vysokaya Hill, one of the most important forts in the defensive ring. From there they could establish their artillery on high ground and were, with impunity, able to shell the Russian Fleet in the harbour.

The Japanese artillery fire was devastating and over the coming weeks four Russian battleships and two cruisers were sunk. The last of the battleships was so badly damaged that she was forced to scuttle herself a few weeks later rather than fall into enemy hands. It meant that by the autumn of 1904 all of the Russian capital vessels in their Pacific Fleet had been destroyed. It was undoubtedly a disastrous state of affairs.

The siege of the city went on, and Russian casualties increased with every attack. On 2 December Russian General Kondratenko was killed when the town armoury took a direct hit from a Japanese shell. Kondratenko, effectively third in charge of the garrison, had been at the heart of the defence, exposing himself to danger every day and leading by example. His death was almost as grievous a blow as that of Admiral Makarov.

Later in the month, when a relieving army failed to get through Japanese lines and was forced to retreat, it left the Russian garrison commander, Major General Anatoly Stessel, with an unpalatable choice. Faced with a dilemma that would have destroyed men of less moral character, Stessel paced the earthworks night after night and pondered his options.

Then, later in December, Japanese troops dug and exploded several underground mines beneath the Russian perimeter. The result of this hugely effective tactic gave them possession of the more important parts of the defensive line. And so Stessel made a decision that many later condemned but which he clearly took on humanitarian grounds.

As far as Stessel was concerned, there was no purpose in defending the city now that the Pacific Fleet had been destroyed. All that was happening was the mindless killing of more Russian and Japanese soldiers. On 2 January

1905, unexpectedly and without consulting the czar or any of the other military leaders, he surrendered.

The Japanese commanders were astounded but more than happy at this sudden turn of events. They had expected weeks of hard fighting, but the Russian surrender of a port and garrison that had seemed to have meant so much to them caught everyone by surprise. Even Togo, still patrolling out in the Yellow Sea, was amazed at Stessel's action.

It was an action that later earned Stessel a court martial and the death sentence, showing how seriously Czar Nicholas took the defence of Port Arthur. Losing it to a horde of Asian savages was not to be tolerated. For a while there was a real possibility that the sentence would be carried out, but eventually Stessel was pardoned for the twin crimes of poor leadership and disobeying orders.

* * *

In the months between the death of Admiral Makarov in April 1904 and Stessel's unexpected surrender at the start of 1905, confusion reigned in Russia and in all parts of the empire. Makarov's end in particular was the most serious blow the Russians had yet suffered. The loss of the battleship *Petropavlovsk* was hard enough to bear but it was unlikely to prove fatal. The death of the popular and charismatic commander, however, was something else entirely.

If Makarov could perish at the hands of a man who, in the minds of many Russians, was already starting to assume demonic proportions, it surely could happen to anyone. What price now the security that could previously be found in the iron warships of the Pacific Fleet?

Many sailors and soldiers believed that to sail out of Port Arthur or Vladivostok and knowingly come under the waiting guns of Admiral Togo and his terrifyingly efficient sailors was like signing your own death warrant. The death in action of General Kondratenko simply added to the uncertainty of the Port Arthur defenders.

After the death of Stepan Makarov, command of the Pacific Fleet had passed to Admiral Wilgelm Vitgeft. Obeying orders from St Petersburg, he began to plan for offensive action. It was not easy but he did eventually manage to get out into open sea. Many observers and critics thought it was a major achievement just to leave the besieged port, but Admiral Togo knew exactly what he was doing. Like a cat playing with a mouse, he stood off, waiting, allowing the Pacific Fleet to get clear of Port Arthur before he turned to strike.

On leaving Port Arthur, Vitgeft was intending to steam for Vladivostok to join up with the Russian squadron that had been held for some time at the northern port. Unfortunately, on 10 August 1904, before he could make the rendezvous, he ran into the waiting ships of Admiral Togo.

Both fleets opened fire at the range of eight miles, the greatest distance thus far ever documented for gun duels between warships. Spotting and control of shot were still in their infancy and the majority of sailors, on the Russian side at least, related more to the short range broadsides of the Napoleonic wooden walls than to the intricacies of modern gunnery.

The Battle of the Yellow Sea lasted for several hours, something of a miracle given that the Russian fleet was experiencing problems before action even began:

> At 11.50 the flagship hoisted the flag K. This meant "Ship not under control". We stopped engines and waited for the defect to be put to rights ... At 12.20 the *Papiela* hoisted flag K and hauled out of line; again a delay. Meanwhile the enemy had already joined hands and formed in line.[7]

Togo crossed the 'T' of the Russian Fleet in a classic naval manoeuvre worthy of Horatio Nelson himself before the ships eventually closed to a range of just four miles. From that short distance both sides could now use their secondary armament as well as their main weapons.

The battle was, for a while at least, evenly contested but at 18.30 hours two shells from Togo's *Mikasa* struck the bridge of the *Tsarevich*, Vitgeft's flagship. The newly appointed admiral was killed instantly. The *Tsarevich* was disabled but still afloat and swung away out of the line of fire. She might have been intact but the senior officers had all been killed and there was now nobody in command of the ship or the fleet. It seemed only a matter of minutes before Togo closed in to finish off the battered *Tsarevich*.

With the admiral dead, Prince Pavel Ukhtomsky on the battleship *Peresvet* attempted to take charge, but when the ship's foremast was brought down by enemy shelling she could no longer hoist signals. Ukhtomsky attempted to fly the flags from the bridge superstructure but they could not be seen by the other vessels and utter confusion reigned in the Russian fleet.

It was time for individual action and at that moment Captain Eduard Schensnovich on board the *Rotvizan* made a madcap solo charge at Togo's battle line. In many respects it was a suicide charge. Schensnovich intended to draw the Japanese fire away from the *Tsarevich* even if it cost him his ship and his life.

With the range reduced to less than three miles, shells were now bursting all around the *Rotvizan*, making it difficult for the Japanese range finders and gunners to accurately judge the fall of shot. Eventually, however, a shell burst on the bridge of the Russian battleship and Schensnovich fell, seriously wounded in the stomach.

Schensnovich's senior officers turned the *Rotvizan*'s bows away from the enemy, and with camouflaging smoke billowing from her funnels she sped off southwards. Her smokescreen had, however, saved the Russian flagship from destruction and the *Tsarevich* was able to limp away after her comrades.

Confronted by this disaster, the rest of the Russian Fleet promptly turned tail and headed back towards Port Arthur. In the process of escaping Togo's guns they lost two ships, with several more sustaining damage and having to find refuge in neutral ports where they were promptly disarmed and interned.

The remains of the fleet – five battleships, one cruiser and a number of destroyers – managed to reach the comparative safety of Port Arthur, but it was something of a poisoned chalice for the Russian sailors. Denied effective leadership, they would sit, inactive and useless, until eventually meeting their own nemesis later in the year at the hands of the Japanese generals and their artillery.

The small Vladivostok squadron had sailed at the same time as Vitgeft with a view to making a rendezvous somewhere off the coast of Japan. Just a few days after the Battle of the Yellow Sea this force met Togo's cruisers. The Battle of Ulsan was short and sharp, one Russian ship being sunk, the others turning tail and fleeing back to port.

The Russian Navy had been humiliated and defeated once again and Togo's stock shot up, in Japan and in the rest of the world. But there was worse to come. Togo Heihachiro seemed to have something of a magic touch in depriving Russia of its admirals. He had nullified Stark and Alexeev before the war began and then killed off Makarov and Vitgeft with his ruthless but effective tactics. Moreover, the effect of those deaths on Russian morale, along with the loss of supposedly all-powerful battleships, shook the czar's regime to the core.

* * *

It was difficult for a totalitarian and autocratic dictatorship like Russia to accept being overpowered in any form of military confrontation. Defeat in the Crimea in the 1850s – where the enemy had been the western nations of Britain and France – had been bad enough, but this time the opposition came from the despised Japanese. It could not be tolerated.

It is tempting to say that such a dismissive attitude came directly from the opinions of the czar but this is unlikely. The czars, like all of Russia's ruling class, were distant and self-contained and as remote as the dark side of the moon. They had almost no contact with the people; one of the reasons why revolutionary ideas grew so quickly in the country.

It was a cultural and sociological problem. Most Russians, whatever their class or position in life, looked down on the Japanese as being inferior, even sub-human, and had done so for years. It was racism of the most invidious sort, but now this third-rate nation was destroying the cream of Russian military might. Something had to be done and it had to be done quickly.

Soon after the death of Admiral Makarov in April 1904 the czar decided he would send out reinforcements, not to defeat Togo or secure control of the Yellow Sea but to help save Port Arthur. He was quite specific about this. Port Arthur represented a toehold for Russia in the Far East. It was the only Russian port that was open and usable all year round and was, therefore, a vital asset in Russian foreign policy.

At the time the Port Arthur garrison was still holding out and Nicholas, like most military strategists of the era, continued to regard the port and harbour as a possession of huge significance. As a consequence the place remained central to Russian thinking. Port Arthur was Russia's 'window on the world' and everything humanly possible should be done to keep it in Russian hands.

Harbours and ports, of course, needed ships to fill them and, as with most of the great Western powers, Czar Nicholas held firmly to the opinion that a powerful navy was not only a valuable weapon of war but also a status symbol that guaranteed prestige and high standing. Britain's Royal Navy, just a stone's throw away from the Baltic, was a prime example of how a powerful fleet could enhance a nation's position in the eyes of the world. Both Nicholas and Kaiser Wilhelm looked on it with envious eyes.

In order to maintain his own empire's position, Czar Nicholas had, some time before the war, ordered the building of four new ironclads, a group of battleships known as the Borodino class. They were fast and powerful vessels, all well-armed and well-protected with armour plating, and the epitome of modern warship design.

The Borodinos were intended for service with the Baltic Fleet where they would offer significant threat to the Royal Navy. Now, however, as they neared completion, Nicholas decided he would 'borrow them' for duty in the Far East. Togo and his staff knew that the four new warships were on their way and, thanks to the efficient Japanese spy network, a careful watch was kept on their progress from the moment they were launched.

By the autumn of 1904 the ships were out of the building yards and moored at Libau, the base of the Baltic Fleet. According to Togo's agents they were taking on supplies and ammunition, crews were drilling and the four much-vaunted vessels were almost ready to sail. Togo knew there could be only one destination; the Far East.

Czar Nicholas, normally indecisive and unsure, at first decided that his new relieving fleet would be reinforced by as many ships from Russia's Baltic Fleet as could be spared. Ignoring the more prescient opinions that these old ships would be nothing more than a hindrance to the relieving force, he stuck rigidly to his beliefs, convinced that he was in the right.

Saving Port Arthur was the only thing that really mattered to the czar. If possible, there should also be a resounding defeat for the Japanese Navy, but saving Port Arthur was the main purpose. Everything, Nicholas decided, would be sacrificed to this end.

And so, as he paced the echoing halls of the Winter Palace and prowled along the quayside at Kronstadt, he reconsidered. The situation in Europe seemed to be in his favour. With cousin Wilhelm of Germany thinking of himself as a virtual ally and Britain still licking her wounds after the Boer War in South Africa, there was little danger in the Baltic or around Russia's western territories.

The debate, within the czar's head and amongst his advisors, went on for several weeks. What was the point of maintaining a strong force in the west if the ships and colony at Port Arthur were facing destruction? Deal with the problem in hand, Nicholas repeatedly told himself; extinguish the Japanese threat before it became insurmountable. Why not send the whole Baltic Fleet out to the Far East? It could be renamed the 2nd Pacific Fleet, and with the four new modern battleships as the central pivot of the force it was, Nicholas thought, guaranteed to bring quick and easy victory. No one ever liked to oppose the decisions of the emperor, and so the staff at the Admiralty in St Petersburg meekly agreed.

In the end Nicholas took eleven battleships, including the four new Borodinos, and numerous support craft from the Baltic Fleet. That created a powerful relief force for Port Arthur, but left just two capital warships to defend western Russia from any potential attack. It was a gamble, but it was one that he felt more than justified in taking.

When he shared his intentions with Cousin Willy, the German Emperor was, naturally enough, all in favour. A mighty, unbeatable naval force was a show of military strength that appealed to the Kaiser and a clear indication that Russia and its leaders were not to be trifled with.

Nicholas was happy, feeling fully supported and encouraged in his actions. As far as Czar Nicholas was concerned the Kaiser was far more experienced than him in politics and in the whole concept of militarism. His help and advice were worth having, particularly when they coincided with the czar's own ideas.

The German Emperor, whose dreams of glory knew no bounds, was still signing his correspondence to the czar as 'Admiral of the Atlantic'. Victory at Port Arthur would underline the significance of Nicholas's own Wilhelm-designated and carefully crafted title 'Admiral of the Pacific'.

Despite his dislike of the Kaiser, Nicholas had always been happy to watch the German at work. Wilhelm's posing and posturing made him a charismatic figure, especially to the naïve Nicholas. The czar was an uncertain man who needed support wherever he could find it, and together he and Wilhelm made something of an unholy alliance.

Wilhelm was not just making mischief, though he would do anything to upset the British. He had a genuine desire to form a German-Russian alliance to oppose the recent British and French entente. Helping his somewhat reluctant cousin to make decisions that would ultimately work in Germany's favour – and possibly Russia's as well – was one way of doing exactly that.

Just to make matters neat and tidy – something that concerned the czar and his advisors far more significantly than the practicalities of the situation – the ships currently being shelled out of existence in Port Arthur would now be known as the 1st Pacific Fleet. The new armada that would soon be unleashed on the Japanese would, as planned, be christened the 2nd Pacific Fleet. It was confusing, and ultimately of little material value, but the ends needed to be tied together and the reorganisation at least left Czar Nicholas happy and content.

When the two fleets united and then sailed north to join up with the squadron at Vladivostok there was, the czar thought, not a power on earth that could deny them. As far as numbers were concerned, he was right, but as he and the whole world were soon to discover, wars were not won by numbers alone.

Having made the decision to form a new Pacific Fleet, Czar Nicholas next turned his mind to what was arguably the most important move of all. He needed to appoint an admiral for the new squadron. He considered many of his most respected fleet commanders, but with Makarov already out of the reckoning, the choice came down to just one individual. Nicholas did not have to search far to find the man he wanted: Zinovi Petrovitch Rozhestvensky.

Chapter 3

Rozhestvensky

Zinovi Petrovitch Rozhestvensky came from the Russian capital of St Petersburg. He did not have a naval background, being the son of a physician rather than a sailor, but had always expressed an interest in nautical matters. He was born in 1848 and joined the Russian Navy at the age of seventeen, specialising in gunnery and, in time, making himself the premier Russian expert in the field.

He rose steadily through the ranks, serving in a variety of commands under renowned figures like Stepan Makarov and experiencing combat on a number of occasions. He survived a scandal when he admitted to falsifying a report during the Russo-Turkish War of 1877–78, but the affair did little to harm his career. Much decorated and seconded to the Bulgarian Navy for a short period, Rozhestvensky also spent two and a half years as naval attaché in London.

He served for a time as commander of the Artillery Practice Unit, the Russian academy for the education and training of gunners, and in December 1898 he was promoted to rear admiral. By March 1903 the czar had appointed him Head of the Naval General Staff.

A well-known figure in court and in naval circles, Rozhestvensky cut a handsome figure at balls and receptions, often appearing with members of the royal family at the Winter Palace. He was particularly renowned for two contradictory traits of behaviour. Firstly he was an inveterate womaniser. Despite being happily married to a woman who seemed to understand him, or would at least tolerate his infidelities, Rozhestvensky's liaisons were famous throughout St Petersburg. In a city that thrived on gossip and the cult of personality, Rozhestvensky could always be relied on for a little bit of scandal and social intrigue.

One of his more renowned affairs was with Capitolina, the beautiful wife of Admiral Makarov, which made relations between Rozhestvensky and the admiral somewhat difficult. After her husband's death, Capitolina remained Rozhestvensky's friend, confidant and, possibly, lover right to the end.

After months of prevarication, when he did finally sail for the Far East in 1904 Rozhestvensky's latest flame, Natalia Sivers, was appointed to the post of head nurse on board the *Oryol*, the fleet's hospital ship. The nurses on the hospital ship were mostly volunteers; women from society who needed a little excitement in their lives. If there were two things Rozhestvensky loved they were women and ships and now he seemed to be getting the best of both worlds. There is, however, no record of how Rozhestvensky's wife responded to the appointment.

Rozhestvensky was also renowned for his fiery temper, which was often vented on ratings and junior officers alike. He was not averse to using his fists on subordinates who had let him down or, in his opinion, had performed badly. He was known throughout the navy as 'Mad Dog'; not that anyone would call him that to his face.

One of his more engaging traits was the habit of throwing his binoculars over the side of the ship when he was in a temper or whenever things did not go his way. It was at least better than pitching his sailors overboard.

Rozhestvensky once hurled his glasses into the sea while engaged in a gunnery demonstration for Kaiser Wilhelm II of Germany. Despite this foible, which amused rather than angered the kaiser, Wilhelm was apparently impressed by the accuracy and rate of the Russian gunfire. He made the comment to his colleague, Admiral Tirpitz, that he wished his own ships were as efficient in their fire as the Russians. Tirpitz nodded his understanding and made a careful note of his master's opinion.

Rozhestvensky's moods and habits were well known to his sailors who, if possible, tried to laugh at them rather than take offence. 'When his battleship fleet set sail in 1904, Rozhtestvensky's staff ensured that his flagship *Knyaz Suvorov* had a good supply of binoculars on board.'[1]

And yet, despite his temper, he could be extraordinarily generous and caring towards his men. If he did not inspire love in them he certainly created a feeling of awe and more than a little respect. Once, docking in the German port of Kiel, he hired workmen to load coal onto the ship because he felt his sailors were too tired to carry out the task. Coaling the ship was a hated job in every navy in the world at that time and 'Mad Dog's' compassion was greatly appreciated by his sailors.

This, then, was the man who Czar Nicholas decided would take the 2nd Pacific Fleet halfway around the world – a journey of 18,000 miles – to relieve the beleaguered Port Arthur. A determined leader and strict disciplinarian, like Togo he suffered from rheumatism but never once allowed it to get in the way of his duty. He was also the best gunnery officer in the navy. As far as Nicholas was concerned there was no greater or more qualified candidate and in June 1904 the Higher Naval Board confirmed the czar's choice

* * *

For the next three months Zinovi Rozhestvensky threw himself into the task of organising his fleet. Despite grave personal reservations about his mission – he was convinced that Port Arthur would have fallen long before he reached it – nobody could accuse him of lack of effort in his attempts to make an efficient force out of a hotchpotch of men and ships.

Even so, all the while he was preparing his fleet Rozhestvensky was hoping that the czar would realise the impossibility of the task and change his mind about despatching it to the Far East. It was a forlorn hope; the czar's hatred of the Japanese would not allow him to back down, no matter what the cost.

And so Rozhestvensky worked eighteen hours a day and sometimes went two or three nights without sleep. He demanded supplies, men and equipment and violently cut his way through the reams of red tape that cluttered the Russian military services. He may have made himself the most unpopular man in the navy, but he invariably got what he wanted.

When he had time to sit and consider his task – which was not often – Rozhestvensky can only have been appalled. He was expected to command a fleet of some forty disparate ships ranging from the new Borodino-class battleships to some of the weirdest auxiliaries ever to take to the sea.

Most of the fleet was made up of out-of-date battleships, ancient cruisers, tiny destroyers and a motley collection of supply and repair vessels. He was to take those ships around the world to face an inscrutable enemy whose admiral had already proved to be a world-class commander. And yet never once did Rozhestvensky flinch from his duty to his country and to his emperor.

If the journey was successful it would be the longest coal-powered voyage ever undertaken by ironclad battleships. Rozhestvensky was vain enough to relish the thought of such an achievement, but it could only be done with huge amounts of effort and luck.

> Coal fired warships were not intended for 18,000 mile journeys without the benefit of extensive dockyard facilities along the way. Their reciprocating engines pounded themselves to pieces over

long periods of time, unless run at their slowest speeds, and were prone to breakdowns.[2]

As Rozhestvensky knew only too well, the dockyard facilities of neutral countries and the British Empire would be denied to him all the way to the Far East. Russia had no ally to offer friendly ports or safe anchorages along the way. Even Kaiser Wilhelm seemed to be as hamstrung as his Russian cousin when it came to finding dockyard and repair facilities for his navy. France was perhaps Rozhestvensky's best hope of support but the French nation was, at best, mercurial in its responses and much would depend on the mood of the government and people at the time.

The only option Rozhestvensky could see was to carry out repairs as they went. Repairing the mechanical breakdowns of ironclads while at sea had never been done before. It would require the technical support of essential repair ships to actually complete whatever work needed to be done.

It was the same problem with coal. Britain, which since 1902 had been an official ally of Japan, had the monopoly on coaling bases in the southern hemisphere while Russia did not possess a single naval base or harbour anywhere along Rozhestvensky's intended route. It was estimated that at least 500,000 tons of coal would be needed to make the voyage and therefore all coaling, like repairs, would have to take place at sea. That would have been a difficult task for skilled and experienced sailors; exactly what Rozhestvensky did not have.

Forty ships needed forty crews but most of the better quality Russian seamen were already serving in the Far East, or lying dead at the bottom of the Yellow Sea. What Rozhestvensky got were mainly conscripts and peasants of low intelligence and limited experience of life. These were backed up by old reservists or merchant sailors forcibly transferred from the Mercantile Marine. Even worse, some of the men who now made up the fleet had been recently released from prison before being summarily added to the roll. Even the best and most intelligent of Russian sailors had poor technical knowledge and skills; for these men they were practically non-existent.

When the crews began to assemble it was also discovered that many of them were active or, at best, incipient revolutionaries and Marxists. Their chief interest in the expedition seemed to be to ensure that it failed, with the result that sabotage and deliberate destruction were common occurrences on most of the ships.

The engineer commander of the *Oryol*, a man by the name of Vasilieff, owned a large library of left-wing literature which he was happy to loan out to anyone who displayed an interest in the topic. The 'library' was well used. The call for revolutionary reform in Russia was already strong: on board a self-contained and isolated warship, miles from home and safety, the feelings were twice as powerful. '"If we gained a victory over the Japanese," one of them (the crew) wrote, "we should hinder the revolution, which was the only hope of the country."'[3]

Despite Rozhestvensky's best efforts a sense of depression and gloom soon settled over the 2nd Pacific Fleet. Much of it was centred on fear of the British and the power of the Royal Navy. It was apparently so strong, hanging like a shroud over the Kronstadt Naval Base and St Petersburg, that most of the sailors developed the firm belief that while the czar and their admiral might be full of hope, they knew they would not be returning from this voyage.

It was a time of rumour and gossip, most of the stories having just enough credibility to make them possible. Britain had built six torpedo boats for Japan, said those 'in the know', and since the outbreak of war those vessels had disappeared. Obviously they were lurking in remote inlets along the Swedish coast, ready to sweep out and attack Rozhestvensky's great armada as it lumbered past.

Some of the stories were so bizarre as to be unbelievable; except that they were believed by dozens of uneducated and naïve Russian sailors. Japanese officers hiding on rocky headlands with portable torpedoes that could be launched from the shore; briquettes of coal with holes for explosive charges to be dropped inside; squadrons of Japanese torpedo boats and destroyers waiting and showing no ensigns or colours in the ports of Britain and Sweden: those were just some of the more imaginative tales.

Laughable in hindsight, in 1904 the stories appeared to be very real. The thought of adding pieces of coal stuffed full of explosives to red hot and blazing furnaces was enough to make any engine room stoker blanch with fear.

Secret agents or spies, most of them amateurs operating on a 'no information, no fee' basis, happily supplied these lurid scare stories. Most of the information originated in the local taverns or dockside cafés. Invariably they centred on a potential ambush by Anglo-Japanese torpedo boats in exotically named places like the Red Sea, the Indian Ocean or the waters off Alexandria. There was even the fear of a combined British-Japanese attack in the Baltic. How the Japanese, resourceful as they were, had managed to sail tiny torpedo boats halfway around the world – in record breaking time – was never explained, but it made a good story, and while it may have been utter nonsense the Russian sailors heard it, repeated it and believed it to be one hundred per cent true.

Even experienced officers who should have known better were consumed by fear and, more importantly, were not averse to sharing their opinions. Just before departure Captain Bukhvostov of the *Alexander III* addressed well-wishers with a few doom-laden words: 'There will be no victory. I am afraid we will lose half the squadron on our way to the Far East. If this does not happen the Japanese will annihilate us. Their ships are better and they are real sailors. I can promise you one thing: we will all die but never surrender.'[4]

It was all depressing stuff but not half as worrying as the fleet that had been hastily cobbled together. In total, Rozhestvensky had forty-two ships, a number that, on paper at least, seemed more than capable of defeating Admiral Togo. The number went up and down as the expedition progressed and ships were left behind or discharged. But this seemed to be a reasonable start. It was only when they were looked at closely that the deficiencies of the fleet became apparent.

Even the four new Borodinos were not quite what they seemed. Armed with four massively powerful 12-in guns set in turrets fore and aft and backed up with dozens of small calibre secondary or close range weapons, Rozhestvensky's flagship *Suvorov* and her sister ships, the *Borodino*, *Alexander III* and the *Oryol*, appeared at first to be formidable machines of war.

However, during construction Russian designers had added more and more weight to the vessels. Sometimes it came in the shape of new equipment – range finders, wireless telegraphy material and so on – but mainly it could be seen in the form of extra officers' quarters and accommodation, all above the waterline. Luxurious cabins and saloons for the officer class – most of who came from aristocratic backgrounds – were an important prerequisite in the czar's navy. Ratings could live in squalor, but not the officers.

What that meant for the *Suvorov* and the rest of the Borodinos was an incredible top heaviness that made them unwieldy and, many experts felt, liable to capsize in gales or bad weather. The concern was so great that Rozhestvensky was even advised not to fly too much bunting for fear of what it might do to the stability of his ship.

The extra weight also reduced the freeboard, dropping the battleships deep in the water and consequently ensuring that most of their armour belt now lay below the waterline. Apart from minimising their protection this also reduced their speed and meant that the lower secondary armament of the battleships could not be used in heavy seas. The issue of speed was to become a decisive factor in the months ahead, particularly when it came to battle.

> Admiral Togo had an advantage of six or seven knots over Admiral Rozhestvensky. This enabled him to stay at the greater range at which his gun crews had been trained. Eventually, he was able to execute the classic naval manoeuvre, crossing the Russian "T," bringing all his guns to bear on the ships at the head of the Russian line.[5]

The four Borodinos made up the first squadron, or division, of Rozhestvensky's fleet and came under his direct command. The czar loved them and considered them unbeatable, but from the beginning Rozhestvensky could see their faults. Whatever Czar Nicholas thought about them, Rozhestvensky could sense that they would be no match for Togo and his fleet which had, unlike the Russian vessels, already been in action.

Rozhestvensky might distrust his ships but most of the sailors, particularly the newly enlisted men, were in awe of the large battleships. Even more experienced seamen could not help finding them impressive. Paymaster's Steward Alexei Novikoff-Priboy, a young man who had been present at the Battle of the Yellow Sea, served on the *Oryol* and later wrote a book on the expedition:

> The battleship *Oryol* seemed to me a giant ... It was painted black, not only the armour plate that invested the hull but the superstructure as well. There were twin turrets fore and aft, armed with 12 inch guns, and three turrets on either beam, carrying 6 inch guns ... Two stages higher was a battery deck fitted with 75 millimetre quick firing guns to deal with torpedo boats.[6]

Another relatively new battleship, the *Oslyabya*, was the flagship of Admiral Felkersam who took charge of the 2nd Division. He was supported by the older battleships *Sisoy Veliky* and *Navarin* and the armoured cruiser *Admiral Nakjimov*.

The *Suvorov* and her sister ships, even with the disadvantage of extra weight, were still able to make fifteen knots, which at the time was considered a reasonable rate of speed, albeit far slower than the Japanese battleships which regularly operated at speeds of over twenty knots. However, the ships of Rozhestvensky's 2nd Division were lucky if they could get up to half that speed, even with a following wind and a calm sea.

Four of Rozhestvensky's cruisers were fast and modern: the *Aurora*, *Oleg*, *Zhemchug* and *Izumrud*. Others were considerably older and slower, some of them nothing more than fast yachts with little or no armour or guns. They were placed under the command of Admiral Oskar Enkvist, flying his flag in the *Oleg*. Five auxiliary cruisers and nine destroyer/torpedo boats, each a mere 350 tons, made up the bulk of the fleet.

For most of the voyage, particularly in seas that were likely to be rough – and there would be plenty of those – the tiny torpedo boats would have to be towed by cruisers or even by the capital ships. Even so, they would continually take on water and the process of towing would inevitably reduce the overall speed of the fleet.

In addition to the warships there were more than a few unusual vessels. These included a couple of tugs, an icebreaker, a refrigeration vessel, the repair ship *Kamchatka* and the hospital ship *Oryol*. To avoid confusion with the battleship of the same name, this second *Oryol* was always referred to by the nickname 'White Eagle'.

The Admiralty in St Petersburg wanted to add even more old ships to Rozhestvensky's force, subscribing to the notion that quantity was a lot better than quality. Rozhestvensky held firm. The old coastal battleships that Czar Nicholas and the Higher Naval Board of the Admiralty were intending to bestow on him would, he claimed, simply slow down the fleet. Obtaining enough coal was going to be difficult enough as it was without the addition of even more 'coal guzzlers'.

Coaling at sea would have to be done at least thirty or maybe even forty times during the voyage, and now the friendship of the czar and the kaiser did at last seem to be paying dividends. The Russians soon signed a contract with the Hamburg-Amerika Line, a German shipping company that would supply sixty colliers and coal the fleet, as required, all the way to Port Arthur. The shipping company was well paid for its services, although the coal it provided was not always of the best quality. Friendship clearly went only so far.

> Rozhestvensky was to insinuate his way into neutral ports as and when he could; when this was impossible, the coal was to be shipped, sack by sack, ton by ton, from colliers to warships hove-to on the ocean and to be deposited from the Russian sailors' backs into the bunkers.[7]

With Russia almost totally devoid of allies the idea of Rozhestvensky 'insinuating his way into neutral ports' was soon to be revealed as a pipe dream. More and more the admiral was reduced to coming to a halt at sea and doing the best that was possible in exceptionally trying circumstances.

Rozhestvensky knew most, if not all, of his immediate subordinates. Some had served with him in the past, others had trained with him. Both rear admirals, Felkersam and Enkvist, had passed out from the Naval Academy at roughly the same time as him. Some he liked; others he did not.

One of the latter was Admiral Oskar Enkvist who had gained his command of the cruiser detachment through family influence rather than ability. Although charming and debonair, he was generally considered by his colleagues and by his sailors to be inept. Rozhestvensky considered him a political opportunist and refused to allow him any form of independent command.

Keeping Enkvist close meant that once the voyage began, the man who was supposedly in charge of the cruisers was denied the freedom and flexibility to roam. This was unfortunate and made the cruiser detachment something of a liability as scouting and sweeping the seas for the enemy was one of the roles for which the fast modern cruisers had been designed.

Enkvist and his squadron were even forced to make the long haul down the length of West Africa and around the Cape of Good Hope, along with the battleships and auxiliaries, rather than take the short route through the Suez Canal. Because of his lack of trust, Rozhestvensky was denying himself the advantages that should have been his, had he only considered using the cruiser squadron appropriately.

Rozhestvensky was not particularly fond of Felkersam either. Officially second-in-command of the fleet, Felkersam was short and corpulent. He did not inspire confidence and long before the fleet sailed Rozhestvensky had called him 'a manure sack'. He did not want to leave Enkvist out when it came to abusing his comrades. He was, Rozhestvensky said, 'a vast empty space'.

And so, having gathered together his ships and the crews, there seemed to be little more that the admiral could do. At the end of August 1904 Rozhestvensky boarded the *Suvorov* in the Kronstadt roads off St Petersburg and formally assumed command of the fleet.

* * *

Rozhestvensky was not yet prepared to sail; at least not for the Far East. Despite dozens of messages from the Admiralty and from the royal palace, all wishing him a good voyage and success against the enemy, the briefest of inspections told Rozhestvensky that his ships and crews were still far from ready. It was, however, time to leave Kronstadt.

On 30 August Rozhestvensky and the fleet transferred to Reval. Known to the local Estonians by its traditional name of Tallinn, the city was romantic and beautiful, seeming more like the setting for an ancient fairy tale than the temporary home of the new 2nd Pacific Fleet.

Reval was a peaceful environment and the families and friends of the fleet soon gathered in its hotels and guesthouses for one last meeting before their loved ones departed for foreign climes; officers' families only, of course. Regular shore leave, receptions and farewell parties in the hotels of Reval were soon the order of the day.

Not so for Rozhestvensky. Over the next seven weeks he regularly took his ships to sea on what were known as 'shakedown cruises'; short trips where the sailors were put through a wide range of tests and training. It was late, possibly too late, but he made sure that as much as possible was dealt with in this brief and in-depth period. Everything he could think of was covered.

From steering while under enemy fire to launching lifeboats at sea, from gunnery exercises to releasing torpedoes, Rozhestvensky had the sailors doing it all. He even had his men taking over the jobs of imagined dead colleagues as well as gaining knowledge of semaphore and use of the new wireless telegraphy. The results were not encouraging.

Rozhestvensky worked his crews tirelessly, beginning in the early morning and sometimes not finishing until midnight was long past. It was small wonder that the officers and sailors looked forward to their times off duty when they could take the leave boats to the welcoming town of Reval. Then it would be somebody else's turn to work their fingers to the bone and endure the wrath of the admiral.

If ordinary setbacks annoyed 'Mad Dog' Rozhestvensky and caused him to deposit his binoculars in the ocean the performance of the 2nd Pacific Fleet during these 'shakedown cruises' must have driven him to despair. Keeping on station, moving in close formation, laying mines; all of the usual prerequisites of a sailor's day were skills that were proving almost impossible to grasp. But worst of all was gunnery. The new gunners repeatedly failed to hit their targets and when Rozhestvensky, the doyen of Russian naval gunnery, ordered night firing exercises he almost tore out his hair at the results. What Rozhestvensky and his staff were trying to achieve in a few short weeks normally took sailors years to master; with this lot, one old sailor was heard to remark, it would take a lifetime.

It was not easy to convince senior officers at the Admiralty that the ineptitude of the sailors was no more than mere inexperience. The disobedience, the mistakes, the failure to learn even basic naval tactics and techniques must, the men in the Admiralty believed, be deliberate. They had to be down to the revolutionary elements in the fleet.

At a time of major subversive energy in the empire it was easy to see the hands of revolutionaries in every setback. The views of the aristocratic officer class had not changed but the 'dark masses' were rumbling with discontent:

> The gathering revolutionary momentum had its primary cause in the character of young Nicholas and his inner caucus of diehard reactionaries ... who believed that the uneducated masses were unfit, and should remain unfit, for any sort of responsibility in their own welfare, government and future.[8]

There were times when this judgement by those with power seemed more than a little justified. It was perhaps inevitable in the rigid, rule-laden regimes of the Imperial Navy, particularly for the officers. Even men like Rozhestvensky, whose origins were decidedly middle class, must have been concerned about the growing power of the proletariat, both on and off his ships.

Meanwhile the training continued. A mock torpedo attack against the flagship was launched one night in September as the *Suvorov* lay at anchor off Reval. Rozhestvensky waited until everyone was asleep or bedded down, and then the alarm was sounded. There was no response. Ten minutes later a few sleepy heads emerged from the odd companionway, but by and large still no one had appeared on deck. The crew, officers and sailors were all sound asleep.

Prepared or not, departure could not be delayed indefinitely. After several weeks enjoying the facilities of Reval the fleet sailed back to St Petersburg where, anchored off the naval base of Kronstadt, they began the last stage of preparations; taking on supplies and ammunition.

It took several days to load everything, but eventually all of the salt meat, dried vegetables, biscuits and other provisions were safely on board. So, too, were the shells for the mighty 12-in guns and bullets for rifles and other smaller weapons. Champagne and vodka – for officers' consumption only – were carefully locked into the wardrooms.

Provisioning over, Rozhestvensky set about moving the fleet back to Reval where the formal farewells were to be made. Thousands of men and women gathered on the embankments at Kronstadt to wave Russian flags, sing patriotic songs and shout encouragement. And yet it remained an emotional time. Try as they might, many of the spectators found it impossible to cheer, just as it was impossible to prevent shivers of fear from running down their backs. Haunting and elegiac, the tragic sobs and sighs of departure echoed across the waves.

For some lucky wives and mothers there was the chance of one last embrace. With a little time to waste, pinnaces carried the officers from ships to shore for a few precious extra and unofficial moments of final leave taking. Once again, it was officers only, the ordinary sailors having to content themselves with waving to their recently acquired girlfriends from the local tap rooms and bars. The Kronstadt women had at least made the journey to the waterfront and their presence swelled the crowd enormously.

The ship's whistles soon summoned the men back on board and the last pinnaces cast off from shore, heading out towards the giant warships that were moored like dark, grey phantoms in the centre of the waterway. Then, slowly, the lines between the battleships and the towing tugs grew taut, white water churned at their sterns and the vessels began to move towards the sea.

Rozhestvensky was still not happy. Despite weeks of preparation and training several of his ships were far from ready. He had considered waiting for them but the skills of the Kronstadt dockyard workers did not fill him with confidence and the longer he delayed the greater the chance of desertion. The delayed ships would simply have to catch up with him. There was, however, worse to come.

While the first three Borodinos were towed safely down channel, the battleship *Oryol* somehow managed to run aground on a mud bank. Her captain had apparently not taken soundings, relying on the tug skippers to do it for him.

The grounding was hardly a major calamity and certainly caused little damage to the *Oryol* but there were many in the fleet who viewed the accident as a bad omen. They had not left Russia and already things were going wrong. Rozhestvensky ground his teeth in fury but at least he did not throw any binoculars over the side.

A hasty salvage operation met with limited success and the port authorities were reduced to ordering the crew, all 900 of them, to run from one side of the ship to the other in an attempt to rock the *Oryol* free of the glutinous mud. It failed but the exercise was a moment of surprising good humour, possibly even hysteria for the sailors. As they ran, laughing, from port beam to starboard and then back again many of them shouted to their comrades, telling them not to rock the ship too much in case she fell apart.

The following day the *Oryol* was still grounded. It was twenty-four hours before hastily summoned dredgers managed to finally dig a channel to allow her off the mud bank. Late but not forgotten, the *Oryol* was soon bidding Kronstadt goodbye and chasing her sister ships en route to Reval.

At Reval the sailors were turned to what they usually did in port; cleaning the ships. Regardless of the danger and destruction that lay ahead, the ships of the 2nd Pacific Fleet would at least be well scrubbed and polished. In the words of one sailor: 'Again and again we washed the gangways with soap and water, we scrubbed the bridges, touched up the paint ... cleanliness became a mania.'[21]

This time, however, there was some purpose to the scrubbing and cleaning. Ever mindful of his duty, the czar arrived at Reval, always one of his favourite cities and holiday destinations. He came by train on 9 October, soon after Rozhestvensky had docked, and with his royal yacht waiting for him he visited as many of the ships as possible in these last few hours. Purposefully, diligently, the czar witnessed and inspected everything from battleships to torpedo boats. In all he managed to climb on board no fewer than twenty-two of the vessels and speak to the officers on every one.

Czar Nicholas was exultant, convinced that the rescue mission to Port Arthur would be a success. Even Rozhestvensky's final words to him failed to upset the czar's good humour. On being wished good luck by his emperor the admiral simply stated that by the time he reached Port Arthur the ships of the 1st Pacific Fleet would probably no longer exist. Nicholas might have wondered about Rozhestvensky's state of mind but he said nothing.

Regardless of his words Rozhestvensky certainly cut a fine figure, his powerful frame and salt-and-pepper beard seeming to ooze confidence, whatever he might say and think about the mission with which he had been entrusted. Just to look at him and his fine array of towering warships, Czar Nicholas felt safe and happy. The man and his fleet inspired confidence, not just in the czar but also in the people of St Petersburg and, hopefully, all of the men under his command. Soon the slight that Nicholas had been forced to endure all those years ago in Otsu would be revenged.

In contrast to the admiral, Rozhestvensky's two subordinates – the short and rather corpulent Admiral Felkersam, and Admiral Enkvist, who seemed more concerned about his flowing white beard than about the mission – seemed to fade into insignificance when placed alongside him. According to his advisors and staff officers, who seemed to have their ears pressed firmly to the ground, most of the fleet felt the same: Felkersam was caring but weak while Enkvist was … just Enkvist.

Nicholas spent the night on his yacht and bade farewell to the fleet the following day, not for one minute thinking that he would never see his great warships again. Defeat to him was an inconceivable nightmare, and as an intensely religious man, God would surely be on his side.

As a final gesture the czar and his family presented the ships with religious icons while the Dowager Empress left mother-of-pearl crosses for those men who would be in the most exposed positions on the main deck and behind the guns during the battle. The crosses supposedly came from the church at Golgotha in Jerusalem.

The day after Nicholas departed Rozhestvensky also left Reval, heading now for the port and city of Libau. Once again there was a huge crowd gathered to see them off and once again there were tears and weeping from the anxious relatives whose emotions had only been heightened by the seemingly never-ending series of farewells.

It took Rozhestvensky two days to reach Libau, the final piece of Russian territory that the fleet would touch on its epic voyage. It held a significance for the men of the 2nd Pacific Fleet, a symbolism that reared like a giant mountain peak through the mist of Mother Russia.

The voyage so far had been more like a triumphal progress than the beginning of a trek to war and Rozhestvensky was glad when the seafront of Libau loomed up over the horizon. Some of the delayed ships finally caught up with him and his vessels took on more coal and provisions. It was the last opportunity to restock their supplies in friendly territory.

They had intended to leave Russian territorial waters on the afternoon of 15 October but two further accidents delayed them. Firstly, and much to the chagrin of the admiral, on the way out from port the flagship herself managed to hit the sea bottom. Rozhestvensky cursed and fumed, calling Libau 'an infernal harbour'. It was not a major problem, more of an embarrassment than anything else, but the *Suvorov* still had to be checked over for damage. Then the old battleship *Sisoy Veliky* lost her anchors and the fleet was forced to settle down for another night in Libau while the anchors were recovered and repairs made. Admiral Rozhestvensky, seemingly forgetting the mishandling of his flagship, fretted and paced the deck in fury while officers and crew made sure they stayed out of his way until morning.

Libau was a crowded anchorage and the Russian fleet was a very large one, herded together like frightened animals. The ships rocked in the swell, rubbing against each other in what somebody called a friendly embrace. Friendly embrace or not, this was the fleet's last encounter with its homeland. From here on danger would be a constant.

Very few of the ship's captains allowed their crews shore leave that night, fearing that with enough vodka or ale in their bellies most of the men would not return and simply head for home. They were probably quite correct in their assumptions.

For nearly everyone involved dawn could not come soon enough. There was a sense of anti-climax in the air as Rozhestvensky waited and his officers worried. 'Months of preparation and they still could not get it right', the admiral thought, but as with any great enterprise, waiting for it to begin was the worst part. Having got this far he had an all-consuming desire to be off and under way.

The 2nd Pacific Fleet, under a lowering sky and with a fine drizzle dampening the sailor's hats and new blue uniforms, finally left Libau on 16 October. There was no ceremony, and unlike their departure from Kronstadt and Reval, very few people stood on the shore to watch them go.

They sailed in four distinct groups. At the head Admiral Enkvist led out the cruisers, followed by Admiral Felkersam with the older battleships and Captain Yegoriev with the transports and auxiliary vessels. The final and most important group was made up of Rozhestvensky and his four new battleships.

Ahead of them stretched the unknown. Nobody knew when they would set foot on dry land again and, with the reports about ambushes still lingering in their minds, everyone wondered if Togo's battleships, cruisers and torpedo boats were out there waiting over the horizon. It was not a comforting thought..

Chapter 4

Early Disaster

On 18 October the 2nd Pacific Fleet anchored close to the Fakkjeberg lighthouse at the entrance to the Great Belt Straits. The Straits were the easiest way out of the Baltic to the North Sea, but the waterway was narrow, ideal for an attack by torpedo boats.

These were Danish territorial waters, but as Denmark was one of the few countries that were at least understanding of the Russian position it was an acceptable spot to pause. As everyone knew, the Dowager Empress Maria Federovna, Czar Nicholas's mother, was Danish and she was actually on holiday in her native country at this time.

This was the age of agents and interlopers; the days when men like Reilly, Ace of Spies first made their reputations. Every nation, small or great, employed spies and secret agents who were loved by their own side and roundly despised by the enemy.

The czar and his government had been receiving regular messages from a host of agents across Europe, notably from a man known by the name of Arkadiy Harting. A mysterious and dubious character, Harting seemed to move freely within the revolutionary and anarchist circles of the time. His real name remains a little unclear. It was either Abraham Hekkelmann or Abe Gekkelmann, but he also sometimes went under the name of Landerson.

This Jewish police agent – an unusual combination at this time of rampant anti-Semitism in Russia and many other European countries – had based himself in Copenhagen and had been officially tasked with protecting Rozhestvensky's fleet. With a fee of over 150,000 roubles a time, Harting knew that his reputation and future career as a secret agent depended on the quality of his information. He needed to make it worthwhile; and riveting.[1]

Consequently, Harting's messages to Nicholas, which were duly passed on to the fleet, and, by default, to the Russian public, were nothing short of disturbing. As ever they centred either on Japanese torpedo boats disguised as trawlers or armoured merchant cruisers pretending to ply an honest trade around the Baltic. As a result, by the time Rozhestvensky had reached the

Great Belt all of the Russian towns and villages along the Baltic Coast were on high alert.

Harting's latest report announced that two Japanese secret agents had recently attempted to hire a boat from one of the Danish ports but had been arrested and detained by the authorities. What these 'agents' were intending to do with the boat Harting did not know, but the czar should rest assured that, he would find out. Admiral Rozhestvensky did not need further warning with such tales. The journey from Libau had been fraught with enough difficulties to terrify any ordinary commander.

His ships were proving to be very unreliable and their crews more than a little truculent. The *Zhemchug* had lost a pair of davits and one of her cutters overboard while the destroyer *Bystry* had rammed the battleship *Oslyabya* when she was closing to pass on a message. The *Oslyabya* was not seriously damaged but the destroyer was forced to return to Libau for repairs.

Before sailing through the Great Belt Rozhestvensky ordered that the entrance to the straits be swept for mines, a difficult task for a fleet that included no minesweepers. However, the mechanics and fitters on the repair ship *Kamchatka* managed to adapt and cobble together fifty grappling hooks and a long length of chain to form a makeshift sweep.

The chain was then stretched between the tug *Roland* and the icebreaker *Yermak* which proceeded down the channel, sweeping the water for mines. Unfortunately, the two ships were poorly matched in power and speed, with the result that they failed to maintain an equal and consistent distance between themselves. Inevitably the chain soon broke. It was repaired and three more attempts were made, all with the same result. Rozhestvensky gave up. 'The passage is to be considered swept,' he signalled furiously to the fleet.

When the Danish port of Skagen was reached there was more bad news. The torpedo boat *Prozorlivy* reported that she had developed a permanent leak in her condensers and the *Sisoy Veliky* was now claiming that she needed serious repairs. Worst of all, however, was the icebreaker *Yermak*, one of the ships that had failed so dismally in trying to sweep for mines in the Great Belt.

Rozhestvensky had, on several occasions, fired blank charges across the bows of ships that had ignored or disobeyed his orders – and there were many such vessels – but the eccentric manoeuvrings of the *Yermak* annoyed him so much that he actually fired live shells in front of the badly commanded icebreaker. It was a dangerous trick to perform but it seemed to work, for a while at least.

At Skagen, Rozhestvensky had time to think and make decisions. He did not need troubles like this so early in the voyage and ordered the *Prozorlivy* and *Yermak* to return to Libau. Their captains needed no urging and headed back to Russia at a speed that made a mockery of their previous progress. It was relief for all concerned to see them go, and for Rozhestvensky and the crews of the two discarded ships in particular.

Torpedo boat sightings and scaremongering continued unabated. For the Russian sailors it seemed as if everyone was against them and all of the oceans of the world were filled with Japanese submarines or torpedo boats. There was even a sighting of two silvery balloons or Zeppelins in the distance, never seen again or acknowledged by any nation. To the Russian sailors, however, they were proof positive that the Japanese were watching their every move, even from the sky: 'The mass hallucinations on the part of the Russian crews are more suitable as the subject of a psychological study than military history. Against this background Rozhestvensky ordered that "no vessel of any sort whatever must be allowed to get in amongst the fleet."'[2] It was an important message, and one that the captains all took to heart. It was also a message that was going to have a dramatic effect on the entire fleet before too long.

While he was at Skagen Rozhestvensky learned, to his delight, that the czar had promoted him to the rank of vice admiral. He nearly did not receive the message as the two fishermen detailed to take the telegram out to the waiting Russian ships were almost blown out of the water by the trigger happy gunners on the *Suvorov*.

Most of the ships took the opportunity to restock on coal while they were at Skagen. Beyond the port lay the North Sea – British-controlled territory – and the last thing any of the ships' captains wanted was to run short of coal in this hostile environment. But just before midnight on 19 October Rozhestvensky ordered all coaling to stop and signalled that the fleet should depart immediately. Japanese torpedo boats had been spotted in the North Sea.

* * *

It was the moment of truth; the news that everyone had been expecting and dreading for the past few months. Nobody questioned the intelligence; they simply accepted it at face value. The Japanese were there and they would have to be dealt with.

Rozhestvensky had divided his fleet into the usual four squadrons, although their order of sailing was different: battleships new, battleships old, cruisers and auxiliaries. The four squadrons were to sail independently across the North Sea and down the English Channel, keeping a distance of fifty miles between themselves, something of a forlorn hope given the inadequacies of the crews. They would hopefully all rendezvous in Tangiers, on the coast of Morocco, but if an attack did come then the dispositions Rozhestvensky had made would mean that at least some of the fleet would survive.

It was an anxious few hours as the ships slowly made their way through the Skagerrak. The night sky was cloudless, the sea beautifully serene and visibility excellent. The further they went without any hint or threat of attack the happier Rozhestvensky felt.

By dawn the four divisions were out of the narrow Skagerrak and into the North Sea but there was no lessening of tension. The reason was simple; weather conditions had changed. The sea was now cloaked in a thick covering of fog and visibility was down to almost zero. At times the officers and watch keepers on the bridge of the flagship felt they were alone in the middle of some dark Russian folk tale. They were able to see their colleagues on the quarter deck only as hazy shadows of their former selves and the most superstitious of the crew quickly crossed themselves and prayed that it was not an omen.

Ship's foghorns wailed out a mournful and discordant wall of noise, bouncing and rebounding off the fog banks like echoes in a mountain pass. They were so loud, so strident, that some of the sailors thought they would surely alert the Japanese torpedo boats. The more experienced men knew better. 'If they can find us in this pea souper,' one old hand remarked, 'then they deserve to put a torpedo into our belly.'

By noon a brisk wind had sprung up, clearing the fog and showing that the first two divisions were certainly not fifty miles apart but were hugging tightly to each other as a way of finding comfort and security. Enkvist's cruisers were out of sight somewhere ahead of the battleships, supposedly scouting out the enemy, and the auxiliaries were trying desperately to keep formation in the rear. The fleet was now scattered across the otherwise empty sea with no torpedo boats and no passing vessels anywhere in sight.

And then the signal that everyone had been dreading finally arrived. The repair ship *Kamchatka*, already beginning to take over the mantle of fleet clown from the discarded *Yermak*, seemed to have disappeared in the night. No one could contact her or raise her, then suddenly the wireless telegraphy on the *Suvorov* crackled into wakefulness. It was the *Kamchatka* and she was signalling frantically: 'Chased by torpedo boats.'

As Rozhestvensky tried to assimilate the news more messages came flooding in from the missing repair ship. The messages were alarming but they were also somewhat vague. Rozhestvensky angrily demanded to know how many torpedo boats were attacking and from which direction they were coming. There was a delay of several minutes before the *Kamchatka* responded with 'About eight and from all directions.'

Rozhestvensky's next request was to know if the torpedo boats had fired any torpedoes. Another pause, then the reply, 'We haven't seen any.' Repeated requests from the repair ship for the *Suvorov* to inform her of the fleet position were refused for fear of the Japanese listening in. Then the *Kamchatka* announced that she was heading east to avoid the enemy. Furious, Rozhestvensky ordered her to turn around and steam westward like the rest of the fleet.

There was a long silence before the Admiral tried again, 'Do you see any torpedo boats?' he cabled. Infuriatingly, the response was brief and confusing, 'We cannot see any.' Rozhestvensky almost beat his head in frustration. What sort of fools had the Admiralty given him, he asked himself, and turned once more to peer into the wall of North Sea darkness. The *Kamchatka* had gone quiet but given her recent history he was not unduly worried. She would turn up in due course, of that he was sure.

Just after midnight, as the fleet began to skirt around the crowded fishing area of Dogger Bank, the fog came back; not the all-consuming curtain that had covered them before but wisps and long tendrils that were strung out like an old man's beard. Rozhestvensky was not sure if it was a blessing or a curse. He knew that English trawlers would be working in the fishing grounds and, if the reports from Harting and the other spies were true, then it would be the ideal spot for the enemy torpedo boats to lurk. With luck the fog might just shield them.

Nagging away at the back of his brain was the incident with the *Kamchatka*. Was she really under attack or was it all a figment of the captain's over-fertile imagination? He glanced across at Captain Vasily Vasilievich Ignatzius, commander of the *Suvorov*, and at Clapier de Colongue, his chief of staff and right-hand man for the voyage. 'Keep your course,' he growled at them, before making his way to the admiral's chair at the back of the bridge. 'Wake me if you need to.' Ignatzius smiled at de Colongue and touched the peak of his cap as Rozhestvensky settled himself down and closed his eyes. The old man would never change, he told himself. No problem with that; at least you knew where you were with him. He had been up on the bridge for almost the whole time they had been at sea, pacing up and down and then catching the odd ten minutes of sleep in his chair. He would probably be still here, doing the same, when they reached Port Arthur.

At 01.00 watch keepers on the bridge of the *Suvorov* saw several boats approaching out of the gloom. They were small and showed no lights. Rozhestvensky, startled out of his doze, ordered an immediate change of course and screamed for the ship's searchlights to be switched on. Long beams of sudden light shot across the sea and up into the night sky.

As the bugles sounded for 'Action Stations' the lights of the other ships joined those of the *Suvorov*. Like rays of sunlight on a summer morning, they split the Heavens, picking out clouds and fog banks, turning the night to day. And then, with a roar louder than a thunderstorm on the Russian Steppes, somebody on the main deck of the *Suvorov* opened fire.

* * *

Within minutes every ship in the fleet was firing her guns, wildly and inaccurately, but firing nonetheless as weeks of pent-up emotion and stress finally found an outlet. Most of the gunners did not know what they were firing at or why. Some, however, later reported seeing dark shapes flitting in and out of view, hurrying between the searchlight beams, then slipping for cover behind other, larger vessels. Whether they were real or simply the product of heightened imagination – mass hysteria, perhaps – was, even then, unclear. For the sailors it did not matter. The Japanese torpedo boats were coming.

Flashes and the dull crump of small explosions told the Russians where shells and machine gun bullets had scored hits on their targets. Mostly, though, the shells simply fell into the sea or flew aimlessly away into the distance. Russian gunnery had clearly not improved since their training cruises off Reval.

Then, in the sweeping beam of the bow searchlight of the *Suvorov*, Rozhestvensky saw the outline of what he swore to the end of his days was a torpedo boat. But when the searchlight stabilised and focused on the target the admiral saw only a large trawler. The lurking Japanese vessel had clearly slipped away in the confusion.

Regardless of what had happened to the 'lurking torpedo boat', the trawler could only be British. Perhaps the other targets that had seemed so appealing to his gunners might also have been British? Rozhestvensky had no desire to create an international incident between Russia and a country that might nominally be an ally of Japan but was then maintaining a peaceful attitude towards his own. Stop while the going was good, he thought.

Rozhestvensky immediately ordered his ships to cease fire. The previously agreed signal to end night firing was to extinguish all searchlights apart from one on the flagship which would be directed upwards. It was effective but it was a slow process that demanded sailors on each ship keeping their eyes on the *Suvorov*.

Slowly, unwillingly, the gunfire stuttered to a stop. Officers and petty officers hauled the men away from the guns, but here and there another burst of firing broke the silence as sailors thought they saw darker shapes against the blackness of the sea. When that happened they fought like demons to get back to their weapons. At last all firing stopped, the silence ringing in their ears louder than church bells at Christmas time. Rozhestvensky breathed a sigh of relief, but the calm was short lived.

Suddenly, searchlights from the west stabbed into the night sky, accompanied by the crash of distant gunfire. Within a few seconds huge columns of water leapt into the air as shells landed alongside the *Suvorov*. Before anyone on the bridge could move, the flagship's 12-in turrets swivelled around and her guns boomed in response. Nobody had given the order but the gunners were clearly not taking any chances.

'Who ordered that?' Captain Ignatzius screamed. 'Who ordered you to fire?'

Even if they heard him no one answered. Then the *Suvorov*'s guns fired again. Whoever the enemy might be, his gunfire was incessant, if inaccurate, and more columns of water shot into the air alongside the long line of Russian ships. All of the fleet was now under attack.

'That's not torpedo boats,' snarled Rozhestvensky, ducking as another fountain of water shot into the air, drenching the bridge and everyone on it. Ignatzius did not answer. Like the admiral, he could see that the incoming shells were from heavy guns. Clearly the Japanese were not just attacking with torpedo boats but were now adding cruisers or even battleships to the fray. Salvo after salvo crashed out as the Russian battleships fired blindly into the night.

Then wireless signals from a clearly terrified Admiral Enkvist were picked up. The supposed enemy weren't Japanese cruisers; they were Russian, part of their own fleet. Enkvist should have been fifty miles ahead of the *Suvorov* but instead he was here, within range of the flagship and adding to the confusion. Rozhestvensky realised that they were firing at their own ships and immediately ordered his gunners to cease fire. Reluctantly, they complied.

A few searchlights from the *Borodino* and the other leading ships still cut into the sky but at least the firing had stopped. Enkvist had ceased firing as well and had now taken up position some two or three miles ahead of the battleships. The Japanese torpedo boats seemed to have disappeared. Maybe, just maybe, they had all been sunk.

The friendly fire between the battleships and Enkvist's cruisers had caused the first Russian casualties of the expedition. The chaplain on the *Aurora* was hit by a shell. As one laconic Russian officer declared, it passed through his cabin and then through him. Another sailor was seriously wounded and later died, but there were no casualties on any of the battleships.

The whole of the Dogger Bank Incident, from firing at what even Rozhestvensky had to later admit were British trawlers to being attacked by their own cruiser squadron, had been utterly ridiculous. It would have been funny if it had not been so tragic. Only the ineptitude of the Russian gunners had limited the damage and kept casualties low. The *Oryol* had fired 500 rounds and had hit precisely nothing. It did not auger well for the future.

The fleet powered on, leaving behind wisps of gunsmoke and shattered fishing smacks, not for one moment considering the damage they might have done to the trawlers which, in everyone's mind, had been simply covering the torpedo boats. Fear of another attack was the main emotion and, rather than close in to look for survivors – from torpedo boats and/or trawlers – Rozhestvensky ordered full speed ahead. He needed to get away from the danger as quickly as possible.

The engines increased their revolutions and as the decks trembled beneath the feet of the Russian sailors there was a palpable easing of tension. Everyone had his own story to tell: the hits he had scored on the Japanese craft; the torpedo trails that had travelled down the side of his ship, missing their mark by inches; the dark shapes of the tiny Japanese vessels as they hugged the sides of the protecting trawlers. The decks of all the battleships, from the *Borodino* to the *Oryol*, were awash with the sound of semi-hysterical voices: 'Not one had seen less than a dozen enemy torpedo boats darting in and out of the shell fire, caught and lost again in the white pin-points of the searchlight beams ... the enemy had attacked in force and had been beaten off.'[3]

The panic that had erupted on all of the ships was immediately forgotten. No one cared to remember that some sailors on the auxiliaries, not used to combat conditions, had actually drawn cutlasses and, wearing life jackets, were running wildly around the decks of their ships convinced that the Japanese were boarding their vessels.

Nobody even gave a second's thought to the claims of some sailors that torpedoes had already smashed into the sides of the battleships. And the rumours that some men from the *Borodino* had actually leapt over the side in an effort to escape from the attacking Japanese were quickly pushed down into the recesses of distant memory.

For the Russian Fleet there was no more action that night although no one slept for fear of another attack. They did encounter another group of trawlers on the edge of the Dogger Bank but powering now at full speed they simply carved their way through the trawls of the fishermen and disappeared over the horizon.

By mid-morning of 23 October the fleet had reached the entrance to the English Channel. There were still fog patches but enough visibility for the sailors to glimpse the legendary White Cliffs of Dover some four or five miles off the starboard beam. Their interest was reciprocated by the thousands of men, women and children who had hastened to the south coast of England to catch a glimpse of the enormous Russian warships they had heard so much about.

News of the attack on the fishing boats had not yet circulated in Britain and the watching crowd was in awe of the fleet that seemed to stretch away, mile after mile, to the east. With their gigantic superstructure and bright yellow funnels, ships like the *Suvorov* were exotic and marvellous. Nobody had ever seen anything like this before and most of the spectators assumed that they would never do so again.

At one point the older battleships from the 2nd Division came to a halt off Brighton's Palace Pier. They anchored alongside waiting colliers, and spent three hours taking on coal. Later in the afternoon the *Suvorov* and her sister ships repeated the performance before hauling in their anchors and disappearing into the mist.

It was another four days before Rozhestvensky and the ships of his 1st Division anchored, as ordered by St Petersburg, at the Spanish naval station of Vigo. Rozhestvensky ordered the older battleships of the 2nd Division and Enkvist's cruisers to sail on and wait for him at Tangier.

It was while he was at Vigo that the admiral first heard the news that had been keeping the people of Europe on the edge of their seats for the past few days. The Russian Pacific Fleet had shelled not enemy torpedo craft but unarmed and innocent fishing boats belonging to the British Empire. War between Russia and Britain seemed highly likely.

* * *

The fishing fleet that Rozhestvensky had attacked – the Gamecock Fleet as it was known – came from the port of Hull. They had left harbour on 19 October and reached their fishing grounds on the Dogger Bank within thirty-six hours. Fishing began on 21 October, with the catch being quickly transferred to the fleet's carrier, the steam vessel *Magpie*, to be taken back to Hull while it was still fresh.

Just after midnight on 21–22 October lookouts on the trawlers reported the lights of a large squadron of warships approaching from the east. The logical assumption was that they were British, the vessels of Charles Beresford's Channel Fleet returning to port after an exercise. But the ships were ignoring the warning lights of the trawlers and even green flares fired from the trawler *Ruff* failed to make the approaching ships change course or reduce speed.

Almost till the last moment the trawler men continued to believe that these were British ships on some sort of training exercise. To watch that for a while would be an interesting and unusual diversion but when the truth dawned it was a rude awakening:

> The faces of the sailors could be seen. I called all hands on deck to witness what I thought was going to be a brilliant spectacle. Then the galley funnel of the *Mino* was hit. Good God, this wasn't blanks. Lie down lads and look after yourselves.[4]

When the searchlights of the Russian Fleet suddenly flashed on and shells began to plummet into the sea around the leading trawlers there was immediate panic on the boats. The trawls were cut and full steam ahead was ordered, direction immaterial; anywhere as long as it was heading away from those all-seeing searchlights. Still the shells came hammering down and some were now finding their mark.

Several fishermen held up large plaice and haddock, shouting and screaming at the tops of their voices, to show that they were fishing boats going about their lawful business. It made no difference, the gunfire continued.

The *Suvorov* was now barely a hundred yards distant from the outer ring of trawlers and even the appallingly bad Russian gunners could hardly miss at that range. The trawler *Crane* was taking most of the fire, her skipper and the third hand being early victims, decapitated by the shells. Out of a crew of nine, all but the skipper's son, who just happened to be making his first voyage, were injured by shells and shrapnel. As the Russian fleet powered away into the darkness, the *Crane* began to sink.

Several of the trawlers had been badly damaged and it was slow progress as the Gamecock Fleet began to straggle away and head back to port. Led by the battered *Moulmein*, they eventually limped into Hull a day later, flying their pennants at half-mast.

The hospital ship of the Mission to Seamen, a vessel by the name of *Joseph and Sara Miles*, had been accompanying the trawler fleet that night. According to the Mission surgeon, Dr Anklesari, the death and destruction on the fishing boats had been horrendous. Before she sank the doctor rowed across to the *Crane* and later described what he had seen:

> I have never witnessed such a gory sight. Two men lay on deck with their heads nearly blown to pieces. In the cabin the scene was more heart rending still when I saw six men stretched about anyhow, bleeding and groaning with the agony of their wounds ... I had them removed to our ship.[5]

With most of the seriously wounded men from the *Crane* and other trawlers on board, the *Joseph and Sara Miles* reversed course and headed for Hull. Her greater speed meant that she arrived in port ahead of the fishing boats. As a consequence, an alerted population had gathered to wait for their sons and husbands on the dockside.

As news of the unprovoked attack spread, a huge wave of anger and indignation began to grow. It simmered, slowly at first, then strengthened and finally erupted amongst the inhabitants of Hull. Soon it had moved on beyond the boundaries of the port to the whole of the British people: 'The surprise attack on the Russian Fleet in the harbour of Port Arthur by Japan, England's ally, angered the Russians. Admiral Rozhestvensky's sinking of British fishing trawlers on the Dogger Bank outraged Britain.'[6]

Almost as soon as they reached port, a deputation of fishermen were gathered together and travelled to London to make an official protest to the Foreign Office. When asked for proof of the attack their response was blunt, 'It's back in Hull, two headless trunks.' The death toll increased to three when a wounded fisherman succumbed to his injuries, but the real damage to the fishing fleet could hardly be measured. Men's livelihoods had been threatened, maybe even destroyed by what was clearly an act of barbarity from a country that nobody had ever trusted.

The press seized on the attack – the 'Dogger Bank Incident' as they named it – whipping up public outrage and demanding retribution, though the British public did not require much whipping up. Newspapers were happy to give as much publicity as possible to the attack. Even King Edward VII was furious at what had gone on. The defeats in the recent Boer War had been bad enough but now it seemed as if everybody felt they could take advantage of the wounded British lion. The Royal Navy would soon exact revenge.

There were demonstrations in Trafalgar Square and the Russian ambassador was soundly booed as he left his residence in London. The same crowds that had originally flocked to Brighton, Dover and other places on the south coast in order to gain the briefest of glimpses of the Russian ships now turned their interest into anger.

What really upset everybody was not so much the firing at the Hull trawlers as the fact that the Russians had committed the outrage and then sailed blissfully away. They did not attempt to search for survivors or offer help in any way. It was the direct antithesis of the British people's view of themselves as charitable, honest and caring individuals.

For the British press and for most of the population such behaviour merely reinforced their image of the Russian Empire, commonly referred to as 'the Russian Bear', as coarse and dangerous. After all, hadn't they been threatening the North West Frontier of India for years? Clearly something had to be done about this uncivilised and loutish lot.

* * *

News of the incident reached the czar when he was out hunting. His initial feeling was that the British were overreacting. Their demand for an explanation and an apology – not to mention an assurance that the officers responsible for the outrage would be detained and dealt with – was, the czar felt, taking things a stage too far. After all, it had been only a few fishing boats, which had, after all, been guilty of an act of war, carefully shielding and concealing Japanese torpedo craft.

Never the most understanding of men when views conflicted with his own, Nicholas soon took to calling the British 'our filthy enemies'. He was in awe of his uncle, King Edward VII but insulting him and his nation – behind his back – was quite acceptable. It was an emotion that was mirrored in the hearts and minds of many Russian soldiers and sailors. Unlike the czar, they did not have to worry about protocol or the political situation:

> The famous North Sea Incident which has just happened and about which so much noise has been made has, in fact, shown that our

apprehensions were well founded, and we offer our most sincere thanks to our brave sailors for the watchfulness they have shown ... Our sailors have always shown a distrust of the English fishermen. It has been seen that the Russian sailors were in no mood for a joke.[7]

And yet, despite his personal feelings, Czar Nicholas knew that he and his country were balancing on the edge of a very steep precipice that led only to a drop of unfathomable depths. It would not take very much to push them all into the chasm.

By 26 October the Royal Navy was on a war footing and had assembled twenty-eight battleships from the Home Fleet, all with steam up. The Mediterranean Fleet had been gathered together from stations all across the 'inland sea' and ordered to assemble at Gibraltar.

Huge pre-dreadnoughts like the *Hannibal*, *Mars* and *Caesar*, pride of the Royal Navy, now threatened Rozhestvensky's fleet. They were fully armed and all of them more than a match for any of the Russian vessels. Dozens of cruisers and destroyers carefully shadowed the Russians down the Channel and across the Bay of Biscay to Vigo, while the battleships lumbered in their wake.

At Vigo, while nervous and angry telegrams, letters and telephone calls flew between the diplomats of Russia and Great Britain, Admiral Rozhestvensky set about preparing to coal his ships. The level of coal in their bunkers was dangerously low and the German colliers waiting at the port were a welcome relief. Rozhestvensky eagerly ordered them to come alongside the battleships.

However, things did not go as smoothly as the admiral had hoped. The Spanish authorities, conscious of the dangerous situation, signalled the *Suvorov* that, in line with international agreements, she and her cohorts would be allowed only twenty-four hours in neutral waters. More significantly, they refused Rozhestvensky permission to take on coal or supplies of any sort.

With the British warships now anchored off Vigo, just a few miles distant from his own warships, Rozhestvensky undoubtedly felt trapped. Even if St Petersburg ordered it, he could not sail out to engage them simply because he did not have the fuel. He had put his head in a noose and now the Russian Admiralty was ordering him to stay at Vigo until enquiries into the Dogger Bank Incident were finished.

Rozhestvensky ordered the colliers to stand by in case they were needed to start transferring coal. Then, on the second day, the Spanish relented.

With the ships of the Home Fleet hovering outside their territorial waters they felt safe in granting such favours. Coaling could begin immediately.

Now that he had time, Rozhestvensky sent a detailed report on the Dogger Bank affair to the czar. His defence was the obvious one, that the fishing fleet had concealed Japanese torpedo boats in their midst. Despite this, he regretted the deaths and the damage he had caused even if it was, as he put it, an action where 'no warship could have acted otherwise'.

Criticism of the Russians continued in the British and world press although it had, by now, assumed a more restrained tone and the call for outright war seemed to have evaporated somewhat. At the end of October *The Times of London*, in an editorial that was critical but not inflammatory, commented that: 'It is almost inconceivable that any men calling themselves seamen, however frightened they might be, could spend twenty minutes bombarding a fleet of fishing boats without discovering the nature of their target.'[8]

Coaling of the Russian ships went on throughout the fleet's second day and night in Vigo, the crews motivated more by the promise of two extra tots of vodka per man than by the message of support that the *Suvorov* had received from Czar Nicholas. Nevertheless Rozhestvensky, conscious of his sailors' morale, ordered the message to be read aloud on each of the ships.

Nicholas was undoubtedly playing a diplomatic game, praising the sailors for their valiant actions but placating the British in whichever way was possible: 'Nicholas II, with one distant war on his hands and no desire to begin a second, quickly wrote a letter of regret to King Edward.'[9]

There was no admission of guilt from the czar, or promises to ensure that such an event never happened again, but the British were placated. It was agreed that an International Committee of Inquiry, made up of admirals and men with experience of the sea, would be set up to discuss the incident. Operating under the remit of the recent Hague Convention, blame, if any, would be apportioned at this meeting.

Meanwhile, guilty officers – three junior officers chosen more or less at random from the *Borodino*, *Alexander III* and *Oryol* – would be left behind in Vigo to act as witnesses. Three lucky men, as it happened, who were more than happy to depart the fleet.

Rozhestvensky also took the opportunity to rid himself of a certain Commander Nikolai Klado who had persistently annoyed him during the voyage. He was Rozhestvensky's chief of naval intelligence on the *Suvorov* and, as befitted his calling, was soundly disliked by most of the officers.

He was a listener, a watcher, a taker of secret notes, and in an autocratic regime like Czar Nicholas's Russia that signified a dangerous man.

He, too, was added to the small group of marooned Russian sailors at Vigo. Klado was not happy to be left behind, even though it meant that, once formal evidence had been taken, he would be sent back to St Petersburg. What he saw as an outrage, even an insult, rankled him, but he would find the opportunity to exact painful and rather cruel revenge, as Rozhestvensky was soon to discover.

Klado's leaving was not without a degree of humour. One of the classic quotes of the voyage came from an unknown officer who watched with relish as the abandoned intelligence officer descended the ladder to the waiting picket boat. He leaned easily against the rail and in a dry, sardonic *sotto voce*, told a colleague who stood next to him, 'I see that this time the rats are leaving the ship before she sinks!'

The Committee of Inquiry duly met in Paris from 9 January until 25 February 1905. The result was something of a whitewash, the report declaring that while the Russian Fleet should not have opened fire there was no discredit to Rozhestvensky, either from a military or humanitarian basis. The Russian government voluntarily agreed to pay £66,000 compensation to the Hull fishermen.

The Hull men were, for a brief period, national heroes. Postcards showing damage to their ships, a number of rather inaccurate drawings of the incident, even photographs of groups of slightly bemused fishermen standing staring at the camera, were soon on sale across Britain. Five of the fishermen were singled out and awarded the Albert Medal for gallantry. King Edward presented the awards at Buckingham Palace in May 1905. It was a singular and well-deserved tribute, but the five men, like their comrades back in Hull, were more interested in when Czar Nicholas's compensation would be paid.

Rozhestvensky and the ships of his 1st Division eventually sailed from Vigo at 07.00 on the morning of 1 November. He was headed now for Tangier where he would join up once more with the 2nd Division and Enkvist's cruisers. The admiral was happy to be at sea once again, well removed from all the publicity and the politicking that he hated. It was time to be a sailor once again. But, even there, the omens glared down on him once again.

The cruisers from Admiral Charles Beresford's Channel Fleet watched him leave port and then increased speed to overtake the plodding Russian ships. They spent the next three days sweeping in, around and across the path of the Russians in spectacular feats of seamanship that amazed everyone who witnessed the spectacle.

Above everything it was an exercise in humiliation, showing what the Royal Navy could have done if the situation had collapsed into war. Rozhestvensky watched the British 'at play' and remarked that these were real sailors. 'If only we had …', he said to Captain Ignatius and Clapier de Colongue, and then stopped himself. The two men knew exactly what he was trying to say.

In particular the skill that the British cruisers displayed when operating at full speed amazed everyone. The Russians stood gaping in wonder as the *Lancaster*, *Hermes* and the others would drop astern, almost casually, and then race back in front of the fleet. Engines powering them at full speed, bow waves creaming up across the hulls like candy floss, the cruisers repeatedly turned on a sixpence, spinning and dancing across the sea. And this was not even the real thing. What would they do if it came to hostilities? The Russian officers and sailors could only gaze in wonder, knowing they could not even begin to compete with such effortless skill and talent. Never had their limited training and inexperience seemed as galling as it did on the trip from Vigo to Tangier.

Sir Ian Hamilton, later to show his own ineptitude on the beaches of Gallipoli, acted as a British observer with the Japanese during the Russo-Japanese War and his reports highlighted what he perceived as the many irreconcilable faults with the Russian military regime. In particular the Russians, he said: 'Had poor intelligence, disregard of cover, disregard of secrecy and swiftness, lack of dash, lack of initiative and lack of good generalship.'[10]

Hamilton was talking about Russian land forces but his comments could just as equally have been applied to the navy. The incident on the Dogger Bank may have been behind them but Rozhestvensky knew that the story of their inept response would follow his fleet like a ghostly albatross wherever it went. At this stage in the voyage, nearly 2000 miles into a journey that no one believed he could complete, Rozhestvensky must have been cursing his bad luck and wondering why he had ever agreed to accept the czar's commission.

Chapter 5

On Into the Wastes

When, on 3 November the *Lancaster*, the last Beresford's cruisers, finally left the 2nd Pacific Fleet to its own devices a mood of celebration settled over the ships of the Russian 1st Division. The British had gone and it was the tenth anniversary of the czar's accession to the throne. During the afternoon many toasts were drunk, both to the czar and to the damnation of the Royal Navy cruisers.

The large amounts of vodka consumed that day helped push the fear and admiration of the British warships out of the sailors' minds. And it didn't matter what the world's press said; they knew they had beaten off a torpedo attack in the North Sea. Now for the Japanese battleships, they thought.

The crews seemed to have gelled together quite effectively since those dangerous moments on the Dogger Bank. It may have been an old adage but the dangers of battle invariably drew men together as nothing else could. It was a universal trend in every navy in the world:

> When I came to my berth I was welcomed by the whole mess more like a brother than a shipmate but this day made us all brothers; feuds and animosities were buried in forgetfulness; and many who had entertained bitter hatred of one another would be seen shaking the hand of friendship together.[1]

The majority of sailors in the new Pacific Fleet were not professional seamen but conscripts. They were peasants and labourers who, until the call came, had spent all of their lives on farms or small holdings. They might have been willing – many were not – but they were still a disparate group of individuals. The action in the North Sea had helped them to start gelling into a team far more effectively than any training or exercise that Rozhestvensky could ever dream up.

The last stage of the passage to Tangier, once the British had withdrawn, was uneventful and soon the spires and minarets of the exotic city began to loom up on the horizon. There was a palpable feeling of excitement as, late in the afternoon of 3 November, Rozhestvensky's ironclads anchored alongside Felkersam and Enkvist's vessels in Tangier Roads. For the sailors there was now the prospect of shore leave and a chance to sample the delights of North Africa. That was what they wanted and believed was their due.

It had been an interesting trip from Vigo, what with the British cruisers and their demonstrations of superior seamanship. The fleet 'clown', the repair ship *Kamchatka*, had of course performed with her usual ineptitude. She managed to get herself separated from the rest of the auxiliary vessels and when she did finally show up her crew were full of their adventures on the Dogger Bank. They claimed to have fired over 300 shells at a group of three Japanese cruisers. In fact, they had been firing at the Swedish merchant ship *Aldebaran*, at a French schooner and at a lonely German trawler.

At Tangier Rozhestvensky quickly disabused his sailors; there would be no riotous night ashore. The fleet was already behind schedule and a gathering of German colliers was waiting to load coal onto the Russian ships. As a sop to his men, Rozhestvensky promised a prize of 1500 roubles to the ship that took on coal the fastest.

It had been decided, long before the 2nd Pacific Fleet even left Russia, that from this point onwards the ships would be split into two groups: one would make the long journey around the Cape of Good Hope; the other would risk the shorter route through the Suez Canal.

First, Rozhestvensky ordered Admiral Felkersam to move his flag from the *Oslyabya* to the older *Sisoy Veliky*. Together with the battleship *Navarin*, three of the light cruisers and most of the destroyer and torpedo boat force, Felkersam would assume command and take this squadron across the Mediterranean, then down the Suez Canal into the Red Sea.

Felkersam's previous flagship, the *Oslyabya*, would join the four Borodinos and Rozhestvensky's 1st Division for the long haul around the tip of Africa. The two units would meet up at Diego Suarez in Madagascar.

The reason for this division of ships has never been made totally clear. Sceptics have argued that Rozhestvensky was prepared to sacrifice his older ironclads to the British by despatching them across what was clearly a 'British sea' but not his newer vessels.

The claim that the Suez Canal was too shallow to take the newer, bigger battleships might have been the official version but even non-nautical men knew that there would have been at least 6ft of grace in the waterway. Fear of a Japanese torpedo boat attack in the narrow confines of the Red Sea, along with a desire to protect the older ships from the rigours of rounding the Cape, were probably more accurate assumptions.

Anxious not to lose a moment, Rozhestvensky ordered the Suez Canal contingent to up-anchor and depart as quickly as possible. They had been waiting at Tangier for some time and were coaled and ready for the next stage of the voyage.

The *Sisoy Veliky* led Felkersam's ships out of Tangier at 21.00 hours that evening. The enormous cloud of black smoke and soot that hung like an umbrella above the vessels could be seen for some time from the deck of the *Suvorov* until the greater blackness of the African night closed in and shut it from view.

Rozhestvensky had intended to leave the following morning but a gale sprang up and prevented a night-time coaling from the colliers. It meant a twenty-four-hour delay before 'Mad Dog' would be finally able to get away. In that time Rozhestvensky would enjoy the hospitality of the Sultan of Morocco, a typical African potentate who cared little for the sensibilities of the Western powers. Rozhestvensky also sampled the delights of Tangier. Much to his pleasure he was even given a seventeen- gun salute as he stepped ashore for a formal visit and reception.

His sailors, denied access to the town, spent their time buying souvenirs from the market traders who had come flocking out to the ships in boats, dinghies or whatever mode of transport they could find. The dealers did great business and for sailors who had spent weeks holed up on board their ships with no one for company but their colleagues it was a welcome distraction.

While they were moored at Tangier several of the slower auxiliary vessels finally turned up. These included the refrigerator ship *Esperance* with a welcome supply of frozen meat and the hospital ship *Oryol* with its contingent of several dozen freshly turned-out Russian nurses.

For the first time since Libau the Russian sailors were able to catch a glimpse of the nurses, albeit from a distance. Russian women here on the North African coast? It was beyond the realms of possibility and the deprived sailors felt like they had been given a lottery prize. They could wave, whistle and shout at the nurses who lined the rails of the 'White Eagle' but for most of them this was as close as they would ever get to the white-clad angels who would accompany the Pacific Fleet almost to the end of its long and fatal voyage. It did not stop them dreaming:

> On board, besides the surgeons, were a number of ladies of high station who had volunteered as nurses. It was the dream of the

common sailors to be transferred to this boat, which they looked upon as a floating palace and a haven of rest.[2]

* * *

That night one or two lucky sailors were able to slip ashore to enjoy the food, the hashish, the wine and the 'ladies of the night' for which Tangier was rightly famous. The majority could only sit back and wish the world was different. Early the following morning the fleet pulled in its anchors and left the roadstead.

The ships were ordered to sail in three columns: the *Suvorov* and the other battleships to starboard, the auxiliaries to port with Admiral Enkvist, and his three remaining cruisers bringing up the rear in an arrow-shaped wedge. Leading the port line was the repair ship *Kamchatka*, not because of her prowess or performance but because Rozhestvensky had had enough of her antics and wanted her where he could see her.

The refrigerator ship *Esperance* and the hospital ship *Oryol* did not join any column. It was deliberately done in order to preserve their neutral status and save them from any potential attack by the Japanese. It also meant that the two ships were exempt from the chaos that was about to take place in Tangier Roads.

Nobody had bothered to pass on to the fleet any specific details about the departure, meaning that vital information such as overall speed when leaving the roadstead and the distance vessels were to maintain from each other were left to the imagination of the various navigation officers. As a result, the leaving of Tangier was another humiliating failure.

Firstly the transport *Anadyr* found that she could not lift her anchor. It had become caught on an underwater obstacle that turned out to be the city's telegraph cable. Try as they might, no amount of effort from the crew seemed able to clear it. At last a furious Rozhestvensky ordered the *Anadyr* to cut the cable, with the result that all telegraph communications between Tangier and Europe were severed for four days.

No sooner had some form of order been established in the two lines of ships than the *Suvorov*'s steering gear became jammed hard to port: 'The bewildered captain of the *Kamchatka* suddenly found the flagship steaming straight towards him. A collision was avoided by a few feet and the other transports scattered.'[3] It took time to reassemble the auxiliaries into some sort of order and to mend the *Suvorov*'s steering gear. Meanwhile the other battleships waited, crews pacing the deck in frustration.

After that things settled down. Destroyers and cruisers from the Royal Navy returned to shadow the fleet for the first few days until it became obvious that Rozhestvensky was heading westwards to clear the African landmass before steering south to the Cape of Good Hope. The Royal Navy did not send the traditional signal of good luck as they first dropped astern and then spun imperiously around to head back towards Tangier. Nobody on the British ships had the heart or the grace to wish the Russian Fleet a successful voyage.

Restricting the fleet's speed in order to preserve coal supplies was Rozhestvensky's first task. The crews grumbled but at a speed of nine knots Rozhestvensky and his newly formed Cape Squadron of the Pacific Fleet ploughed steadily onwards. Once the British had left, the sea was empty. It belonged, the Russian sailors felt, to them.

Their destination now was the port of Dakar in French-controlled Senegal. It was a journey of nearly 2000 miles south from Tangier, skirting the western fringes of the Sahara Desert. Inevitably the weather was blisteringly hot, even out at sea, and with a degree of malice shared by experienced sailors the world over, the old hands promised that there was worse to come.

They were right. The fleet headed steadily southwards, conditions growing more and more unpleasant as the heat became oppressive and then debilitating. Humidity soared skywards. It was not helped by the routines of shipboard life, which effectively replicated a microcosm of Russian society.

Discipline in the navy was harsh and the 2nd Pacific Fleet under Rozhestvensky was no different from any other unit. In fact, as they sailed on, the divide between officers and men seemed increasingly to be as wide as the English Channel.

The aristocratic naval officers were the pride of all Russia; the 'Stars of society' as they were called. On the other hand the crew of the *Suvorov*, *Borodino* and the rest were largely peasants or serfs. Even if they had wanted to, there was no way the two groups could ever mix or relate to each other in any way but as master and servant.

There was no privacy, not even for the officers, though they did at least enjoy cabins of their own. That, the quality of their food, and the vast quantities of alcohol they consumed with their meals were the only perks that they enjoyed. The crews of the destroyers and torpedo boats expected cramped and wet conditions but on the battleships the squalor had been unexpected, and because life at sea was an open book everyone could see the huge difference in standards. In particular men noted that officers always enjoyed better quality food than them.

The further south they journeyed the worse the sailors' meals became. Fresh meat and vegetables taken on at Tangier had lasted only a few days and then crews were soon reduced to eating the refrigerated meat from the *Esperance*. When that ran out there was no option but to eat solonina, meat preserve that looked, smelled and tasted appalling. Officers had their own cooks and all their meals, by comparison with the crew's, were of an altogether higher quality; they were also accompanied by fine wines and spirits.

As the voyage progressed the camaraderie that had so recently built up began to break down under the strain of increasingly appalling conditions and a stubborn refusal to relax discipline or the seemingly mindless rules. This decision to maintain the status quo, in keeping with the inequality of Russian society, was short-sighted and a misjudgement by Rozhestvensky and his captains.

The sailors cast envious eyes in the direction of the officers but everyone knew that they were, for the moment, untouchable. Fellow crewmen, on the other hand, were fair game. Men hid possessions that others might like to acquire, nobody trusted his neighbour and minor thieving was soon a common occurrence.

Arguments and squabbles between crew members grew more common and the petty officers, never liked at the best of times, became hated figures who settled disputes with their fists. Rozhestvensky's Cape Squadron consisted of approximately 7000 men, most of them ordinary sailors who had been forcibly enlisted within the previous few months. As time went on these men, used to the routines of the farmyard or the milking shed rather than life on a giant battleship, felt their insignificance more and more. It was a ticking time bomb.

In a working day that began at 05.00 hours life at sea consisted of two basic ingredients: training and cleaning. Training to improve skills was expected. It might not have been a welcome chore but it was not hated in the way that cleaning the ship most certainly was.

Every day decks were swept and washed, then swept and washed again. Brass was polished until it gleamed like crystal in the blazing sunshine; but for what? Disaster was all that waited ahead. What did it matter if a man went to his grave on a well-polished and beautifully cleaned ship or a filthy one?

The little luxuries of life for officers and men, things that made the interminable voyage somewhat more bearable, were starting to disappear.

Tobacco – rolling tobacco for the men, pre-rolled cigarettes and cigars for the officers – was soon at a premium. Soap had also become scarce and what was available refused to lather in salt water.

Everyone slept naked in an effort to ward off the crippling humidity, many spending their off-duty nights on deck where there was a fresh breeze to cool their sweating bodies. Some officers, in the privacy of their cabins, even stayed naked during their off-duty hours.

Clothes quickly became soaked through by sweat and would not dry. Everyone was constantly thirsty, some of the crew resorting to the traditional Russian peasant practice of making bread cider in order to quench the longing.

Worst of all, however, was the increasing tendency of ships to break down. When this happened the result was that the whole squadron had to heave to and wait until repairs had been completed.

Breakdowns were hated by the sailors. Apart from anything else they meant that ships would have to lie idle, engines on dead stop for three or four hours at a time with the result that there was no cooling breeze blowing along the decks. Sitting and rolling in the waves like a child's wooden yacht on the boating pond meant, of course, that they were vulnerable to sudden attack. Nobody knew whether or not the Japanese torpedo boats were lurking on the coast but everybody could use their imagination.

Tolerance disappeared, lost in the haze of heat that hung like a shroud above the ships. Tempers were short and no one had a worse temper than Rozhestvensky. He was back to his old bad behaviour and had developed a wide range of expletives to describe his officers and ships. Admiral Enkvist was the 'Slutty Old Geezer', while Captain Serebrennikov of the *Borodino* was 'the Brainless Nihilist'. The cruiser *Aurora* he called 'the Whore' and the luckless *Kamchatka* was labelled 'the Lecherous Slut'.

Such language and behaviour was unacceptable but it was, perhaps, a way of releasing the tension and stress inside the admiral. Whatever the reason, Rozhestvensky was certainly driven to the edge of desperation by the inadequacies of his subordinates. The Captain of the *Oryol* once took an hour and a half to decode a semaphore message from the flagship and then deliver an almost unintelligible reply.[4]

Communication was a major problem, just like it was in far off Port Arthur. It was not just the practicalities of the process; it was also the emotional effect that troubled men most. They were, they felt, cut off from the rest of the world. If that was an important issue in the morale of the men in Port Arthur, it was a major concern for those on board the ships of the 2nd Pacific Fleet, isolated from their friends and family and heading into unknown dangers and difficulties. It was no wonder that morale began to drop and everyone started to fear the worst.

* * *

When Rozhestvensky finally arrived at Dakar, early on the morning of 11 November, he was faced by a charming interlude followed by news of the most unpleasant sort.

In order to celebrate the admiral's fifty-sixth birthday – which just happened to be 11 November – a luncheon for the officers of the fleet and for civil dignitaries from Dakar was arranged on board the *Suvorov*. One of the guests was none other than Natalia Sivers, Rozhestvensky's beautiful nurse and courtesan who had been brought across from the hospital ship. Rozhestvensky was idyllically happy and it was immediately apparent to everyone that the admiral was infatuated with this blue-eyed blonde. During the luncheon he had eyes for no one else.

This was followed by a sudden and potentially crippling reality. At first the French governor had been happy to welcome the fleet to Dakar and had left the luncheon full of wine and good cheer. He was more than content with his visitors who, he was sure, would enliven the social life of this remote and rarely visited piece of colonial France.

However, later that afternoon he was back with new instructions from his government. The Russian ships were now forbidden to take on coal. As there were ten colliers just off shore, waiting to begin the transfer of fuel into the bunkers of the Russian warships, it was an unwelcome change of heart.

France was the closest Russia had to an ally in this campaign but the British had been active in trying to persuade them that allowing Rozhestvensky to coal in their territorial waters could be a breach of their neutrality. Annoying Britain was not high on the French agenda. They needed the power of the Royal Navy to act as a deterrent against the Kaiser's belligerent posturing in neighbouring Germany. Whatever they really felt, keeping Britain sweet was a lot more important than openly pandering to Russia's needs.

Rozhestvensky, furious that his good mood should be ended in this manner, hit the roof. He had had enough. He informed the governor that he was intending to take on coal, despite the French edict, declaring, 'Unless your shore batteries intend to prevent me.' The French governor responded with a typical Gallic shrug and told Rozhestvensky that, as he could surely see, there were no shore batteries at Dakar.

Both men laughed and filled their glasses with champagne. Each of them had done their duty and honour was satisfied on both sides. The French had no way of enforcing the ruling in this tiny and insignificant colony and what the authorities in Paris did not know, the governor thought, would not harm them. Another few glasses of champagne and the governor soon departed. Within minutes of his launch casting off from the admiral's ladder at the side of the *Suvorov* the colliers came alongside the Russian ships to begin coaling.

After that it was a matter of trial by coal dust. Rozhestvensky intended that his battleships should take on over 2000 tons of the precious fuel. As their bunker capacity was just 1100 tons the idea presented something of a problem. The danger of overloading the already top-heavy ironclads was temporarily forgotten in the drive to load more and more coal.

Rozhestvensky's decision was something that had been forced on him. Unknown to everyone apart from his closest advisors, Clapier de Cologne and Captain Ignatzius, the French had forbidden him to coal at Libreville, his next port of call. The double load of coal from the colliers waiting at Dakar was not a luxury but a necessity.

For the Russian sailors the whole world now turned into one of black: black dust, black clothes, black nuggets of coal that, unless handled carefully, would fall to crack fingers and crush toes. Every waking second was devoted to shovelling and hauling bags of the unwieldy lumps of fuel along the tiered and uneven decks. Officers and crew worked together, all distinctions of rank abolished in the need to load coal onto the ships.

Coal was stored in any space that was available. It was shovelled into gangways, into bathrooms, even into the cabins of the disgruntled officers. It was stored in engine rooms, in workshops, on deck and in the turrets of the mighty 12-in guns. Wherever men turned, it seemed, they were faced by mountains of black coal.

There were a few exceptions, notably in enclosed areas in the bowels of the ships where men were liable to suffocate and in the cabins of any officer above the rank of commodore; but that was it. The more coal that was loaded, the more coal dust settled like a filthy blanket of black ash across the ships:

> It hung about in clouds in the still damp air … in the gangways, mess decks, shafts and passages and cabins in which it was stacked,

creating an atmosphere like that of a mine shaft in a heatwave. For four months Rozhestvensky's crews worked, ate and slept with the bitter, nauseating fumes of coal in their nostrils.[5]

It was a nightmare from which there was no escape. Coal dust clung to every surface and found its way into food, clothes, even into the pores of the skin. To the sailors it seemed as if they would never be free from this cloaking film of dust. The ships were hidden in a perpetual black mask through which the sun burned a distant yellow like a child's naïve painting. To some it was romantic; to most it was eerie and the more superstitious crew members shuddered, crossed themselves and wondered what this portent signified for the fleet.

Along with the coal dust there was, of course, heat and humidity. Men collapsed from heatstroke and exhaustion as they sweated and strained. Several even died in what were later recorded as temperatures of 120°F. Amongst those who collapsed and could not be brought back to life was Lieutenant Ivan Nelidoff, the son of the Russian Ambassador to Paris. It seemed that nobody was exempt from the perils of coaling in such conditions; aristocrat or peasant, eventually the heat and dust would get them all.

Rozhestvensky drove them onwards, night and day, through the pain. He was remorseless; determined to fulfil his mission, even if it killed him. As the crews coughed, choked and spat up black phlegm there were many who would have happily ended his life for him. In the meantime, there was another shovel to be swung, another sack to be picked up or thrown down and, if the men had enough breath left another silent prayer that the agony would soon end.

If anyone collapsed from the heat and strain – and there were many who did – he would receive treatment; of a sort. A bucket of sea water over his head would bring him to his senses and then he was assisted back into the line of sweating, cursing and panting sailors:

> Even at night the temperature never fell. During the day it was like working in a furnace. The men in the holds of the colliers and in the bunkers of the ironclads stripped to the buff. To avoid being choked by coal dust, some stuffed oakum between their teeth while others wrapped cloths around mouth and nose.[6]

For nearly two days the men worked and at last the holds of the supply vessels were empty. The ships of the Pacific Fleet were, by contrast, stacked high with the 'black gold', looking more like North Sea colliers than the warships of His Imperial Majesty, the Emperor of Russia.

Relieved and weary men fell onto the decks with their prized cups of vodka, exhausted and almost blind from the layers of dust that cloaked their eyes and faces. But at least it was over; until the next time. Then the order, thunderous and unwelcome, hammered like the voice of doom in their ears: 'Prepare to clean ships!'

* * *

Almost as soon as the decks were cleared and cleaned, Rozhestvensky ordered the fleet to sea. Dakar was not the healthiest of places to linger, the tiny community being renowned for the high incidence of yellow fever. Not only that, the rumour machine was in action again. Two Japanese spies had been spotted in the town, and three Japanese cruisers were patrolling off the coast. It was clearly time to move quickly.

Never easy to control at the best of times, the overloaded battleships were now more unwieldy than ever. The slightest swell would send water flooding in across the lower decks and everyone dreaded a storm or gale suddenly springing up.

As they ploughed steadily south, mechanical breakdowns continued to harass the squadron, something that should not have been entirely unexpected considering how far they had already come. Troubles and stoppages on the *Malay* became so regular that she eventually had to be taken in tow. Even the newer ships were now experiencing difficulties. The *Borodino* developed major problems with her bearings and could manage no more than 10 knots.

And, then, of course, there was the *Kamchatka*, the fleet comedian; except that sometimes her antics were not in the least bit funny. It was obvious to everyone that by 22 November the repair ship was falling behind the rest of the fleet. Contacted by the *Suvorov*, her answer to a query about her situation was clear and succinct: 'Dangerously damaged so cannot proceed.' Angrily, Rozhestvensky ordered the flag engineer to drop back and examine the problems affecting the *Kamchatka*. Before the engineer got there another message from the repair ship told the admiral that the trouble was trifling and that she was about to resume her position in the line.

Given the mix of personalities and political sensibilities on the ships it was inevitable that the further they went, and the longer they were cooped up like battery hens, disaffection should simmer and grow. Civilian stokers on several vessels, men who had been hired to augment the naval personnel, began to murmur about the discipline to which they were regularly subjected and there were even mutterings of mutiny. Rozhestvensky dealt with the problem in his usual no-nonsense manner and threatened to put the whole lot off in open boats. The muttering stopped; for the moment.

Rain had begun to fall as the fleet left Dakar: hard, driving rain that fell mostly at night. At dawn the heat and humidity returned. The blistering sun burned all day, sailors soon scratching and rubbing at the heat rashes that had become endemic. Nightfall was a blessed relief and men were able to lie under canvas awnings on the decks and gaze in wonder at the stars and constellations. They had never seen anything like them before and everyone strained his eyes for a glimpse of the famous Southern Cross.

Rozhestvensky filled their days with never-ending exercise and training. He had ships changing position, closing up for torpedo attacks, tacking and turning with dizzying regularity. None of it was easy as the ships decks were crammed with mountains of coal. And while it kept the crews busy, it certainly did nothing to improve their seamanship. The sailors, both new and experienced, needed time to learn or refresh their craft, but time was the one thing they did not have. The admiral knew it and drove them even harder, not for his sake but their own.

Rozhestvensky's temper did not improve either. His chief of staff, Clapier de Colongue, was invariably the buffer between him and the luckless officers and crew. The strain was enormous but de Colongue, unlike his admiral, did not thrive on pressure and stress. As the voyage went on he became increasingly nervous, as if all the cares of the world were resting on his narrow shoulders: 'A long thin man who couldn't be more than forty-five years old, the passage of time had tonsured his head, grizzled his beard and wrinkled his forehead.'[7]

On 26 November the fleet anchored in the mouth of the Gabon Estuary, just outside French territorial waters. The land to either side of the estuary was green and lush, a welcome change from the rolling, empty sea. Now, for the first time, sailors were allowed shore leave, but Libreville, the capital of this French province, was not the most enticing of places. Neither was the immediate countryside.

The town of Libreville held no more than a few hundred white Europeans. The local native king and his six wives were often drunk, more usually fast asleep, whenever any of the Russians stopped by. And stop by they often did as there was little else to amuse them in this desolate region. The elderly dowager queen usually appeared stark naked, holding her hand out for money.

(*Above*) An artist's impression of the attack on *Tsarevich Nicholas* by one of his samurai guards.

(*Right*) Japanese warships through the ages.

THE GROWTH OF THE JAPANESE NAVY.

1. 1860; War-Galley of the Prince of Wasima.
2. 1848; War-Galley.
3. 1861; War-Junk.
4. 1881; The Gun-Boat *Tsukushi*.
5. 1901; A Torpedo-Boat Destroyer.
6. 1869; The Paddle-wheel Battleship *Kangsoo*.
7. 1867; The Corvette *Tsukuba Kan*.
8. 1871; The Iron Ram *Stonewall*.
9. 1906; The *Shikishima*.

(*Above left*) Inside the opulent Winter Palace in St Petersburg.

(*Above right*) Russian soldiers camping in the snow during the Russo-Japanese War.

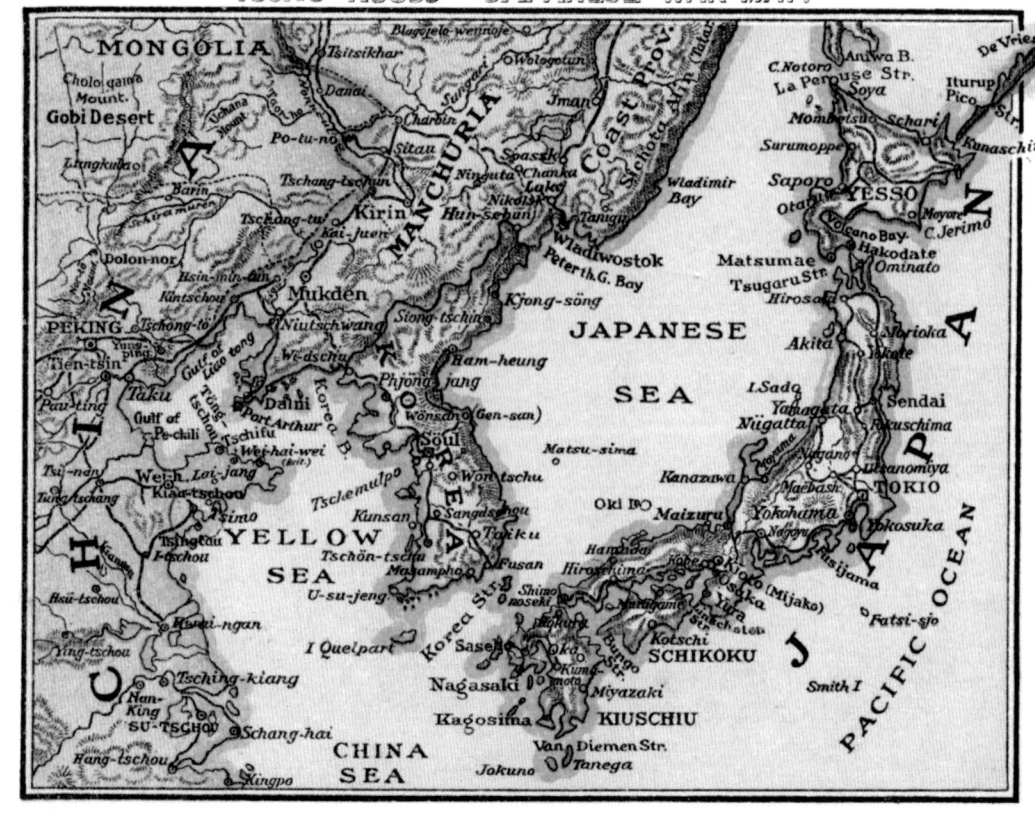

(*Below*) A general map showing the area that was fought over, on land and sea, during the war.

The giant battleship *Suvorov* during her fitting out.

Torpedo boats and searchlights: a new weapon of war.

Les torpilleurs japonais attaquent les Cuirassés russes au mouillage de Port-Arthur.

Torpedo boats attack.

(*Above*) Admiral Makarov, heavily bewhiskered, as fashion of the time dictated.

(*Above left*) Operating at night, the fear of a sudden and deadly attack from enemy torpedo boats was strong, on both sides.

(*Left*) Another torpedo boat attack.

The disaster at Port Arthur; sunken Russian warships litter the harbour.

BOTH COMMANDERS AT THE SITE OF INTERVIEW, SHUI-SHIH-YING, WITH THEIR STAFF OFFICERS. 5TH, JANUARY, 1905.

(*Above*) The Russian and Japanese delegations pose for a formal picture at the surrender ceremony. Japanese General Nogi sits centre left in the middle row; General Stessel is centre right.

(*Below left*) Admiral Togo, the 'Nelson of the Orient'.

(*Below right*) A man with worries enough to sink the world, Admiral Rozhestvensky.

ADMIRAL TOGO.
IN COMMAND OF THE JAPANESE FLEET.

(*Above left*) The oil tanks at Port Arthur on fire.

(*Above right*) A Japanese warship of the time.

(*Left*) Interest in Japan and all things Japanese grew rapidly during the war.

The Russian outrage: British trawlers are attacked in the North Sea.

Damaged trawlers after the Russian attack.

Public outrage at the Russian attack almost brought Britain and Russia to war.

Some of the surviving trawlermen.

The Battle of the Yellow Sea, Togo opens fire.

(*Above*) Rozhestvensky's flag ship *Suvorov*.

(*Left*) Vice Admiral Nebogatov.

(*Below*) Map showing the route of Rozhestvensky's fleet, and the detached ships of Admiral Felkersam who took his squadron through the Suez Canal.

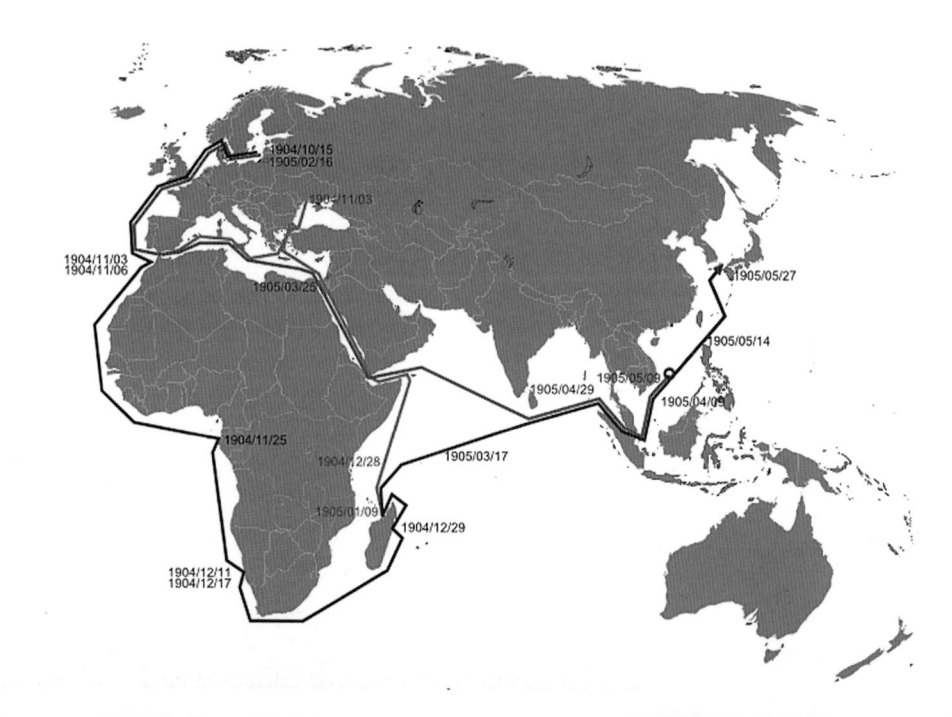

It did not take the world's press long to ridicule the antics of the Russian Fleet, as this cartoon from *Punch* shows.

Calling the Admiral in the morning was a mission of some danger.

Another *Punch* cartoon.

Togo's flag ship *Mikasa*, seen here from the stern.

15,200 Tons; 15,000 H.P.; Speed, 18 Knots; Length 400 ft.; Beam, 76 ft.; Draught, 27 ft. 3 ins.; Built, Barrow. Armour Belt, 9 ft. 6 ins.; Gun Pos. 14.6. Deck, 3. Guns; 4 12-in. 14 6-in. Q.F.; 20 12-Pdrs.; 8 3-Pdrs.; 4 2½-Pdrs.; Torpedo Tubes, 4 (Sub.). Coal, 1,400 Tons. Crew, 935.

"MIKASA," JAPANESE 1ST CLASS BATTLESHIP.

An illustration of the *Mikasa*.

Admiral Togo and his staff on the bridge of the *Mikasa*.

Der russisch-japanische Krieg. "Seeschlacht."

Battle is joined; a Japanese postcard.

The Baltic Fleet, led by the *Suvorov*.

(*Above*) The opposing Japanese fleet.

(*Below*) The famous Z Flag, hoisted by Togo as the battle began.

(*Above*) The end of the *Suvorov*.

(*Left*) Russian Vice Admiral Vitgeft.

(*Below*) A contemporary postcard showing the various types of Japanese warships.

TYPES OF THE JAPANESE FLEET.

The Battle of Tsushima was short and bloody with little quarter asked or given.

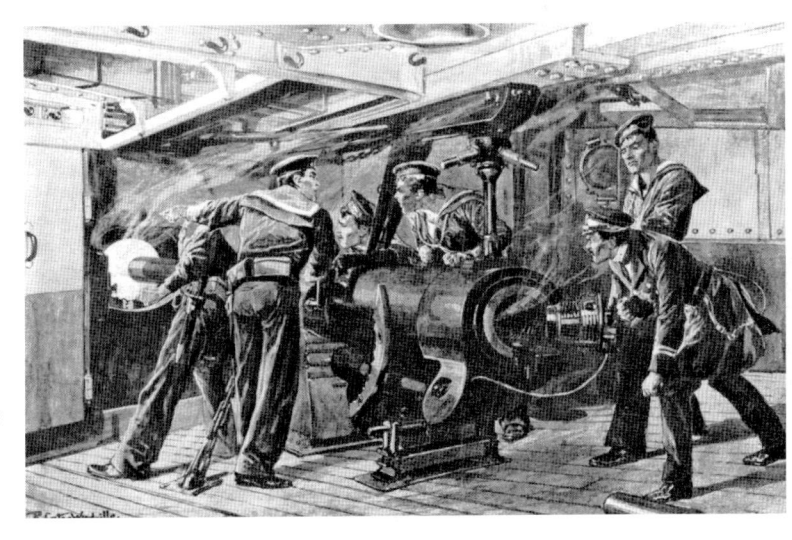

Japanese gunners: the quality of Japanese gunfire was far superior to that of the Russians, just one of the reasons for the Japanese victory.

The Japanese cruiser *Mizuno*.

"IDZUMO," JAPANESE 1ST CLASS CRUISER.

PUNCH, OR THE LONDON CHARIVARI.—November 16, 1904.

AVE, CÆSAR!

(*Left*) Yet another cartoon, this time honouring the fallen at Port Arthur.

(*Below*) Shell damage to one Russian ship.

RUSSIAN CRUISER "OLEG".

The Japanese fleet in action.

The cruiser *Aurora* was one of the few Russian ships to escape destruction. She is now moored in St Petersburg as a floating museum.

A rather romanticised image of the battle.

(*Above*) The Treaty of Portsmouth is signed, bringing the Russo-Japanese War to a close.

(*Left*) The Japanese warship *Hatuze*.

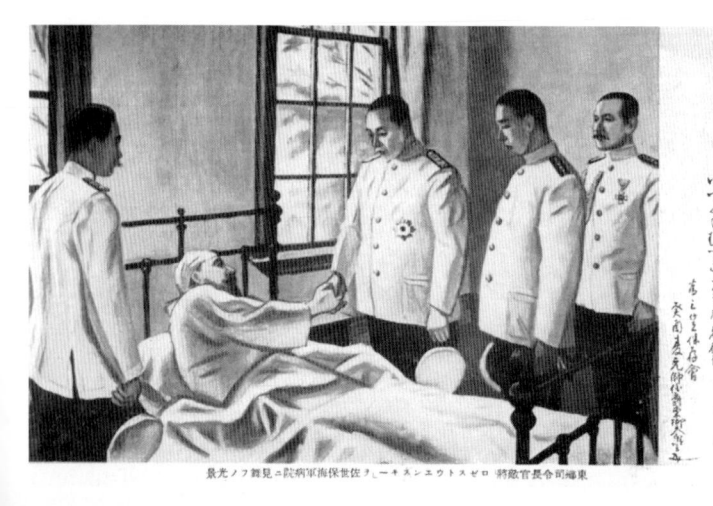

Admiral Togo visits the wounded and dispirited Rozhestvensky in hospital.

The one thing that did fascinate the visitors was the proliferation of wildlife. The sea was home to sharks and turtles, the jungle full of monkeys and deadly snakes. Parrots and other exotic birds with plumage of every imaginable colour continually shot past the ships, diving with seeming impunity into the thick jungle vegetation. However, the Russians learned early on in their stay that it was not wise to venture too far off the beaten track: 'Six weeks before, the cannibal blacks had slain and devoured four French elephant hunters in the forest just behind the coast off which we were lying.'[8]

The stay in Gabon was most memorable for what Rozhestvensky saw as a serious breach in discipline. Despite his own infatuation with Natalia Sivers, the admiral was acutely conscious of the attraction which the *Oryol* nurses held for the men of his fleet and was determined to limit the contact. As a consequence he banned all passage between his ships after 17.00 hours.

One evening while the fleet was in Gabon, the captain and officers of the cruiser *Dmitri Donskoi* decided to invite one of the nurses to dinner. She was an attractive woman by the name of Miss Klemm and also a renowned amateur singer. It promised to be an entertaining evening, but as the meal did not even begin until 18.00 hours Rozhestvensky's order presented the officers of the *Donskoi* with a significant problem. How could they get the nurse back to the *Oryol* without being noticed? Should the event be cancelled?

In the end, regardless of the admiral's order, Captain Ivan Lebedev decided that his officers needed some relaxation. He was a fun lover himself and wasn't going to allow some petty regulation stand in the way of his – and his crew's – enjoyment. Things would go ahead as planned.

The dinner and Miss Klemm's singing were an undoubted success and when the evening's events finished sometime after midnight three rather drunken junior officers were entrusted with the task of ferrying her back to the hospital ship. The sailors were in a light-hearted mood and, fuelled by copious amounts of vodka, champagne and brandy, were hardly the quietest of rowers.

In an attempt to cover his tracks, Lebedev had already made a formal and totally false request to the flagship, asking permission to bring back a number of crew members who had become stuck on the *Oryol* after coaling. The request, which fooled no one, was refused and Rozhestvensky instantly became suspicious.

The searchlight of the *Suvorov* soon picked out the long boat and its occupants. Furious that his order and recent instructions had been disobeyed,

Rozhestvensky's wrath was so great that it even managed to penetrate the befuddled brains of the intoxicated officers. Their boat was taken to the stern of the flagship where it remained, with the sailors left squatting on the duckboards for over an hour. It was a traditional Russian sign of displeasure but the angry words of the admiral, when the three officers were eventually allowed onto the bridge, scared everyone; even those who were simply on duty, watching and listening.

The following day brought retribution. Lieutenant Vaselago, Midshipman Varzar and Midshipman Selitrenikoff were sent to Libreville to wait for the next transport to Russia where they were discharged from the service for disobedience. It was a harsh punishment, but in light of future events the three men were probably not unhappy with the way things turned out.

Miss Klemm did not escape punishment either. She was banned from visiting shore for the next three months. Captain Lebedev went to the *Suvorov* to explain that it was his idea and that the punishment should be meter out to him, not the three junior officers. Rozhestvensky would not even see him and the punishment remained in place.

The fleet left Gabon at the end of November, heading towards what they thought was the Equator. In fact they had already crossed the Equator line before arriving at Gabon but a mistake by the navigating officer of the *Suvorov* had given them the wrong location. The formal 'Crossing the Line Ceremony' was therefore held on 2 December.

It was a moment of pure relaxation, something that was greatly needed by the sailors who increasingly believed themselves abandoned and forgotten by the world:

> Our boats were like homeless vagabonds. No-one was willing to offer us shelter ... The foreign world had come to the conclusion that the power of the Russian Empire, with its population of one hundred and fifty million, was a myth.'[9]

Now, however, there was a day of fun and laughter to be enjoyed. It would take everyone's minds off the realities of their voyage. Dressed as devils and satyrs, savages and creatures from some far off region of Hell, the experienced crewmen led their victims – those who had not previously 'Crossed the Line' – to the huge canvas bath that had been erected on the forward 12-in gun. There they were met by King Neptune, suitably clothed and armed with his trident, who would sit in judgement on the victims.

Inevitably, they were coated in soap and lather, unceremoniously shaved with an enormous 2-ft wooden razor, and then dumped into the bath.

Nobody was exempt, even Captain Ignatzius finding himself a more than willing victim of King Neptune's whim. Admiral Rozhestvensky escaped a ducking but, like everyone else on board the flagship, he was still soaked by the streams of water that Neptune's followers sprayed from the ship's fire hoses.

Meanwhile the battle against the elements continued. It was, in many respects, an uneven contest for men more used to snow and ice than the sweltering humidity of the tropics:-'intense heat, pallid sky, the atmosphere that of a steam bath, our clothing drenched with sweat. Shower baths were rigged on deck.'[10]

The introduction of showers on the open decks of the large warships gave only minor relief and was one of the few considerations made by senior officers. Even pith helmets were denied the men, most of whom had to cope with the effects of the sun by wrapping wet cloths around their heads.

* * *

Some measure of relief did eventually come; not from Rozhestvensky or his officers but from the elements themselves. Between the Tropic of Cancer and the Equator temperatures had remained high but now, once over the Equator, they started dropping. Humidity decreased and soon the temperature reached a comfortable and acceptable level, in the mid-twenties centigrade. Perhaps, everyone thought, the great King Neptune had been pleased with their celebrations and offerings.

The fleet's next destination was Great Fish Bay, a Portuguese colony that was as distant and remote as any they had yet encountered. Portugal had regarded itself as an ally of Britain since the campaigns of the Peninsula War in the eighteenth century and Rozhestvensky knew, even before his ships entered the bay, that he would find little solace in this Portuguese enclave.

Defended by a single gunboat, the *Limpopo*, Rozhestvensky looked on with amusement as the tiny vessel, her single gun trained on the flagship, steamed out to challenge him. As expected, he was told that he would not be allowed to load coal and other supplies in Portuguese waters.

Rozhestvensky's reply was simple. As the bay was just over six miles wide he would remain in the tiny strip of international waters that lay between the two fringes of Portuguese territory and take on coal from there.

The lieutenant in charge of the *Limpopo* nodded his agreement and remarked that he had better do exactly that, otherwise he would be forced to take action. Even Rozhestvensky found it impossible to supress a grin and the moment the gunboat began to head back to shore he started to take on coal from the waiting colliers.

There was no shore leave for crewmen but officers were allowed to sample the delights of Great Fish Bay. It was, they reported, just miles and miles of sand but the beaches were full of gorgeous shells and strutting pink flamingos.

The fleet remained in Great Fish Bay for just one night. The moment coaling was completed they weighed anchor and departed, much to the relief of the crew of the *Limpopo* who were undoubtedly preening themselves, believing they had frightened away the Russian interlopers.

Chapter 6

Felkersam's Fleet

When Rozhestvensky left Great Fish Bay he was headed for the German colony of Angra Pequena in what is now Namibia but was then known as German South West Africa. This remote and wind-swept sanctuary was likely to be the only friendly port that the fleet would see before reaching the island of Madagascar on the east coast of Africa. At Madagascar they had been promised a good welcome and safe anchorage by the French, but first they had to reach the place.

Temperatures might have fallen but now there was another hazard to overcome. Within a day of leaving Great Fish Bay a heavy storm blew up, ferocious winds and mountainous waves crashing into the hulls and superstructure of the battleships.

Rozhestvensky sat huddled in his chair on the bridge of the *Suvorov* listening morosely as the wind screamed like howling wolves through the rigging and stay-lines of the battleships. Like some demented beast, the gale plucked at the heaps of coal on the decks of the larger ships and tossed the smaller vessels about as if they had been made of matchsticks.

Battling the storm all the way, the fleet reached the German base of Angra Pequena on 11 December. There, Rozhestvensky anchored alongside the narrow promontory that split the bay into two distinct parts. The ships hugged the rocky outcrop but relief from the elements was a forlorn hope and they swung and rocked alarmingly in the wind.

Angra Pequena was a worthless piece of territory, until diamonds were discovered in the hinterland some five or six years after Rozhestvensky's visit. It had been annexed by Germany as part of their post-Bismarck drive to establish colonies in Africa. The British were in possession of a few small islands off shore and now the representatives of the British Empire on these islands braved the elements to make an official protest to the governor about the Russian presence.

The governor, a major in the German army, looked disdainfully at the British delegation, and then rose to stare out of his window. The promontory completely shielded the Russian Fleet, enabling the major to give a wonderful

Nelsonian response, 'I see no ships!' When it was suggested that he should take a boat and go see for himself his reply was equally as trenchant. He was, he declared, a soldier and he was not prepared to patrol the coastline in a native dugout.

The weather remained appallingly bad, and with the bay at Angra Pequena offering little protection from a storm that quickly grew to near-gale proportions, it was obvious to everyone that this coaling was not going to be easy. Rozhestvensky intended his battleships to take on board another 2000 tons, enough fuel to see them around the Cape of Good Hope and reach Madagascar without touching land. Much of South Africa was British territory, where the welcome would be less than friendly, but now even the weather seemed to be against them.

When the *Suvorov* made the first attempt to transfer coal into her bunkers the attendant collier was simply picked up by the waves and hurled against the flagship. One of the *Suvorov*'s 12-lb gun barrels pierced the collier's side like a knife going through butter, damaging the battleship's gun and adjacent torpedo booms in the process. The collier limped away and the attempt at coaling directly from the supply ships was immediately called off.

In desperation Rozhestvensky ordered up small boats to ferry coal from the colliers to the *Suvorov* and her sister ships. It was a dangerous and time-consuming process, which involved a double handling of fuel, from the colliers to the lighters and then from the diminutive lighters onto the waiting warships.

Many of the sailors involved in the operation later claimed that it had been harder going than the much-talked-about coaling at Dakar. Just like the Dakar affair, it also involved loading twice the amount of coal as originally intended.

It was three days before the storm eventually died. Only then was the German governor able to get out to the fleet. He brought with him disquieting news about the siege of Port Arthur.

Vysokaya Hill – '203-m Hill' as it was sometimes known – had been attacked and captured by the Japanese. Commander Semenov, a veteran of the Russian campaigns in the Yellow Sea and at Port Arthur and now serving on the *Suvorov*, gave Rozhestvensky a final summation. The hill, he said, overlooked the harbour, the roadstead and the town of Port Arthur. From a military perspective it commanded everything that was in range below it.

From this strategically crucial hilltop the Japanese could bombard and destroy ships, troops and emplacements at their leisure. Its capture, Semenov declared, could well mean 'the end of Port Arthur as a fortress.'

The news did not shock Rozhestvensky; he had expected the port to fall long before he reached it. But it was positive evidence that the Russian forces in the Far East were in serious trouble. The 2nd Pacific Fleet was heading into a war zone and it was looking increasingly as if they were in over their heads. It was a depressing climax to the stay at Angra Pequena.

* * *

In October Admiral Dmitri von Felkersam had left Tangier with his detached squadron of older ships, knowing that while his journey would be shorter than Rozhestvensky's it was likely to be just as dangerous. The Mediterranean was effectively a British enclave with strong naval bases in places like Gibraltar, Malta and Alexandria. If the Royal Navy did not act against him themselves they would certainly turn a blind eye to any Japanese moves. Only the waters around Greece – a country always friendly towards the Russian Empire – promised anything like safety and security.

Felkersam's squadron was hardly the most powerful part of the 2nd Pacific Fleet. His flagship, the *Sisoy Veliky*, was overdue for scrapping while the *Navarin* had been as good as obsolete long before she even left the builder's yard. Two of his cruisers were little more than armed yachts. And yet those were the least of Felkersam's problems.

The rear admiral was terminally ill with cancer. By rights he should have been at home in front of his fire in St Petersburg, but this strange little man, overweight and with a high-pitched voice and girlish walk that many mocked, had one character trait that was admirable: he had a sense of duty and he would do that duty, no matter what it cost him.

Felkersam's squadron reached Soudha in Crete at the beginning of November. Despite his fears, it had been an uneventful voyage and Felkersam, a kindly, considerate man, felt that his sailors deserved some rest and recuperation. He granted shore leave, but the sailors responded by getting very drunk in the bars and taverns and then becoming involved in a series of brawls with the locals.

There had undoubtedly been fights but they were nothing like the full-scale riots gleefully reported by the world's press. The media machine would have liked nothing more than another Dogger Bank Incident but, as Felkersam explained, scuffles in and around the bars and brothels of any port was nothing unusual for men who had just spent the last two months at sea.

The squadron soon left Crete and proceeded carefully towards the Suez Canal. The canal itself did not unduly worry Felkersam, but after they had finished with the waterway the Russian ships would be faced by the Red Sea, and that, everyone believed, was the perfect place for a Japanese ambush. The sea was narrow and, according to Russian spies, enemy agents and ships had already been spotted lurking in the environs.

As it happened, Felkersam's passage through the Suez Canal and the Red Sea was as uneventful as the voyage across the Mediterranean. What he did encounter, however, was a series of contradictory messages from the Admiralty back home in Russia. British and Japanese pressure on the French had unnerved Russia's tentative allies and now France was refusing to allow the fleet to anchor and rest at Diego Suarez on Madagascar.

Diego Suarez was too public, the French declared. They still wanted to help the Pacific Fleet and the alternative they now suggested seemed, to them and to Felkersam, a great deal more appropriate. The large bay on the tiny island of Nossi-Be on the north coast of Madagascar (Nosey Bay as it was often called) was considerably quieter and hidden from prying eyes. What did Felkersam want to do, St Petersburg asked? Rozhestvensky had been sent the same message but had failed to respond, leaving the decision for Felkersam to make.

Another message informed Felkersam that Captain Leonid Dobrotvorsky had recently left Libau with cruiser reinforcements and could be expected to link up with him soon. It was a surprise that he had not been expecting, but when told of the ships in the new detachment Felkersam was reasonably pleased by what he heard.

Dobrotvorsky's squadron was made up of ten more or less modern vessels, including two new armoured cruisers, the *Oleg* and the *Izumrud*. There were also two auxiliary cruisers, five torpedo boats and the training ship *Ocean*.

An opinionated and highly ambitious officer, Dobrotvorsky was nothing if not an adventurer. Steaming down the English Channel he had to decide on either Le Havre or Dover as a port of call, where he could take on fresh water. Surprisingly, he chose Dover, anchoring off the town and nearly colliding with an ocean liner in the process, then sailing away again with his water tanks full. There was no interference or objection from the British government.

Plagued by storms and hounded by continual breakdowns – even in the newer ships – Dobrotvorsky and his cruiser fleet struggled across the Mediterranean. They had intended to spend just two weeks at Soudha on Crete, but the need for repairs and spare parts extended their stay to a month. By the time they finally sailed, the sailors had exhausted the pleasures of the town's red light district and were more than happy to move on.

Through the canal and calling at Djibouti, the Russians again became stuck, waiting for spare parts. The sailors spent their time counting the sharks that cruised around their ships and enjoying whatever shore leave they could persuade their captain to give them:

> The town had just a handful of decent wooden houses belonging to the French. The miserable huts of the locals appalled the Russians. The 'Hotel des Arcades' served oysters but the very first feast, predictably enough, ended in mass food poisoning.[1]

Meanwhile, Felkersam, ahead of Dobrotvorsky in the Red Sea, remained in something of a quandary. Before he could make a decision about where to go he received another cable forestalling any move he might choose to make and effectively making the decision for him. The cable instructed him that he would, without argument, proceed to Nossi-Be, which, he was assured, was undoubtedly a fine, sheltered and safe anchorage. Felkersam might be caring of his crew, but he was not the man to protest against orders. If the Admiralty back in St Petersburg told him to proceed to Nossi-Be then that was where he would go.

At the end of December he reached Madagascar. There he anchored his ships in the beautiful Nossi-Be and settled down to wait for Rozhestvensky and the relief ships of Captain Dobrotvorsky. His crews immediately began to enjoy the lush green forests and cool waters of the bay. It was almost like a holiday.

Dobrotvorsky was finding things a little different. By this time morale on his ships was low, partly due to the heat and partly to enforced stays in foreign ports that had little to recommend them. The constant work to repair damaged engines was grinding men down and the fear of dysentery that might be picked up on shore visits was both real and unrelenting.

Dobrotvorsky had neither the compassion of Felkersam nor the iron fist of Admiral Rozhestvensky. Despite his ambition, as a fleet commander his methods were sadly lacking, falling between the two extremes of the experienced admirals. The result was a wishy-washy approach to discipline that left his crews unsure and increasingly unhappy.

When they did eventually leave Djibouti on the final leg of their journey Dobrotvorsky's crews were so low-spirited that nobody even thought of organising the usual sailors' ceremony of 'Crossing the Line'. Dobrotvorsky himself was in a low state and did not insist on the traditional performance. What Neptune thought about the insult has not been recorded.

At the beginning of February 1905 Dobrotvorsky and his cruisers reached Dar es Salaam. It was a brief stay and none of the officers or crew were particularly taken by the colony or the town. When the Russian officers were trying to find rooms in the town's only hotel they discovered that the place was packed out with visitors from a German squadron that had recently docked. The son of the kaiser was part of the squadron and the German sailors were intent on celebrating his birthday. They were boisterous and opinionated and the Russian sailors felt totally intimidated.

With all of the rooms in the hotel already allocated to the Germans the Russian contingent were forced to sleep on the veranda where drunken singing from the streets and a plague of mosquitoes kept most of them awake all night. The fleet left early the next morning.

On 14 February Dobrotvorsky, after many fruitless attempts, managed to finally make wireless contact with Rozhestvensky and a few hours later his lookouts spotted the smoke of the admiral's ships out practicing at sea. Felkersam was already anchored off Nossi-Be and now, with Rozhestvensky located, the most difficult part of his journey had been completed. Contact had been made.

* * *

Sailing around the southern tip of Africa, Rozhestvensky and his squadron had endured the worst of the Cape storms. For days on end they put up with huge rolling seas. Waves of over 50-ft high constantly swept in to crash down with all the fury of a battery of 12-in shells onto the decks of the battleships. How the smaller vessels survived was a mystery that nobody cared to ponder for too long.

Twice, three times, the *Suvorov* was broached, lying helpless and side on to the elements for what seemed like hours before the helmsman was able to turn her bow back into the storm. Nobody had ever seen anything like it before; even the old hands who had sailed the oceans of the world simply held up their hands in horror.

When, one night, the tug *Roland* disappeared the natural assumption was that she had foundered and gone down with all hands. She was followed into the blackness by the old *Malay* whose engines had broken down yet again. Nobody had time to even think of searching for the missing ships.

At the height of the storm the *Kamchatka*, always to be relied on for inappropriate responses to any difficult situation, signalled Rozhestvensky asking for permission to throw its stock of useless coal overboard. The admiral screamed out a negative reply, stating that all of the ships used the same coal, the *Suvorov* included, and that there was nothing wrong with it. He followed up his message with the vague threat – or maybe not so vague – that only those who attempted to ditch their coal would go over the side.

Not content with this interlude, a little later the *Kamchatka* signalled once more, 'Do you see torpedo boats?' A general alarm was sounded across the fleet before the *Kamchatka* was in touch again, this time claiming that the signalman had made a mistake. He had used the wrong code. What he should have said was 'We are all right now.' Nobody, least of all Rozhestvensky, found the *Kamchatka*'s antics funny any longer.

When the storm finally died the Russians were able to examine their ships. Apart from the missing *Roland* and *Malay*, most of them had sustained considerable damage with loose gear and railings swept away by the giant waves. More worryingly, three of the battleships had now developed trouble with their steering gear. It was a relief when, with the Cape and its dangerous waters behind them, the *Suvorov* finally spotted the southern shores of Madagascar.

There was a brief stop at the little island of Sainte Marie where the crew were supposed to start coaling once again. It was an unpropitious port of call, however, being run by the French as an overflow prison for Devil's Island. Bad weather prevented coaling and the French governor suggested a more sheltered spot; an estuary on mainland Madagascar five or six miles to the north. The move was duly made and another 2000 tons were loaded onto the battleships as the men cursed and groaned beneath the sacks. It seemed as if their lives had been completely taken over by the constant need to load fuel.

The one redeeming factor of their stay in this part of Madagascar came when they heard that, against all the odds, the tug *Roland* and the *Malay* had somehow survived the storm. Both ships were now steaming to rejoin the squadron.

Coaling was followed by the approach of a collier bearing a message from Admiral Felkersam. The message was simple but it was infuriating: he had reached Nossi-Be, as instructed by St Petersburg, and had begun to decommission several of his ships, ready for repair and overhaul.

Rozhestvensky was furious. 'What happened to Diego Suarez?', he wanted to know, his anger flowing as wildly as the recent storm over the decks of the *Suvorov*. His rage was directed both at the Admiralty in St Petersburg for giving orders to his subordinate without his approval and at Felkersam for taking and acting on those orders without consulting his chief.

There was worse to come. Before he could order his ships north to Nossi-Be to drag Felkersam off towards Diego Suarez – as he fully intended to do – the tug *Rousse*, which Rozhestvensky had ordered to scout ahead of the fleet, returned with even more distressing news. Port Arthur was about to fall.

The news that the end had finally come was confirmed when the hospital ship *Oryol* returned from detached duty at Kaapstad. The Japanese had taken control of the port and the 1st Pacific Fleet in its harbour had been totally destroyed by the enemy gunners on the hills. There would be no help now for Rozhestvensky's fleet.

The fall of Port Arthur was a traumatic event, not just for the men of the relieving fleet but for all of the people in the vast Russian Empire. At first there was disbelief, but when they were finally able to assimilate the news everyone remained stunned. 'How could such a tiny nation – little more than two islands – and such an insignificant people defeat the might of Imperial Russia?' they asked. The defeat was emotionally and psychologically devastating, but there were also military consequences: 'A vast quantity of military supplies was thus acquired by the Japanese, including 546 artillery pieces and 35,000 rifles … the Russian public was devastated.'[2]

More significant for the men of Rozhestvensky's command was the loss of the 1st Pacific Fleet. Within minutes the news was relayed to every deck on every one of Rozhestvensky's ships and righteous anger was soon replaced with depression and fear. The whole purpose behind this idiotic cruise had been to join up with the ships in Port Arthur and make one single, unbeatable force. Now that was impossible. Nobody even thought of turning about and heading back to Russia, but almost everyone, from the lowest stoker to the admiral himself, knew instinctively that most of the sailors in the fleet would never see their homes and families again.

However, what really hurt Rozhestvensky even more than the defeat at Port Arthur was the news that, on the orders of the czar, a 3rd Pacific Fleet had been formed and would soon be on its way to join him. It was news that he had been dreading ever since his fleet had left Russian shores.

The first detachment of this new 3rd Pacific Fleet, consisting of four ancient ironclads – the *Emperor Nicholas I*, *Senyavin*, *Ushakov* and *Monomakh* –

and the cruiser *Rus*, had been placed under the command of Admiral Nikolai Nebogatov. Rozhestvensky knew the ships only too well and had even served on board one of them in the dim and distant past. They were no better than coastal defence vessels, woefully short on fire power and speed, as Rozhestvensky remembered. To match them against Admiral Togo would be nothing short of suicide.

The first ships would be in Djibouti by the end of February, the Admiralty cabled, and the second half of the squadron would depart in May. Rozhestvensky was to wait at Madagascar until Nebogatov's Fleet caught up with him – a delay of at least two months – and then sally out to attack Togo.

The formation and despatch of the 3rd Pacific Fleet was no accident or sudden whim by the czar. It was in fact the culmination of a long and vengeful campaign waged by Commander Klado who Rozhestvensky had sent back to Russia in the wake of the Dogger Bank Incident.

Always a high profile figure, Klado had made himself doubly visible in the weeks after his return. For a brief period he became a much valued naval expert and an icon in the salons of St Petersburg. He was a familiar figure at court and had always been something of a favourite with the Romanovs. He had even acted as tutor to two of the family, the czar's brother Michael and his cousin Kyril, who had been standing alongside Admiral Makarov when he had been decapitated and killed.

Klado was not universally popular, however; the czar's Uncle, Grand Duke Alexei, disliked him intensely and labelled him a 'newspaper hero'.[3] Despite this, Klado did have the ear of the czar and in Russia under Nicholas Romanov that was the most important factor in any debate or discussion.

Klado had championed the formation of a 3rd Pacific Fleet, but Rozhestvensky, knowing all that was left in Russia were old, out-of-date warships, simply did not want them. They would, he declared, just slow him down. Klado insisted – and convinced the czar – that this old 'sink themselves fleet', as someone immediately labelled them, would at least draw the Japanese fire away from the newer battleships. It was sweet revenge for Klado who must have felt that he had achieved a moral victory over Rozhestvensky.

As if this was not bad enough, there was a final sting in the tail for Rozhestvensky. Just a few weeks before, as he was battling his way down the coast of Africa towards the Cape, Czar Nicholas had appointed Admiral Nikolai Skrydlov commander of the small fleet based at Vladivostok.

He had been despatched via the Trans-Siberian Railway and was now with his squadron at their base.

Skrydlov, the so-called 'fighting admiral', had never seen combat, but he was superior in rank and position to Rozhestvensky and that meant the man who had dragged his fleet halfway around the world would have to relinquish his command to someone he detested and loathed for his total incompetence. The Vladivostok Squadron might be tiny when compared to the 2nd Pacific Fleet but Skrydlov's rank and position were all that mattered.

Skrydlov, eager for the chance to acquire fame and glory, had no intention of waiting until Rozhestvensky reached Vladivostok to take over command. He immediately telegraphed asking for a date and place where he and 'Mad Dog' could rendezvous.

Even to someone who had not yet been in combat it must have been obvious that Admiral Togo and the Japanese Fleet had total control of the seas in the area. Whatever port or anchorage Rozhestvensky designated Skrydlov had no hope of reaching the rendezvous point. Such knowledge gave Rozhestvensky little satisfaction.

Rozhestvensky was clearly driven to the end of his tether and felt that his only recourse was to beard the dragon in his den. He dictated his resignation to Clapier de Colongue and ordered the chief of staff to send it to St Petersburg. Not surprisingly, within a few days there was a fulsome and placatory reply. His resignation had been refused. It seemed that the admiral could not even be allowed to fall on his sword with dignity and grace. More than anything he felt totally betrayed and let down by the czar and by the Admiralty. After all he had achieved on this impossible mission it was like being kicked in the teeth by the very people he had believed were his supporters.

Depressed and beaten, Rozhestvensky ordered a course to be set for Nossi-Be where he would join up with Admiral Felkersam at last; he had no alternative; Nossi-Be it would have to be. Then he retired, ill and confused, to his cabin.

The voyage along the eastern coast of Madagascar was an uneasy one. Charts of the area were, for the most part, unreliable and the reports of Japanese cruisers and torpedo boats in the area were arriving with almost monotonous regularity. Captain Ignatzius ordered that no lights were to be shown at night and that the guns were to be constantly manned. He was not going to be surprised by a sudden attack, particularly with the admiral confined to his bunk.

The only relief came towards the end of the journey when they met the cruiser *Svetlana* which had been sent by Admiral Felkersam to make contact with Rozhestvensky and lead him to Nossi-Be. The cruiser was carrying mail for the sailors; messages from home that brought relief, happiness and more than a few tears. It was the first contact with their loved ones that they had been given in over two long and distressing months. The downside was that the *Svetlana*'s escorting torpedo boat *Bodry* promptly broke down and led to yet another angry outburst from the cabin of the still-suffering Rozhestvensky.

* * *

The anchorage to the south of the island of Nossi-Be was, as the French had indicated, remote, beautiful and secure. The entrance to the bay where the Russian ships would anchor was through a series of channels that took them around and between small islands. It was a route that needed careful navigation and steering. Everyone soon realised that here there was little chance of the sudden and unexpected attack in which Togo specialised. Even Rozhestvensky seemed reasonably happy with the arrangements that had been made for his fleet.

The town of Hellville – perhaps appropriately named, considering the chaos the place was soon to see – had many of the usual amenities. There were small shacks, a few bars, three restaurants and shops. Within a matter of days, tradesmen, entrepreneurs and shop owners had flocked to the place and before long it was equipped with everything the Russian sailors could need or desire.

Dockyard workers had been sent from Diego Suarez and all of the facilities for repair that the fleet so urgently required were also there, waiting for the ships. At first glance it seemed that the French decision to relocate the base had been a good one.

The Russians had celebrated Christmas Day (according to the Russian calendar) as the fleet skirted the eastern coast of Madagascar. It had been a subdued celebration, but when, on 10 January 1905, Rozhestvensky stood on the bridge to oversee the difficult entry to their new anchorage, he seemed to have recovered at least some degree of good spirits and hope for the future.

Admirals Felkersam and Enkvist came on board the *Suvorov* to confer with Rozhestvensky the moment the flagship anchored. The three men had lunch together and Rozhestvensky told them of the 3rd Pacific Fleet that had been formed at Libau and was now on its way to join them. Like the commander-in-chief, neither of the two men was much impressed.

This meeting was one of the few occasions during the voyage that the three leading members of the expedition came together, face to face, for discussion and planning. It should have been a key moment, but far from being an informative and mutually beneficial gathering Rozhestvensky told them absolutely nothing about his plans or their future movements. The two rear admirals left the flagship considerably more bemused and uncertain than when they had arrived.

Rozhestvensky neither liked nor totally trusted his two subordinates, but the real reason for his reticence was that he simply did not know what they were going to do next. He knew that all of the ships needed overhaul but there was also coal to be taken on board. Not only that, the ships were in desperate need of provisioning and the crews were equally as desperate for rest and recuperation.

He still had hopes of leaving Nossi-Be within a few days, knowing that his only chance against Togo was to move quickly. He had to catch the Japanese admiral before he had time to refresh and prepare for battle. For a few days he turned the notion round and round in his head before coming to his decision. Rozhestvensky had to catch the Japanese somewhere and this seemed like the best opportunity.

Togo and his fleet had been almost continually at sea for the past twelve months. Like the Russians they too would be in urgent need of refitting and a little rest. Rozhestvensky knew that the only way forward was to catch them while their guns were in poor condition, while the bottoms of their hulls were fouled with weed, while supplies were low and while the men were tired from almost constant sea duty.

The reinforcing 3rd Fleet, with its ancient and decrepit ships, would be no earthly good to him. Speed was their best asset, not numbers, and so Rozhestvensky signalled the Admiralty with his new suggestion. 'Let me sail now', he pleaded, 'and break through to Vladivostok. Then, with Skrydlov's small but undamaged and untried squadron added to the main fleet, we might stand a chance of defeating the mercurial Japanese Admiral.' He cabled that it did not matter if he or Skrydlov was in command; with Port Arthur gone the only aim of the enterprise was now beating Togo, and that would not happen by waiting for the slow and obsolete 'self-sinkers'.

St Petersburg refused the request, falling back on the czar/Klado plan for a 3rd Pacific Fleet. For some time now – in newspaper articles and in private consultations with the czar and with members of the Admiralty –

Commander Klado had been actively promoting the theory of might and size being the only way to get the better of the Japanese.

Togo had been victorious so far, Klado stated, only because he had been able to pick off small Russian units one by one. Put together a huge fleet, confront Togo with an overwhelming force and the Japanese would have no chance. Hence the importance, as far as Klado's theory was concerned, of the 3rd Pacific Fleet linking up with Rozhestvensky before sailing to meet Togo.

Objections sent by hand and by wireless telegraphy to St Petersburg failed to bring any change to what Rozhestvensky thought were foolish orders. The admiral tried over and over again without getting what he wanted. Technically he held an independent command, but like all generals and admirals, the czar's approval for any request was essential.

The negative response to Rozhestvensky's repeated requests might have been expected. He began to think that Czar Nicholas did not like him any longer. His paranoia grew, but fulminate as he might, and for as long as he wanted, Rozhestvensky was not permitted to leave Nossi-Be. He would have wait for Nebogatov before he proceeded any further.

More disappointment came a few days after the fleet arrived at Nossi-Be. The vital colliers had always, as the admiral knew, been potential targets for the Japanese. No colliers meant no coal, and no coal meant no Russian fleet. So far they had not come under attack, but now the captains and owners of the Hamburg-American Line colliers found themselves faced by a distinctly threatening message from the enemy: proceed any further and it will be at your own risk. To make matters worse the Japanese weren't even their enemy; *Russia* was at war with Japan, not Germany. The colliers were, as their crews were only too well aware, vessels of an independent and neutral country that was not technically involved in the conflict.

So far they had supplied Rozhestvensky's ships wonderfully well, but now, with Japanese-controlled territory almost in sight, the risks had suddenly become much greater. Now they had become real and the prospect of death, blood and disaster held little appeal for the collier captains.

All of the previous threats of attack on Rozhestvensky's ships had been exactly that: threats. With distance between them they could only ever be little more than rumour and fear. Now the fleet was within range of Japanese torpedo boats and battleships and when they did finally set sail for Vladivostok it was clear to everyone that combat would not be delayed for long.

That was not the whole concern. The colliers had been operating as allies to the Russian Fleet. If anything was liable to challenge their neutrality it was the simple fact that they had been aiding and abetting the Russians, albeit at a price. And now they had been given a direct warning from the Japanese navy. It was a dose of sudden and harsh reality, and one that they were certainly not intending to ignore: 'Any colliers discovered in the vicinity of the Russian squadron would be instantly fired on and destroyed.'[4]

In light of such a warning the collier crews felt that it would be foolish – not to say suicidal – to continue supplying coal to the Russians. They, in turn, now faced Rozhestvensky with what was not so much an ultimatum as a blank refusal. They would not proceed across the Indian Ocean.

As if he had not suffered enough disappointments, this was the last straw for Rozhestvensky. He already felt isolated and betrayed. Now his ships were going to be deprived of the one thing they could never do without: coal. For the second time in the month he retired to his cabin, sick at heart and sick in body. Clapier de Colongue, the chief of staff, told the *Suvorov* crew that the admiral was suffering now from neuralgia and did not need to be disturbed.

While Rozhestvensky lay in agony on his bunk, the 2nd Pacific Fleet lay equally as immobile and impotent at its anchors in their safe anchorage on Nossi-Be. With boilers tamped down, ensigns furled and decks, as ever, immaculately scrubbed, they looked like dummy ships on a dummy lake. Only the ripples of their reflections in the waters of the bay told lookers-on that these were real vessels, powerful men-of-war just waiting for the call to action.

The voyage so far had taken the Russian sailors thousands of miles away from their homeland. It had been a journey fraught with difficulties, frustrations and mistakes. Now it seemed as if the whole enterprise had stalled.

Chapter 7

A Stagnant Pause

Despite Rozhestvensky's illness and the fears of imminent disaster that seemed to spread like a forest wildfire through the decks of every ship, there was still work to be done. Before anything else the sailors had to face the inevitable rigours of coaling.

It promised to be the last and many sailors, particularly the revolutionary minded ones, were quick to grumble to their colleagues. 'What was the point?', they asked, the fleet wasn't going anywhere. But orders were orders and the men were cajoled and bullied into finishing the hated task. The problem with the colliers was not their concern, the petty officers repeatedly shouted; that was down to the admiral and his staff to sort out.

Coaling took four days, in heat that was as bad as any the Russian sailors had yet encountered. Several men died from heatstroke and accidents, two of them sailors who had been overcome by fumes and suffocated to death in a dark companionway on the *Borodino*. By now all of the crews, even the new recruits, had grown used to the process of coaling. It was a vile task, made all the more unpleasant by the fact that their clothing and equipment were far from appropriate:

> The men, in their torn shoes, laboured with a will. When their feet were torn, too, they tied them up with rags. To spare their caps, they wrapped their heads in clouts. They looked like ragged stevedores ... The cloud of black dust which enveloped the ships was pierced by the shouts of the coaling parties and the rattle of crank chains.[1]

Lack of proper equipment for what was known throughout the navy as a labour-intensive process hindered the coaling at every stage. The biggest problem men faced came in the shape of the very things that were supposed to make the job easier; the sacks in which the coal was meant to be transported and stored:

> On the *Oryol* there were thousands of them but they were flour sacks, too long for the job. A couple of men would hold a sack open

at shoulder height, while a third man filled it. But this was a slow business; and the sacks, being frail, were constantly tearing.[2]

When this happened the coal spilled out across the deck. The only way to recover the precious fuel was to sweep it up into piles and then shovel it into another sack which, just like the first one, was more than liable to tear and spill coal once more across the wooden decking that had recently been so pristine and clean.

After coaling, cleaning the decks should have been next on the agenda. However, Rozhestvensky was lying in his cabin and not overseeing the process. It was something of a blessing, the crew decided, and this time the planking was left dirty and stained.

The next task was the loading of stores. Thousands of tons of supplies – everything from potatoes, meat and vegetables to crate after crate of champagne and vodka – were man-handled onto the waiting ships. Petty officers patrolled the decks to make sure that none of the supplies, the alcohol in particular, made its way into the lockers of the sailors.

And then, finally, it was time to relax. The little town of Hellville, previously sleepy and laid-back, suddenly mushroomed into a loud and vibrant community where the primary occupation of the sailors was enjoyment in whatever form of debauchery they could find. The residents of Hellville, both temporary and permanent, were determined to give it to them.

Many of the officers took the opportunity to hunt in the tropical rainforest that encircled the bay. Taking quinine to guard against malaria and wearing thick leather boots up to their knees to prevent fatal snake bites, they spent hours in the jungle. A lake in the centre was full of crocodiles and beyond it ran a river, also heavily populated with crocodiles. It was cool, and a great spot for swimming, but the ever-present crocodiles made this a dangerous pastime.

For most of the ordinary sailors, and for a large number of the least imaginative officers, the town of Hellville provided them with all the entertainment they required. They might visit the jungle occasionally to see exotic wild animals, but the bars and restaurants of the town held considerably more interest than mosquito-infested jungle where the options of death by crocodile bite or snake venom were all too real.

After the coaling and resupplying of the fleet had finally ended, what followed was a long, protracted and often torpid stay on Nossi-Be. On other occasions the stay was also riotous, even dangerous. While Rozhestvensky lay silently on his bunk and pondered on the fate of the expedition his sailors decided that if they were heading towards oblivion, as seemed likely, they might as well enjoy what little time they had left.

A complex of brothels was quickly established on the shoreline; local girls for the ordinary crewmen and imported French prostitutes for the supposedly richer officers. Even in matters like 'bought sex' it seemed that the class divides still existed.

Regardless of their origins, the girls, and the establishments in which they were based, did a roaring trade. Homemade signs were hastily pinned up outside the bars and shops declaring things like 'Purveyors to the Russian Fleet'. One satisfied brothel owner put up a sign changing the name of his bar-cum-brothel to 'The Parisian Café', declaring, 'After you lot leave I'm going to retire and settle in Paris on my proceeds.'

At first cheap alcohol was readily available, much of it local hooch brewed in the shacks of the original town:

> Drunkenness increased. The officers ordered what they wanted from their own canteen. The men got liquor clandestinely when they went ashore or bought strong drink from the bum-boats. Crazed by their potations, they behaved like lunatics ... Prices soared. A bottle of beer cost three francs and a bottle of champagne from forty to sixty. Nobody bothered about the cost. Our men despaired of escaping from the war with their lives, so they drowned thought in drink and dicing.[3]

Drink was one thing but the real curse of Hellville lay in gambling shacks where sailors could throw away their money for the fun of seeing the dice fall or the right card turn over. And where there was gambling there was inevitably fighting over the results, even if men did not care about whether they won or lost; they were all going to die so what the hell.

The deteriorating discipline on the ships soon led to outbreaks of disobedience and petty theft. Insubordination was rife and there were attacks on officers and petty officers who tried to prevent men from getting too far out of hand. Even officers took to using their fists when a superior's command prevented them from doing what they wanted. And some of the things they wanted were bizarre in the extreme.

Everyone took the opportunity to acquire for themselves a wide range of pets. Keeping these animals had become a craze and everything from parrots and poisonous spiders to monkeys were brought on board every ship in the fleet. The decks ran wild with dogs and hares and more exotic creatures such as porcupines and chameleons.

Sometimes the so-called pets were not just unusual but downright dangerous. A crocodile was discovered on one ship, a venomous snake on another. The snake, concealed in bales of straw, emerged and bit one of the ship's engineers with the result that his leg swelled like a balloon and the surgeon thought he was going to die. In the end he survived, but the snake was consigned to the water, much to the chagrin of his owner.

Forcing monkeys, wild pigs and dogs to get drunk on champagne – a regular event on some of the ships – was perhaps one thing: making them then fight one another and gambling on the result was something else entirely.

Rozhestvensky, alone and despairing in his cabin, seemed unaware of the anarchy that had taken over control of his fleet. Unaware or uncaring, it hardly mattered and men like Clapier de Colongue and Captain Ignatius began to despair of what might happen next.

Things eventually grew so bad that, despite the prosperity the fleet was bringing to Nossi-Be, the local French administrator was forced to complain about the behaviour of the Russian sailors. Some of them had become so drunk and out of control that they began tearing down native shacks just for the fun of it. Such behaviour was, apparently, setting a bad example and the administrator feared what might happen when the fleet left.

If there was one positive result from the Russian excesses ashore in Hellville – and, perhaps more significantly, of the administrator's reluctant complaint – it was that it managed to rouse the supine and despairing Rozhestvensky from his sick bed.

The admiral was furious. He knew that he had been derelict in his duty, no matter how unwell and depressed he might have been. It was time to make amends. He could not stop the gambling and drinking but he could limit the opportunities of his crews to over-indulge.

Much to the indignation of the sailors, he immediately put an end to shore leave, except on Sundays and Feast Days. Even officers, apart from specially selected and approved individuals, were limited in the number of times they could now venture ashore to enjoy the pleasures of Hellville.

As for the collection of wild animals that Rozhestvensky literally fell over the moment he stepped out of his cabin, they were immediately to be thrown overboard, or taken ashore and dumped. The resentment was palpable and it was clear that serious difficulties now lay ahead. Rozhestvensky saw that and knew it would take all of his iron-fisted discipline to keep the sailors in line.

* * *

A revitalised Rozhestvensky quickly decided that an idle Russian seaman was a dangerous Russian seaman. He set the crews to cleaning their ships, polishing away the dirt and grime of many weeks of neglect. They worked, reluctantly, until the brass and decks once more sparkled like jewels in the tropical sun. Then the admiral began taking the ships to sea for training.

Training was perhaps the wrong term. It was far too late for that. Very quickly it became apparent that the ships could not steam in anything like a battle line and their gunnery was exceptionally bad. In one exercise the target was missed by every ship in the fleet while in another the *Suvorov* did eventually manage one hit: on the bridge of the cruiser *Donskoi* which was actually towing the target.

Torpedo firing exercises were just as bad. On one occasion seven torpedoes were launched: out of the seven, one jammed in its tube, two shot off to starboard and another to port; two simply missed the target while the last one kept going round and round in circles and causing utter panic on the ships of the fleet. Rozhestvensky despaired: 'If, after four months cruising, we have not learned the principles of concerted action, what likelihood is there that we shall have mastered them by the date God has chosen for our encounter with the enemy?'[4]

The early months of 1905 brought a renewed flurry of cables between Rozhestvensky and the czar. The admiral was now more determined than ever to leave Nossi-Be as soon as possible; Czar Nicholas was equally as determined that he should stay to wait for Dobrotvorsky and Nebogatov.

The one consolation for Rozhestvensky was that, thanks to diplomacy back in Russia, combined with what little pressure he was able to exert on the collier captains, the dispute with the Hamburg-Amerika Line was settled. The colliers would continue to coal the fleet as long as they could travel separately and their safety was guaranteed. There was no explanation as to how this was to be achieved, but if any of the supply vessels were damaged or sunk there would be a massive compensation payment from the Russian government. Rozhestvensky was not happy at being held to ransom, as he saw it, but he had no option other than to agree.

Meanwhile the climate was beginning to exact a dreadful toll as tropical diseases and disorders spread from one ship to another. The hospital ship

Oryol was full of sick men with hardly a bed to spare, and there was little chance now of Rozhestvensky finding Natalia Sivers free for a light lunch.

The death rate among sailors rose alarmingly and almost every day there was a burial at sea. The pattern had now become a ritual. A destroyer would come alongside the ship where the death had occurred and transfer the corpse. With ceremonial gunfire, flags at half-mast and bands playing mournful dirges, the dead man would be taken to his last resting place on the ocean floor. Many of the old hands remarked that the dead were the lucky ones; they were well out of it.

It was not only serious illness that afflicted the fleet. The seemingly innocuous complaint of prickly heat drove men wild, scratching at the irritation one minute, wincing in pain the next:

> I suffered much from prickly heat, my whole body being covered with irritable, itching and smarting vesicles. It was not bad enough to lay me up but it interfered greatly with rest and, as it did not actually put a man on the sick list, the surgeon paid no heed to it.[5]

The arrival of Dobrotvorsky's squadron, with men whom many of them knew from back in Russia, brought some relief. It also brought mail and newspapers from home. Letters from loved ones were welcome; the news of events in Russia, gleaned from papers that were originally intended for officers only, was certainly not. It seemed that revolution had broken out.

* * *

In early January 1905, at the annual ceremony to consecrate the River Neva, a live artillery charge was unfortunately used instead of a blank in one of the saluting cannons. The subsequent explosion wounded many dignitaries and convinced everyone that it was an attempt on the life of Czar Nicholas. The original explosion had been an accident but, rather than elicit support or sympathy for the czar, a mood of rebellion spread rapidly across the country. It was as if the bomb in St Petersburg, combined with the military defeats in Korea, had been a signal that ignited the revolutionary spirit in Russian peasants and workers.

Within a matter of days there were strikes, protests and demonstrations in the capital and in many other recently industrialised cities across the nation. The czar's government reacted as it always reacted to protests: with force.

Unlike the later revolution of 1917 this earlier uprising was very much an accidental revolt. It was brought about by the incompetence of the czar's government and the total lack of leadership it provided, but was ignited by an incident that nobody had expected. That did not mean that it was not wanted or wished for by the proletariat. In fact it was just the opposite.

In 1902 the writer Leon Tolstoy had penned what he called 'An Open Letter to the Czar', detailing the conditions and persecution under which the Russian people lived:

> Prisons were overflowing with convicts innocent of any real crime, the city streets were full of soldiers ready to shoot the people on a whim, and the censor's power stretched everywhere denying freedom of religious and political expression ... Tolstoy's depressing conclusion was that it was impossible to maintain this form of government except by violence.[6]

He might not have been advocating open revolt but Tolstoy's views were confirmed by the events of 22 January, a day that quickly became known as Bloody Sunday. If the bomb explosion earlier in the month had galvanised the revolutionary forces, this violent bloodletting cemented the left-wing opposition to the czar.

Only the day before Bloody Sunday a General Strike had been called and the mood in St Petersburg was sullen and dangerous. Bloody Sunday was the catalyst that saw that mood spill over from one of resentment into dramatic action.

Father Georgy Gapon, a man much influenced by Tolstoy's writings, led a march of several thousand workers and their families to present a petition to the czar at the Winter Palace in St Petersburg. The petition begged Nicholas to use his position and authority to help relieve the terrible conditions in which the people lived.

The marchers got to within 200yds of a defensive line of troops standing with loaded muskets outside the palace. A company of Cossacks sat on their cavalry mounts alongside them, swords drawn, silently watching the marchers. And then, without warning or reason, the horsemen charged. Gapon later described the attack in some detail:

> A cry of alarm arose as the Cossacks came down on us. Our front rank broke before them, opening to right and left, and down this lane the soldiers drove their horses, striking on both sides. I saw the

swords lifted and falling, the men, women and children dropping to the earth like logs of wood.[7]

Estimates place the number of dead at around 200, all of them innocent marchers who believed implicitly in the power and justice of the czar, the man they knew as the 'Little Father'. Now that faith had been challenged in the most brutal and bloody fashion. Even though Nicholas had not been present at the Winter Palace on Bloody Sunday, and certainly did not order or condone the massacre, he was the man who sat at the top of the regime; therefore, people believed, the slaughter was entirely his fault.

The leader of the Bloody Sunday march, Father Gapon, was an Orthodox priest from the Ukraine who had an uneasy and troubled relationship with his church. He was at the centre of much of the revolutionary activity in St Petersburg, working tirelessly to help and encourage the urban poor that he encountered in his missionary work in the city.

Even before the march, Gapon had organised the Assembly of Russian Factory and Mill Workers of St Petersburg; in effect an early trade union that attempted to protect workers' rights. Unfortunately, the assembly was supported and encouraged by the secret police who were clearly working on the premise that it was better the devil you knew than the one you didn't.

The police were happy to keep the organisation running, to monitor its business and all the while gather information from its members. Gapon was well aware of the links, but he firmly believed that dual loyalty would help rather than hinder the development of worker solidarity and progress.

Gapon was distraught after the Bloody Sunday massacre; appalled at the death of so many innocent people. He became vocal in his criticism of the czar and the way his government was running the country, and soon he was forced to flee abroad. In Switzerland he came into contact with revolutionary leaders such as Lenin and other Bolsheviks. He did not stay long in Switzerland, but his socialist ideas and beliefs were confirmed.

After he returned to Russia Gapon's end was tragic and sudden. He was murdered by members of the Socialist Revolutionary Party who had become aware of his secret and somewhat shady involvement with the police. Unlike Gapon they could see no justification for it. In 1906 the priest disappeared while on his way to a secret rendezvous and a few weeks later his body was found hanging in a remote cottage outside St Petersburg.

Regardless of Father Gapon's dubious methods Bloody Sunday led to more violence and further strikes in cities like Sevastopol and St Petersburg. At the same time, terrorism became rife in the countryside. It was the real start of the 1905 Revolution. Czar Nicholas was infuriated by the revolutionary activity, writing to his mother, 'It makes me sick to read the news, nothing but strikes in schools and factories.'

Despite fears of a repeat of the massacre at the Winter Palace, students remained unbowed and paraded down the Nevsky Prospect in St Petersburg, waving red flags and singing revolutionary songs. The brutal killings in front of the palace combined with the successive defeats by Japan on land and at sea had provoked open and bitter criticism across all parts of Russia.

A railway strike in October 1905 brought chaos to the country and Nicholas had no choice but to begin a process of bringing in basic civil liberties. The October Manifesto of that year promised liberal reform and the calling of a Duma (or parliament). The next few years saw almost continual feuding and problems as each successive Duma – Nicholas called and suspended them more or less at will – fought for equality and acceptance.

By contrast, the czar clung determinedly to his position of autocratic power. In 1914 the outbreak of war with Germany brought a temporary halt to the arguments, but successive defeats and a slowly worsening of living conditions led to an unworkable situation. In March 1917, with the situation untenable, Czar Nicholas II abdicated, bringing to an end hundreds of years of autocratic Romanov and Czarist rule.

* * *

On the ships of Rozhestvensky's Pacific Fleet the developments back home in Russia were viewed with mixed emotions: horror and fear in some sailors, jubilation and thanks in those with revolution in their hearts. Perhaps inevitably, rumours of a planned revolt amongst the sailors soon spread throughout the ships and it did not take long for those rumours to become reality.

It started with suicides and deserters, men desperate to escape the certain death that awaited them if the fleet ever got around to sailing. Leaping over the side was an easy way out. Few of the sailors could swim and by the time a boat was launched to look for them the doomed men were already dead. For those who did make it ashore the lush forests around the bay provided an ideal hiding place until the fleet finally left.

Fear – real corrosive fear – was stalking the fleet. It was a different type of anxiety from the fatalism that had been present for many months.

This was sheer terror; an emotion that was hard to place and even more difficult to eradicate.

The Japanese, of course, watched carefully and continued to fuel the Russian paranoia. The message was simple: the Japanese were coming and they made damned sure that their enemies knew it. One message in particular – a warning that originated from the Japanese prime minister, Count Katsura – was whispered everywhere: while the Russians had not encountered any Japanese torpedo boats in the North Sea, they would certainly come across them in the Indian Ocean. The feared was thus racked up another notch.

Mutiny began on the battleship *Admiral Nakhimoff* where the officers were a particularly aristocratic and distant group. They were also inefficient and uncaring about the welfare of their crew. Lazy and indolent, the officers were more concerned about their own pleasures, both in their wardroom and during their times ashore in Hellville.

Unlike most other battleships in the fleet, the *Nakhimoff* did not have a bakery, with the result that none of the sailors had tasted fresh bread for over two months. Dry biscuits that had acted as substitute bread rations were now turning mouldy in the hot, humid atmosphere of the tropics and the mood of the sailors was poisonous:

> A spirit of revolt spread throughout the ship. If the officers had been less unobservant they would have noticed the angry sentiment that prevailed. They were taken by surprise when that evening, the biscuit distributed for supper was flung over the side.[8]

Gathering courage and determination, the mutinous crew surged onto the upper deck. They were about to rush the bridge when the captain appeared. He pointed out that the 12-in guns of the *Suvorov* had swung around and were now aimed directly at the *Nakhimoff*. If they did not instantly submit to his authority the flagship would open fire.

It was no idle threat; Rozhestvensky would certainly have shelled them. The mutineers knew it and promptly surrendered. Fourteen of the ringleaders were sent back to Russia on trial for their lives; several more were sentenced to detention. Harsh punishment perhaps but mutiny was a serious affair on any ship in the Russian Navy and for one in a war zone it was doubly dangerous.

That was just the beginning of the revolutionary outbursts and the admiral's repression. Courts martial became commonplace for what were often minor offences and they seemed to work. Almost every day a court was in sitting on one or other of the ships, dispensing drastic punishments that quickly quelled any thoughts of rebellion or revolution in the minds of the sailors.

If the threat of outright mutiny had, for the moment, receded, insubordination and disobedience continued unabated. One officer on the *Ural* beat his captain half to death and the assailant was dismissed from the service. On the *Suvorov* sailors stole a crate of wine, hid it in the engine room and then, when attention was diverted elsewhere, drank themselves insensible. They were sentenced to detention for three years.

Soon, even Rozhestvensky had reached the end of his tether. There seemed to be no end to the disturbances fomented and often run by the revolutionary elements in the fleet. It was time for even more drastic action.

The *Malay*, with her constant mechanical breakdowns, had been causing problems for long enough and had been lucky to survive the trip around the Cape of Good Hope. Now the admiral decided to take pity on the old vessel and still get valuable use out of her. He loaded the battered steamer with the worst offenders, many of them being those with clear revolutionary ideals, and prepared to send her back to Russia.

Before the *Malay* could sail, however, a mutiny broke out on board. It was a serious outbreak and officers were attacked, beaten and locked below decks. It took a boarding party from the *Suvorov* – officers and sailors armed with cutlasses and pistols – to regain control. Several shots were fired, many heads were broken and casualties incurred on both sides, but the uprising was quelled. A few days later, with the mutineers chained and added to the ranks of the prisoners, the *Malay* set sail. She also carried with her two dozen of the seriously sick, many of them having developed tuberculosis in the wet and humid conditions on board ship.

The rainy season had now set in and conditions on the ships at Nossi-Be became almost unbearable. Rain storms erupted every few minutes, beginning and ending with no warning. It was, as Alexey Novikoff-Priboy was to later write, 'as if a tap had been turned on and then off in the heavens.' Yet the heat remained constant: a humid, steamy atmosphere from which the rains gave no relief.

Things were not made any easier when a breakdown in the refrigeration units of the *Esperance* presented Rozhestvensky with a serious problem. It would take time to carry out repairs and in the meantime the frozen food was rotting: 'The frozen meat on board began to putrify, and was dumped out at sea. But the winds and waves carried it back into the harbour, where it gave off the intolerable smell of carrion.'[9]

The half-defrosted, rancid carcasses of cows and sheep rocked easily in the swell and proved an inevitable draw for what seemed like every shark in the Indian Ocean. Soon the ships in the fleet were surrounded by sweeping schools of grey and ghostly killers, their fins cutting through the waves like the sails of yachts.

The presence of the sharks and the fervour with which they devoured their unexpected meals chilled the whole fleet to the bone and sent a shudder of fear up everyone's spine. It was, the superstitious declared, an omen of bad fortune; as if there hadn't been enough already on this voyage into oblivion and disaster.

There was some relief for Rozhestvensky in the person of Natalia Sivers. Almost every other day, she came for lunch on the *Suvorov* and made a huge impression on the ship's crew, not only because of her beauty but because of the admiral's closed cabin door when the meal was over. The mere sight of the closed door brought on an almost indescribable longing in the sailors. Rozhestvensky's niece, also a nurse on the *Oryol*, invariably came with Natalia Sivers, but when the cabin door closed she was left outside, which only heightened the feelings of envy and anger of the women-hungry sailors.

Communications between Rozhestvensky and St Petersburg were now at their most tense. One minute the admiral was insisting that he was not going to wait for Nebogatov, the next he was refusing to make any contact at all with the Admiralty.

The jungle tom-toms were soon in action yet again. As with any group of frustrated men who could see their moment of glory racing swiftly past, the 2nd Pacific Fleet was a hotbed of rumour. By the beginning of March the rumour that the fleet was soon going to sail had taken hold, but this time it was not just idle chatter; there was evidence to support the belief.

Divers had been put over the sides of the ships and were busy attempting to clean the hull bottoms as best they could, prior to getting underway. Cleaning the hulls of weed and molluscs, gathered during the voyage and the enforced stay at Nossi-Be, would not only give Rozhestvensky's ships greater speed, it would also reduce coal consumption.

Unfortunately, cleaning the hull bottoms of large warships like the *Suvorov* was a difficult task. It really required the attention of a good dockyard where the vessels could be hoisted out of the water and scraped clean. Whatever the divers managed to do was better than nothing, but it was really only the best of a very bad job.

Divers being dropped over the side and working all day and night in the shark-infested waters was not the only hint that something would soon happen. Somebody noticed that the officers' wardrooms, even on the smaller vessels, had taken on extra supplies of perishable foods while colliers and lighters full of coal were seen milling around in the bay. The older hands nodded sagely: preparations for departure were certainly well underway.

The Admiralty in St Petersburg had been unable to obtain a response from Rozhestvensky for some time. Despite their orders that he should remain at Nossi-Be, officials and statesmen in St Petersburg could see that Rozhestvensky was in no mood to meekly accept their ruling. He was, they were sure, thinking about taking independent action, disobeying the czar and setting sail for Vladivostok.

Things were not made any easier when negotiations with various countries in Latin America for the purchase of several new armoured cruisers broke down. It had always been something of a long shot but it had given hope when everything else seemed to be against the fleet. Czar Nicholas had promised that he would buy these ships for Rozhestvensky, but now it was clear that this would not happen. The admiral was being left only with the old 'self-sinkers' that he despised so much.

Felkersam had expected to find these promised new ships when he joined Rozhestvensky in Madagascar and was equally as disappointed as his commanding officer to find them not there. Like Rozhestvensky, he felt let down and abandoned to his fate.

The fatalistic attitude of many officers and crew began to grow once again. The failure of the czar to buy them new vessels was a real 'gut grinder' for men who had been promised so much but had been given so little: 'One of the midshipmen, losing control, exclaimed in maudlin tones "They are sending us to Golgotha but if I don't want to be crucified, what then? Will they drag me to the cross?"'[10]

Rozhestvensky had already declared that with Port Arthur gone the only possibility of victory was to get to Vladivostok as soon as possible and link up with the squadron there. St Petersburg did not disagree with that assessment but, as ever, the devil was in the detail.

Thanks to Commander Klado's influence the Admiralty was insistent that Rozhestvensky must wait for the 3rd Pacific Fleet. Rozhestvensky's hatred of the old 'self-sinkers' was equally as well known and his personality was such that, if pushed too hard, he could easily head off to confront Togo without them.

The thought of such an event terrified the autocratic St Petersburg government, particularly at a time when unrest was growing in the country. They certainly did not need their fleet commander out in the Far East taking matters into his own hands. They had fought, and were continuing to fight, the revolutionaries at home; they were certainly not going to allow the admiral of the 2nd Pacific Fleet to hold them to ransom.

Unfortunately, the Admiralty had precious little to fight with, but in retaliation to Rozhestvensky's attitude the St Petersburg government decided they would throw their toys out of the pram. They refused to pass on news of the whereabouts of the 3rd Pacific Fleet.

It was a puerile response, and it annoyed Rozhestvensky. The delays and disputes, the repeated refusal of his requests, and a growing feeling of disillusionment had already put Rozhestvensky's fearsome temper on a short fuse. This unhelpful decision from the Admiralty simply pushed him over the edge. Rather than force Rozhestvensky to comply with their wishes it merely strengthened his resolve to go his own way. They clearly did not know their man.

It was perhaps to be expected that both sides would stick to their principles, something that certainly did not ease the problem but which made Rozhestvensky's decision almost inevitable. In the end it was an unofficial report from one of the French officers stationed at Nossi-Be that finally determined the date and time of Rozhestvensky's departure.

According to the Frenchman, the 3rd Pacific Fleet had already crossed the Mediterranean and its ships were now coaling at Crete. Rozhestvensky realised to his horror that Nebogatov was closer than he had thought and could be reasonably expected to reach Madagascar within a few short weeks.

The fact that the Admiral had to learn the news from an officer of a foreign nation – albeit a friendly one – underlined the ridiculous nature of St Petersburg's decision to keep Rozhestvensky in the dark. The news made Rozhestvensky's decision for him. The redoubtable Clapier de Colongue was summoned to the admiral's cabin and informed that the fleet would sail the following day, 16 March 1905.

It was the logical move before the ancient 'self-sinkers' arrived to hinder the fleet. It was logical and it was also the wisest tactical move. And yet, de Colongue and the other members of the admiral's staff knew only too well that Rozhestvensky was about to commit not just an act of insubordination but one of actual mutiny.

Chapter 8

Togo Waits, Mad Dog Moves

By March 1905 it was clear to everyone that Admiral Togo Heihachiro was in supreme control of the waters around Japan and the Asian mainland. He was the only senior naval officer, on either side, with experience of commanding big gun warships in combat and was already the victor in three battles against the Russian Empire. Two of these had been fleet to fleet actions at sea. He might have been excused for being confident – or even over confident – but that was not Togo's way.

He had always been a careful and consistent planner and he was not going to change now. Two of the Japanese admiral's greatest virtues at this time were experience and patience. Experience was probably the most important of these.

Togo knew that, despite claiming victory at the Battle of the Yellow Sea the previous year, he had made crucial mistakes during the action. Firstly, he had split his gunfire rather than concentrate on one or two ships with the result that, overall, Japanese shelling was too loose and too poorly directed. The effect of this mistake was gunfire that was largely sporadic, ineffective and poor. This erratic performance had allowed the Russian cruisers to intervene when their battleships were in difficulties and draw away enemy fire. At the same time Togo was acutely aware that several of the Russian ships were not attacked at all during the seven-hour battle and had been allowed to escape with no damage.

Secondly, Togo had opened fire at far too great a distance when the possibility of claiming hits – let alone effective hits – was minimal. It was simply a waste of ammunition. Japanese gunfire had been considerably more efficient when the range had been closed to just four or five miles. Close the enemy before opening fire was to be Togo's maxim from now on.

Togo knew that he had been lucky in the Battle of the Yellow Sea. The shot that killed Admiral Vitgeft was what had decided the battle, disheartening the Russians and forcing them to turn and flee. He could not hope for such good fortune again and, therefore, this time it would have to be skill and courage that would bring him victory.

As for patience it was a quality that the Japanese admiral possessed in vast quantities. He had displayed this during his blockade of Port Arthur when it would have been all too easy to charge into the roadstead and fall victim to the shore batteries of the town. He had waited then and he would wait now. He could allow himself the luxury of watching to see what his opponent would do.

In fact, every day that went past was a bonus for Togo. As Rozhestvensky knew, his fleet had been at sea for twelve months, patrolling the waters around Korea and Japan, and, like the Russians, his ships were in desperate need of maintenance. Weed coated their hull bottoms, greatly reducing their speed, while guns and engines also required urgent overhaul.

Due to the recently laid minefields, which claimed two Japanese victims, Togo's strike force of six battleships had been reduced to four, and while these new French-built vessels were still the most dangerous part of his fleet, they would all benefit from short periods in dockyard.

This was something that Togo was able to facilitate on a rolling or rotating basis, his spies and a watching detachment of armed merchant cruisers keeping him well informed about enemy movements. With one or maybe two battleships in dock at any one time it would be easy enough to recall them if Rozhestvensky decided to leave port.

The longer the Russians delayed the more effective the repair and cleaning process would become. In dry dock the ships could be hauled clear of the water and cleaned of weed and other encumbrances, unlike Rozhestvensky's vessels which had had to make do with the near-impossible task of divers attempting to clean their hulls while the ships were still afloat.

As days turned into weeks and weeks into months Togo waited, wondering why the Russians had not yet come. His intelligence sources told him that their ships were still at Nossi-Be; knowledge that pleased and suited Togo very well indeed. If they delayed even longer, he told his staff, engineers might be able to raise and repair the Russian ships destroyed at Port Arthur. To turn these against Rozhestvensky would be a triumph in itself.

By the end of February, while Rozhestvensky was still sitting, fretting and fuming in Madagascar, all of Togo's ships had received their refits and his fleet had regrouped. They were now waiting patiently in Chin-Hei Bay on the south-eastern coast of Korea. Being close to all the sea routes north to Vladivostok, it was the perfect place to lay up.

Togo's four battleships – the *Mikasa*, *Shikishama*, *Fuji* and *Assaki* – were French-built pre-dreadnoughts, constructed on the same lines as the new British King Edward-class vessels. They were each armed with four 12-in guns, fore and aft, backed up by large numbers of 6-in secondary weapons and by smaller quick-firing guns.

From a logistical point of view the Japanese battleships were at least the equal of the *Suvorov* and the other Borodino-class battleships of the Russian fleet, even if they were fewer in number than the enemy. That was not Togo's greatest strength, however. From the perspective of professional seamanship and experience the Japanese hand was infinitely superior.

The Japanese battleships were backed up by the armoured cruisers *Nisshin* and *Kasuga* and by a large number of protected cruisers, destroyers and torpedo boats. In total, Togo had over sixty ships under his command.

More significantly, Togo had insisted on his crews practicing gunnery on a regular basis. The Russians, by contrast, had hardly fired their weapons since the Dogger Bank Incident:

> The Japanese also used mostly high-explosive shells with shimose (melinite), which was designed to explode on contact and wreck the upper structures of ships. The Russians used armour piercing rounds with small guncotton bursting charges and unreliable fuses. Japanese hits (would) set the superstructures, the paintwork and the large quantities of coal stored on deck on fire.[1]

Not only that, Togo ensured that his ships were issued with the brand new Barr and Stroud FA-3 coincidence rangefinders. That gave them a 2000-yd advantage (6000yds compared to 4000) over the Russian ships with their Liuzhol rangefinders which dated from the 1880s.

Togo's strategic preparation was equal to his logistics. On their charts he and his staff sectioned the Sea of Japan and the Korea Straits into more or less equal squares. Each had its own number, thereby easily indicating the location of any approaching enemy ships, and this would then be passed on by the new wireless telegraphy to Admiral Togo on the *Mikasa*. Each square was patrolled by the armed merchant cruisers of what was termed the Special Service Squadron and by the fast light cruisers of the Japanese Navy.

Togo's main battle fleet was divided into first and second squadrons: the first made up of the four battleships and the second comprising the powerful 8-in gun cruisers of Admiral Kamimura. The destroyers and torpedo boats, nearly fifty of them, operated as separate units.

Apart from regular exercises when the two squadrons went to sea for gunnery practice, Togo was content to wait in Chin-Hei Bay. He had prepared as fully and as effectively as he could. Now it just needed the Russian Fleet to appear.

* * *

Rozhestvensky weighed anchor shortly after 13.00 on 16 March and slipped quietly out of Nossi-Be. The *Suvorov* was followed by the other vessels of the 2nd Pacific Fleet and soon only the irrepressible *Kamchatka*, which signalled that she was taking water and sinking, remained in the anchorage. The trouble on the *Kamchatka* was traced to a broken pipe in her engine room and before long she had set off in pursuit of the fleet.

Rozhestvensky then seemed to disappear off the face of the earth for three solid weeks. There were no sightings of his fleet, no radio messages and no report from any of Togo's watching cruisers. He had simply disappeared. But in that time the Russian fleet covered well over 3000 miles across the Indian Ocean, most of the voyage being out of the sight of shore:

> We took twenty days to cross the Indian Ocean, never sighting land the whole time. The weather was calm, save for occasional flurries ... Our course was set for the Sunda Islands. Some of us were disappointed at not returning to Russia; others, weary and dispirited, felt glad that an end of any sort was approaching.[2]

It had been, in many respects, an easy journey. Then again, perhaps not. There were the inevitable deaths as several sailors, unable to cope with the sheer isolation of the rolling sea and the never-changing horizon, leapt overboard into their own personal oblivion. For most of the men, however, as the fleet ploughed steadily on at speeds of no more than ten knots, those three weeks were a period of quiet calm before the storm.

The fleet coaled five times as they crossed the Indian Ocean; on each occasion carrying out the dangerous and difficult task at sea. There were no friendly ports or islands now available to him so Rozhestvensky was forced to rely on good weather and a lack of Japanese intervention. He got away with it.

Breakdowns occurred with maddening frequency. The *Oryol* set the standard with a stoppage in her port engine within one hour of leaving Nossi-Be. Nothing improved much from there. Given the constant halts for refuelling and repairs, what Rozhestvensky achieved in that three-week period of silence was nothing short of a miracle. He drove, he cajoled, encouraged, and achieved one of the great seaborne journeys of the Twentieth Century.

In that period of relaxation and rest from the world, the sailors went about their tasks cloaked in a torpid drowsiness. They appeared to be almost half-asleep and gave half-hearted, mechanical responses to orders. They had lost interest in where they were going or what their fate might be. It was now simply a matter of living for the day:

> When off-duty we played the concertina or the balalaika. We sang songs, solo or in chorus. Some of the bluejackets, throwing off their fatigue, would dance. We told one another entertaining stories, distracting our minds to the best of our ability.[3]

The fleet finally glimpsed land early on the morning of 5 April. It was the coast of Sumatra. Rozhestvensky immediately formed his ships into two lines, with the colliers and auxiliaries between the warships, allowing the destroyers, which had been towed much of the way by the auxiliaries, to finally cast off their tow lines and shoot out ahead of the fleet in search of enemy vessels.

The main body of Rozhestvensky's fleet sighted Singapore on 8 April. Thousands of locals flocked to the seafront to catch a glimpse of the ships that had destroyed the Hull trawlers and sailed thousands of miles against all the odds to reach this point. Everyone reported that the ships were looking much the worse for wear. The coal on their decks made them appear dirty and untidy and every vessel trailed a foot or two of green weed along its sides.

The Admiralty back in St Petersburg still had no knowledge of Rozhestvensky's position. For two days after he had left they were still sending him cables at Nossi-Be and a spokesman had recently told the press that 'we have absolutely no news of the squadron'. Even allowing for political necessity, it was an amazing statement to make.

Having now appeared off the coast of the British-held port and citadel of Singapore, they – and the whole world – would quickly learn, by default, exactly how far Rozhestvensky had sailed and which way he intended to reach Vladivostok.

As the fleet steamed past Singapore – somewhat reluctantly and certainly with resentment at being unable to use the British facilities that lay so tantalisingly near – they were approached by a launch carrying the Russian consul.

The consul had hoped to board the *Suvorov* and personally congratulate Rozhestvensky on his feat, but the Admiral was in no mood for discussion. He replied to the consul's request to come aboard with the message that it was not possible. He was 'In haste'. Instead of climbing onto the deck of the flagship, the consul was to pass on papers and reports to one of the torpedo boats.

His dignity hurt and now feeling thoroughly frustrated and angry, the consul closed to within hailing distance of the battleships. Through a megaphone he shouted the news that the fortress and town of Mukden in Manchuria had fallen to the Japanese. The Battle of Mukden was a disaster that spelled the end for Russian land forces in the war. The only hope now was for a victory at sea.

The consul also brought Rozhestvensky orders from St Petersburg. He was to sail for Kamranh Bay on the Cochin China coast, where he was to wait for Nebogatov's 3rd Pacific Fleet. No arguments; he would wait there. Rozhestvensky did not even bother to reply.

More worrying for Rozhestvensky was the information that the Japanese Admiral Kamimura and his cruisers had been at Singapore just a few days before and were believed to be heading for Borneo.

Almost as an aside came the news that Nebogatov had left Djibouti and was well on his way to join the 2nd Pacific Fleet. Cursing, Rozhestvensky sailed on, easing his way out of the Indian Ocean and into the South China Sea.

* * *

Rear Admiral Nikolai Ivanovich Nebogatov was fifty-six years old when the czar and Grand Duke Alexei, commander of the Imperial Navy, called him to the Winter Palace to give him command of the 3rd Pacific Fleet. He was not a fighter like Rozhestvensky or a diplomat like Felkersam, he was a mild, gentle man, better suited to a desk in St Petersburg than he was to the bridge of a warship, no matter how old and worn out she might be. But like the other commanders in this naval war, he accepted his appointment and vowed to do the best that he could with the tools he had been given.

He and his 'self-sinkers' made good progress out of the Baltic. They hugged the Dutch coast in order to get safely past Dogger Bank and then moved slowly down the English Channel. As they sailed on, the crews practiced repelling torpedo boat attacks and survived a ferocious storm in the Bay of Biscay. After crossing the Mediterranean to reach Crete,

Nebogatov allowed his crews shore leave. The response was a repetition of Felkersam's experience some weeks before: 'The men immediately got drunk and started fights with the locals and with sailors of other nationalities. The debauchery continued for several nights. British newspapers exploded with well-practiced rage.'[4]

It was while he was lying off Soudha in Crete that Nebogatov learned Rozhestvensky had left Nossi-Be. Nobody, not the Admiralty in St Petersburg nor the French authorities on Madagascar, had the faintest idea of where he was headed or which route he would take to get himself out of the Indian Ocean and into the open sea that led to Vladivostok.

Rozhestvensky had always had several options open to him. First, there was the Sunda Strait between Java and Sumatra; a route that Rozhestvensky had originally favoured. Alternatively, he could take the Timor Strait or skirt the coast of Australia, but, unfortunately, both were long and the Australian coast, with its wide stretches of reef and rocks, was rugged and dangerous.

Admiral Rozhestvensky eventually decided on the Straits of Malacca. He knew that the moment he passed Singapore his route and his presence in the Straits would become public knowledge, but Rozhestvensky did not care. His next move was already taking shape in his head and it was something that neither Nebogatov nor the officials in St Petersburg would be able to do anything about. Meanwhile Nebogatov was inching closer.

While he was at Crete Nebogatov met a Russian officer called Essen who was on his way back to Russia after being a prisoner of the Japanese. The Japanese, Essen told him, were excellent fighters, particularly at long-range firing. Nebogatov immediately set his crews to belated exercises in long-distance firing. After that he took his fleet through the Suez Canal and soon arrived at Djibouti.

Despite repeated requests, St Petersburg could not give Nebogatov information about the location of Rozhestvensky's fleet. It would be several weeks before his position would be revealed and for the moment they remained in the dark. Nebogatov was told simply that he should try to find the fleet, wherever it might be, and if unsuccessful to aim to reach Vladivostok by himself.

Nebogatov ploughed steadily onwards, hoping that somewhere on his travels he might come across news of Rozhestvensky. He knew that the admiral had no time for his 3rd Pacific Fleet and did not want the ancient ships to join the larger squadron. Above all he knew that Rozhestvensky's 'disappearance' was as much a political as a strategic move. Nevertheless, he could do no more than continue his voyage and eventually, when he had found the missing admiral, try to be as much help as he could.

Nebogatov eventually guessed correctly, reached Singapore and there heard the welcome news that Rozhestvensky had sailed past the colony some days before. At the very least it meant that he was on the right track.

* * *

From Singapore Rozhestvensky headed towards the coast of Cochin China. It was not a destination he had decided on through choice. On 13 April the fleet made landfall and the following day steamed through the narrow entrance to Kamranh Bay. They had sailed nearly 4500 miles from Madagascar and Rozhestvensky might have been excused for giving himself a solid pat on the back. In fact the opposite was true: he was suffering from a severe case of depression.

The cause of his troubles had come three or four days before. Not long after passing Singapore, Rozhestvensky had ordered that all ships should report on their fuel stocks. The order puzzled everyone, but for the moment Rozhestvensky did not enlighten anyone.

The reason was actually quite simple. He had been determined to make a sudden and swift dash for Vladivostok, cutting out the need to call at ports in Indochina, and, more importantly, enabling him to reach the Russian Pacific port before Nebogatov and his 'self-sinkers' arrived. But he needed to be sure that all of his ships had sufficient coal to get them to Vladivostok.

His plan was thwarted by the coal stock returns. The *Alexander III*, the ship that had seemingly always led the way in rapid coaling competitions, reported that she had 500 tons less than any other ship in the fleet – small wonder that she had always won the coaling competitions, somebody sagely remarked – and there were no colliers within hailing distance to make up the shortfall.

The discrepancy of 500 tons meant that there had been a gross miscalculation, whether deliberate or accidental, by the *Alexander*'s officers, but the result was that Rozhestvensky's intention of sailing directly to Vladivostok could not now take place. While Vladivostok was only 2500 miles away the *Alexander III* simply did not have enough fuel to get her there. The fleet would have to summon up the colliers, then stop and take on more coal.

Dispirited and defeated, Rozhestvensky gave in and informed St Petersburg that he was, as instructed, heading for Kamranh Bay. Then he retired to his cabin where he lay in darkness, head pounding and his whole body feeling as if it was on fire. Meanwhile his 2nd Pacific Fleet headed slowly towards the coast of Indochina.

The fleet made no more than five or six knots in a desperate attempt to save fuel and to prevent further breakdowns. To officers and crew alike, the journey seemed interminable. Rozhestvensky neither knew nor cared. He was at the end of his tether, though no one, apart perhaps from Natalia Sivers and de Colongue, had any real understanding of his mental state.

When the ships reached their destination and the admiral finally emerged from his self-imposed exile, he was not impressed by what he saw. In fact he was appalled, but the shock at least brought him back to his senses. Kamranh Bay was twenty miles long but only ten miles wide. If Togo carried out one of the lightning-fast assaults for which he was famed it was the perfect bottleneck. There was no room to manoeuvre; no way to escape attacking ships. Even if Togo chose not to attack, he could sit outside the bay and blockade the Russian fleet as effectively as he had blockaded Port Arthur.

Knowing he would have to make the best of a bad job Rozhestvensky immediately ordered two cruisers and several torpedo boats to patrol the approaches to Kamranh Bay. Torpedo nets were to be slung from the sides of the anchored battleships to guard against submarine and torpedo boat attacks and all decks were to be constantly cleared for action.

Kamranh Bay, once a thriving French colony, had fallen into a state of disrepair. Buildings had collapsed as people left and the place was now choked by overgrowing vegetation. Only half a dozen houses were inhabited and a feeling of despair and depression hung over the anchorage. No shore leave was granted and the supply vessels had not yet arrived with fresh food. Morale in the fleet plummeted. But at least Kamranh Bay possessed a telegraph and post office.

Bowing to the inevitable, Rozhestvensky was finally forced to admit his location. '"Have arrived at Kamranh Bay," he signalled St Petersburg, "Remain until the arrival of the 3rd Pacific Squadron," answered St Petersburg once again, adding plaintively this time "And please keep us informed of movements."'[5]

Rozhestvensky knew he was trapped. Until fresh supplies of coal arrived he could not move anywhere. And all of the time Rear Admiral Nebogatov and the obsolete ships of his fleet were drawing inexorably closer.

It was not only Rozhestvensky who dreaded their arrival. The enemy also feared Nebogatov's ships, albeit for different reasons. Admiral Togo was already outnumbered by the Russian battleships and while the additional 'self-sinkers' were, as he knew, old and slow they possessed powerful 10- and 12-in guns. Just one lucky shot and they were all more than capable of causing serious damage to the four remaining Japanese battleships.

If, by some lucky accident or fluke, Rozhestvensky did manage to reach Vladivostok then his hotchpotch of a fleet made up of modern battleships, creaking cruisers and out-of-date coastal protection vessels would pose a real threat to Japan. That threat was not just from a tactical viewpoint. As a bargaining tool this massive array of shipping – somewhere in the region of fifty vessels when Nebogatov finally arrived – could be used to huge advantage in peace negotiations.

Japan had been at war for over twelve months and her resources were now running low. Unlike Russia, she did not have an unlimited supply of men and machinery. Troops needed guns and ammunition, ships required shells, and if the Japanese government did not have the means to purchase them then their new-found 'allies' would soon drop away.

Interest in the progress of Rozhestvensky's fleet had already begun to wane and the world's press had become almost apathetic in its coverage: 'The first flush of surprise and delight over the discovery that Rozhestvensky really possesses an effective squadron is wearing off and people are reverting to a condition bordering on indifference.'[6]

No money, no friendly nations, no glory or world acclaim: the situation for Japan was beginning to look a great deal more parlous than the victories at Port Arthur and in the Yellow Sea might lead people to believe. Togo needed to provide a victory and, more than anything, keep Rozhestvensky away from Vladivostok.

Meanwhile diplomatic pressure on countries that were friendly to Russia, such as France, was stepped up. Even the United States of America (the Russians had now come perilously close to US territories in the Philippines) added her tuppenceworth to the equation and put a number of cruisers and destroyers to sea to watch for Rozhestvensky. It was another annoyance for Rozhestvensky; another niggling problem he had to be aware of; and, more importantly, ensure that none of his trigger-happy gunners started a war with the USA.

Four Hamburg-America Line colliers arrived at Kamranh Bay on 15 April and for the Russian sailors the hated task of coaling ship began again. This time Rozhestvensky made sure that the *Alexander III* made an accurate count of the tonnage she had taken on board.

There was some relief for the sailors, however, when transports and supply vessels also arrived, bringing with them fresh fruit and vegetables.

The hungry sailors from every ship in the fleet seized the vegetables with alacrity and were soon making traditional cabbage soup, the first they had tasted in what seemed like an eternity.

Over the coming weeks, as increasing pressure from Japan and Britain was exerted on the French government, Rozhestvensky was forced into playing a series of annoying but ultimately ridiculous games. The French would complain about his presence in their territorial waters and give him twenty-four hours to depart; Rozhestvensky would move a few miles up the coast until another ultimatum forced him to move again; and so on.

It was a pointless existence, annoying and infuriating, and it inevitably led to trouble in the fleet. After all the complaints about coaling and cleaning the ships, the men were bored and annoyed at their lazy and seemingly valueless stay on the coast of Indochina.

On the *Oryol* mutiny broke out when sailors were issued with a meal of rancid beef from a diseased cow. The meals went over the side and scuffles between officers and men eventually resulted in the captain backing down and fresh meals being prepared.

When Rozhestvensky came aboard the next day he furiously degraded officers and crew and took away eight randomly picked ringleaders. It had become almost the standard performance: Rozhestvensky would arrive, scream and shout, then pick out a few men and depart. By this stage of the voyage it impressed no one and was as much a dramatic interlude as it was a disciplinary procedure.

On the morning of 9 May the smoke from Nebogatov's fleet was finally sighted. It was the moment Rozhestvensky had dreaded, but the sailors of his fleet welcomed the new arrivals; anything to break the monotony. Formal greetings by flag were exchanged and within a few hours the two admirals were standing face to face on the deck of the *Suvorov*.

Rozhestvensky received Nebogatov coldly and in a meeting that lasted just half an hour told him nothing about his plans. Then Nebogatov was curtly dismissed and sent back to his ship. The two admirals did not meet again or communicate directly for the duration of the cruise.

Chapter 9

Towards the Donkey's Ears

The combined Russian fleets, with Nebogatov's ships now known as the 3rd Armoured Unit, left Indochina on 14 May 1905. It was to be the final leg of their long and arduous journey around the world and by any stretch of the imagination it was clearly going to be the most dangerous.

Admiral Rozhestvensky had decided to approach Vladivostok through the Korea Strait, a stretch of water that separated the Japanese islands from the Asian mainland. This deep-water passage was divided into two by Tsushima Island. Known as the Donkey's Ears, after the two high mountain peaks that towered above the island, the whole area was, by any standard, a pretty impressive location; as long as the mist, for which the region was well known, did not hide the view.

The two channels, the eastern and western waterways, again provided Rozhestvensky with a choice and a decision to make. Either route would serve a purpose but the eastern channel was the furthest away from the coast of Korea where Togo was known to be lurking. That was the route that Rozhestvensky chose. There were, however, drawbacks to the channel.

This eastern channel was, at its narrowest, just twenty-five miles wide and was potentially another deadly bottleneck where space to manoeuvre was limited. But it was short and clearly the fastest way to reach Vladivostok which, from the northern end of the channel, lay just 600 miles away. The passage was usually known as the Tsushima Strait.

Rozhestvensky realised that Togo would be guarding the Tsushima Strait, but decided to employ decoys in order to see for certain where the Japanese forces lay. He despatched four auxiliary cruisers to cover the other possible routes: through the Tsugaru Straits between the two main Japanese islands, and the longer and more difficult La Perouse Straits which took ships close to Australia. These ships would, hopefully, also distract Togo's attention from the fleet's real route.

In all, Rozhestvensky despatched ten of his charges – mostly transports and supply ships – under the guise of using them as reconnaissance vessels. In reality he was moving slow, unarmed vessels out of the danger zone.

Everyone knew that battle could not be delayed very long and that Togo was waiting somewhere. The clash, when it came, would be fierce and bloody. It would be no place for unarmed service vessels or for crews who were not prepared to die for the czar.

The dying Admiral Felkersam was now fading quickly as his will to live slipped away. Although he and Rozhestvensky certainly had their moments of disagreement there was a degree of mutual respect between the two men. Felkersam was the second most senior admiral in the fleet and if Rozhestvensky were to be killed or immobilised he would be the man to take charge. But if, as now seemed likely, Felkersam was also dead, to whom should command then devolve?

Rozhestvensky had absolutely no trust or faith in Nebogatov or Enkvist, and as a way around the problem decided that, in the event of his death, command would pass to the captain of the next ship in the battle line behind the *Suvorov*; in this case the *Alexander III*. It would then, if necessary, move to the *Borodino*, then the *Oryol* and so on. In effect he had cut out Admirals Nebogatov and Enkvist, deciding instead to grant seniority to the captains of the newest battleships in the fleet.

Rozhestvensky did not bother to inform Nebogatov of his decision; something that was liable to cause problems in the days ahead. As far as Nebogatov was concerned he was the next in line of succession after Felkersam and so far nobody had said anything to disabuse him of this notion.

Admiral Felkersam died on 24 May. On Rozhestvensky's orders the news was kept secret from the rest of the fleet and the dead admiral's flag continued to fly from the mainmast of the *Oslyabya*. Sailors, as Rozhestvensky knew, were a superstitious breed and, as if there hadn't already been enough bad luck on the voyage, the death of one of the senior men in the fleet would have undoubtedly been seen as yet another bad omen.

Felkersam's body was placed in a zinc coffin and held in the cold storage lockers of his flagship, ready for burial at a later stage. Tragically, it never happened and the body, still encased in its metal coffin, was doomed to go down with the ship a few days later.

By 26 May, with the fleet now well into the Korean Strait and rapidly approaching Tsushima, the gun crews on all of the Russian ships were placed on full alert. Since leaving the coast of Indochina most of them had slept and eaten their meals at the guns, watching and waiting for the Japanese. For the time being there was no sign of them, but everyone knew they were out there somewhere.

Now that combat was close, sailors slotted automatically into their routines. Regardless of skills – or lack of them – everyone at least knew what he had to do: 'It is safe to say that in many shore jobs routine destroys initiative ... but it is not so in the navy where a routine job builds up his (the sailor's) character.'[1]

At night all lights were extinguished. There were now two hospital ships, the *Oryol* having been joined by a second white-hulled vessel, the *Kostroma*, which had been part of Nebogatov's fleet. Only these two ships showed any illuminations at all, as laid down by the generally accepted rules of war. These demanded that hospital ships should be lit up at night so that they would not be confused with warships. As a consequence, compared to the other vessels in the fleet, the two ships stood out like festive Christmas trees against the dark night sky.

On the battleships, decks had been hosed down with holy water, and all wooden items from mess decks and wardrooms – things that could easily catch fire or throw splinters in any direction – had been hurled unceremoniously over the side. Despite the danger, ammunition was stockpiled alongside the guns, ready for easy access. Everyone knew that hostilities were only a few hours away. Rozhestvensky and his fleet were about as ready as they could possibly be for battle.

To begin with the ships travelled in one continuous line, stretching for nearly five miles astern of the flagship. Then Rozhestvensky got it into his head that two columns would be better and more effective. It was hardly the wisest move; from whichever direction the enemy approached half of the Russian fleet would not be able to fire for fear of hitting their own ships.

Rozhestvensky soon realised that his commanders could not organise anything as complex as forming up in columns while the fleet was at sea. The chaotic response to his orders – at one stage the *Alexander* was actually steaming in the opposite direction from everyone else – brought about a change of heart and, in despair, he ordered a return to the single line formation.

Again, though, there was chaos and the single line had hardly been thought about, let alone put in place when, in due course, the Japanese fleet was finally sighted. By that time Rozhestvensky had once more changed his mind about dispositions and ordered his battleships into yet another formation. This time they were to form up line abreast, with all twelve big-gun ships facing the Japanese.

As might be expected, the manoeuvre was beyond them and chaos ensued once more. Reluctantly, the move was abandoned so that when the two fleets did eventually come face to face, the Russians were still organised in two columns.

Rozhestvensky, in the *Suvorov*, led the right-hand column: Nebogatov, in the *Zhemchug*, was slightly astern and leading the left. It was not the wisest of moves, for if the Japanese were to attack from port quarter the powerful 12-in guns of the newer battleships would be rendered impotent.

* * *

From the moment he had entered the Korea Straits, Rozhestvensky had believed that Admiral Togo was already at sea. He had taken at face value the earlier reports that Japanese battleships had been sighted in and around Singapore. In fact the reports were wrong. The cruisers might have been out scouting but Togo was lying peacefully in Chin-Hei Bay on the Korean coast, waiting for his cruisers to report their first sightings of the Russian fleet.

While he believed that Vladivostok was still the likely destination for Rozhestvensky's ships, Togo had to guard against a Russian landing somewhere on the coast of China and the opening of a second front. That made Chin-Hei Bay, from where he could proceed in almost any direction he chose, by far the best option for a fleet that was about to fight a defensive action.

By the morning of 26 May Rozhestvensky was making good progress through the Korea Strait. So far he had seen nothing to cause him alarm, not even the tell-tale columns of smoke that would indicate Togo's scouts were near. Several of the officers began to believe that they had evaded the Japanese admiral and were now on the home run.

The sailors were not so hopeful. Following Russian tradition they changed into clean underwear – in case they were called to meet their God – and wrote final letters home, even though there was no chance of them being posted until, if they were very lucky, the fleet reached Vladivostok.

That evening a thick mist descended over the sea, covering the Russian ships like a blanket. Captain Ignatzius on the flagship smiled to himself, knowing that a heavy fog like this was their best form of protection. It would, he hoped, last for the next forty-eight hours.

By dawn the next day the mist was still there, but now it was more patchy and sparse. Soon a slight drizzle of rain added to the discomfort of the watchkeepers. The sea began to rise in a heavy surging of white-capped rollers.

Visibility varied between eight and nine miles one minute, a few thousand yards the next. Soon the looming peaks of the Donkey's Ears began to appear ahead of them, solid and almost touchable before they slid away into an all-concealing fog bank. If they could just get into the Tsushima Strait, Rozhestvensky and Ignatzius told themselves, their chances of reaching Vladivostok unharmed would be so much greater.

And then disaster struck. A lookout high above the deck of the *Suvorov* screamed out a warning; an unknown ship was approaching from starboard. The mist broke momentarily, and through their binoculars the men on the bridge were clearly able to see the long, almost delicate shape of the Japanese auxiliary cruiser *Sinano Maru*.

At the same moment the cruiser heeled over and, as the fog closed in once more, disappeared from view. Togo's scouts had found them.

* * *

The *Sinano Maru* had actually spotted the lights of the hospital ship *Oryol* during the night and orders were given to close and investigate. By 04.30 the two ships were almost within hailing distance, and Captain Narukawa, commander of the cruiser, could see that the Russian ship carried no guns. He recognised her as a hospital ship and therefore immune to attack. However, where there was a 'mercy vessel' like this there were bound to be warships close at hand.

For some strange reason, the *Oryol* mistook the *Sinano Maru* for a friendly vessel and actually signalled that there were other Russian ships in the immediate area. That was all that the Japanese captain needed to know.

The *Sinano Maru* surged away until well out of range and then began to signal her report to Admiral Togo. The new wireless telegraphy was certainly proving itself invaluable. It gave more or less instant communication where only ten or fifteen years before Togo's scouts would have had no option but to return to base in order to pass on the message. Now the air was red hot with the news that Rozhestvensky had been spotted.

The danger, however, was not over. Suddenly, out of the darkness, Captain Narukawa saw the ghostly shapes of at least a dozen ships, each of them faithfully following in the wake of the *Oryol*. If he needed more proof of the Russian presence this was it.

At that time Togo was still on the coast of Korea, but the message he received, at 05.00, galvanized him into action and he immediately ordered the fleet to sea: 'The whole crews [sic] of our fleet leapt to their posts.

The ships weighed anchor at once, and each squadron, proceeding in order to its appointed place, made its dispositions to receive the enemy.'[2]

By 07.00 the Japanese ships had left port, but Togo's orders were clear. The fleet would stay well away from the Strait of Tsushima until Rozhestvensky was firmly into the narrow channel. In the meantime the *Sinano Maru* was to continue to shadow the Russian fleet. Reinforcements would be despatched.

As full daylight came grudgingly to the Korea Strait other cruisers joined the *Sinano Maru* and a whole series of intercepted radio messages back to Togo made it abundantly clear to the Russians that this day, 27 May, was going to be one of destiny for the two opposing sides.

The cruiser *Idzumo*, the first Japanese vessel that the Russian sailors recognised, soon appeared from the north-east, swinging around to sail on a parallel course to the 2nd Pacific Fleet. The *Idzumo*, like the other watching vessels, took care to stay well out of range of the secondary armament on Rozhestvensky's battleships.

For the moment the main Japanese fleet also continued to keep its distance. Admiral Togo, in his later 'Report on the Battle of Tsushima', mapped out the difficult weather conditions but also made it clear that Japanese observation of the enemy movements was being maintained and reported back to him every few minutes:

> Though a heavy fog covered the sea, making it impossible to observe anything at a distance of over five miles, all the conditions of the enemy were as clear to us, who were 30 or 40 miles distant, as though they had been under our very eyes.[3]

The morning drew on, the mist clearing a little but the sea remaining disturbingly high. On several occasions waves swept over the decks of the battleships and the rolling of the giant vessels became more alarming by the minute. The more pessimistic of the officers stole surreptitious glances at the towering and top-heavy superstructure of their ships and wondered if the words of the Job's Comforters back in St Petersburg might be about to come true.

Observers from the bridge of the *Suvorov* took some perverse comfort from the way the destroyers of the squadron pitched, rolled and shipped gallons of water every second. The watchers greeted the sight with a mixture of admiration and relief that at least it wasn't them getting the soaking.

It was not just Rozhestvensky's smaller ships that were suffering. Togo had been forced to order his torpedo boats to remain close to the shore as there was considerable risk of them foundering in the heavy sea. As his one area of tactical supremacy over the Russians, the torpedo boats were an essential element of the Japanese fleet. Their time would come, but as he repeatedly told himself under his breath, not yet. For the moment it was better to keep them distant and safe.

On the Russian ships a mixture of emotions ran like wildfire through the crews. Many were glad that the final reckoning was now close; others hoped against all logic that they had managed to evade the shadowing Japanese fleet. They had seen no battleships. Perhaps they had slipped past them in the fog? Either way, the ordeal that had lasted for the past six months was almost over.

For the next hour or so a regular succession of Japanese cruisers kept appearing on both the port and starboard beams of the Russian fleet. They were always out of effective range and always signalling back to Togo with messages that could be intercepted but never understood.

The watching cruisers were as infuriating as wasps or hornets in summer. But unlike the insects that everyone remembered from glorious July and August days back home in Russia, these irritants could not be brushed away or crushed beneath a foot.

Meanwhile, the fleet powered on, its speed now increased to a regular eleven knots. Iron plates creaked demonically and the wind howled through the stays, but nobody had the time or the inclination to take note of such poetics. Up on the bridge all eyes were fixed on the horizon or, when they emerged out of the mist, on the dancing enemy ships.

The island of Tsushima gradually slid astern as Clapier de Colongue, Captain Ignatius and other members of Rozhestvensky's staff counted off another hazard that had been faced and passed. Soon they would be out of the Tsushima Straits and into open sea with room to manoeuvre. Then it would be a case of signalling for top speed and making a quick dash for Vladivostok.

On board the *Suvorov* that morning there was a Thanksgiving service, held on the bare and pitching after-deck of the flagship. With the ship now cleared for action the deck was empty of everything, apart from the ranks of sailors who stood, trying to retain their balance as the *Suvorov* rolled and dug her bow into the waves.

The flag of St Andrew was solemnly and ceremoniously raised at the stern and the masthead while the ship's chaplain, in full canonical garb, conducted the service. The wind was just cold enough to cause discomfort but no one seemed to notice.

The service was being held to mark the anniversary of the czar and czarina's coronation and was soon being replicated on every ship in the fleet. Surprisingly, it was an emotional moment for all of the crews, each knowing that within minutes he could be called upon to fight and die for the Russian ruler and for the empire he commanded.

For just a moment, patriotism – love of a regime that most of them had cursed since childhood – swelled like the rising tide in all of their breasts. Parades and good wishes from the czar could not create such feelings, but the prospect of sudden death certainly could. Perhaps just as welcome was the tot of vodka that was given to every man following the Thanksgiving service.

Just after midday the fleet swung to the north-east and set course for Vladivostok. They were through the Strait of Tsushima with its shallow waters and dangerously narrow channel. Sanctuary, such as it was, now beckoned.

The officers of the battleships hurried below for luncheon and for several desperately needed glasses of champagne. On the *Suvorov* Rozhestvensky stood in the wardroom and gave the toast to the emperor, the empress and to Russia. At that moment, before the glasses could even be drained, there was the roar of gunfire and 'action stations' sounded throughout the ship.

Chapter 10

Battle at Last

The first shots of the Battle of Tsushima were fired almost by accident. During the morning of 27 May the shadowing Japanese cruisers had been joined by a number of destroyers that whipped in and out of the cruiser formation, seeming to dance like horsemen across the waves. There was a fear on all of the Russian battleships that these fast little vessels might sweep ahead of the fleet in order to drop mines across their path.

Such a tactic was indeed a possibility; the Japanese had already used mines quite effectively in the war. And yet, up on the bridge of the *Suvorov* nothing seemed to be happening. Rozhestvensky appeared to be paralysed, turned to stone like Lot's wife. No one could see why he had not immediately ordered an attack on the destroyers.

Eventually Captain Yung of the *Oryol* took matters into his own hands. A salvo from *Oryol*'s 6-in secondary armament brought up everyone's head in amazement. The *Oryol* was using smokeless powder and nobody knew the origin of the gunfire. The gunners on the nearest Russian ships assumed the salvo was a signal from the *Suvorov* and they immediately opened fire on the distant enemy ships. Dozens of broadsides crashed out, all of the shots falling harmlessly into the sea, well short of the enemy cruisers.

It was several minutes before the 'cease fire' signal began to flutter from the mast of the flagship. Rozhestvensky knew the Japanese cruisers and destroyers were well out of range. 'Do not waste ammunition,' he signalled and then ordered all the crews below decks for dinner.

As the Japanese cruisers disappeared into the mist, the Russian sailors poured joyfully down the companionways to their mess decks, all of them boasting that they had frightened away the enemy. The comparison to the jubilation after the Dogger Bank Incident was lost on the sailors, who were concerned only with the present action. This, many declared, was going to be easy.

When, a little later, the enemy cruisers and destroyers appeared again, this time ahead of the fleet, Rozhestvensky attempted to get his battleships into line-abreast formation. The result was utter chaos and the ships were allowed to slip back into their two columns. Rozhestvensky remained at the head of the right-hand line, slightly ahead of Nebogatov.

In the wardrooms and on the bridge, discussion and debate ran wild. Perhaps this was the moment for the final confrontation? Why did they not take out the light reconnaissance vessels? That would be the logical move. To wait was surely playing into Togo's hands, but now, before the Japanese battleships appeared, the cruisers would be easy meat for the squadron.

Even as the Russians studied the enemy through their binoculars, all of them willing Rozhestvensky to order 'Open Fire', the Japanese cruisers turned away once more and were soon out of sight. What game was Togo playing? Where the hell was he?

At last, just before 13.40, the two main battle fleets sighted each other. The sudden appearance of Togo's fleet was almost an anti-climax. It was the sight that the Russian sailors, had been hoping for, or dreading, for days. Now that the moment was here it seemed almost surreal. However they viewed it, this was the moment of truth and even the most irreligious of them muttered a silent prayer as he went almost gleefully to his task.

The sight of the Japanese fleet was as expected as it was alarming. Lookouts reported that they had identified four battleships and eight armoured cruisers seven miles to the north-east of Rozhestvensky's leading ships. One of them was Togo's flagship *Mikasa* and she, like the other vessels, was sitting menacingly in the intended path of the Russian fleet: 'At around 13.55 Togo ordered the hoisting of the Z flag and issued a predetermined announcement to his entire fleet: "The Empire's fate depends on the result of this battle. Let every man do his utmost duty."'[1]

The Z flag was the Japanese equivalent of Nelson's message to his sailors on the day of Trafalgar in 1805, exactly one hundred years before. Indeed, there was a distinctly Nelsonian touch to almost everything the Japanese admiral did that day, from raising the Z flag to his poetic rallying cry to his crews urging them to do their duty.

Togo had long expressed his admiration of Lord Nelson – something he had picked up during his training on HMS *Worcester* – and in the forthcoming battle he was more than happy to use tactics that Nelson himself would have used (if he could have been suddenly transported into the twentieth century). Not for nothing was he later given the epithet of 'The Nelson of the Orient'.

Rozhestvensky was pleased that the Japanese were approaching from the north-east. It meant that his most modern battleships would not be restricted by the presence of the older, slower vessels and would be able to use their heavy guns. All of the manoeuvring and chaotic responses of the morning had been due to a desperate need to ensure the *Suvorov* and her sisters were in the van of the Russian attack. More by luck than judgement, it seemed that Rozhestvensky had played his cards perfectly.

As soon as the Japanese fleet was sighted the senior officers on the *Suvorov* and the other battleships retired to the conning towers of their vessels. Cramped, barely 10ft in diameter, the conning towers held duplicates of all of the equipment needed to control and steer the ship. On all of the Borodino-class vessels the conning towers were located directly below the forward bridge and just above what was known as the lower fighting position.

Heavily armoured for greater protection, the conning towers were the customary positions for senior officers during any combat situation, but now on the *Suvorov* Rozhestvensky decided to remain for the time being on the forward bridge. This was the place where the admiral had spent so many hours during the voyage and unlike the conning tower, which had limited views of the sea ahead, gave him an excellent prospect of the approaching Japanese and his own, still-disordered, fleet. The Russian ships were struggling to form themselves into some sort of order and the admiral knew that it was his last-minute tinkering with the dispositions that had caused the problem. Reluctantly, Rozhestvensky finally left the bridge for the conning tower. He had seen enough.

Unlike Rozhestvensky, who was struggling to understand what was happening, Admiral Togo, on the bridge of the *Mikasa*, was able to make a realistic and accurate appraisal of his opponent's dispositions:

> As expected, his right column was headed by four battleships of the Borodino type, his left by the *Oslyabya*, the *Sisoy Veliky*, the *Navarin* and the *Nakhimov* ... The *Zhemchug* and *Izumrud* were between the two columns and seemed to be acting as forward scouts. In the rear, obscured by fog, we indistinctly made out the *Oleg* and the *Aurora* with other second- and third-class cruisers forming a squadron.[2]

Togo had formed up in a single line-astern formation: battleships at the head, followed by Admiral Kamimura's heavy cruisers. They ranged across the horizon, the complete Japanese fleet, and even at a range of seven to eight miles they looked frighteningly formidable; exactly as Togo intended. Now it was time for his great 'Nelson gamble'.

* * *

'Crossing the T' was a time-honoured and recognised tactic in naval warfare. Nelson had used it against the Franco-Spanish Fleet at Trafalgar in 1805, knowing that it was a risky manoeuvre, just as Togo knew it was still a risky tactic one hundred years later. Even so, Togo was clear that battles were not won by being too conservative. It was a risk the Japanese admiral was willing to take.

Essentially, crossing the T meant a commander taking his battle fleet through or ahead of the enemy line, changing the direction of the attack and enabling all of his guns to bear as the crossing took place. In the days of Nelson's slow-moving wooden walls it was potentially a battle-winning tactic. It was also one that could easily lead to disaster. Nobody had attempted the manoeuvre now that steam and iron had replaced sail power and wood, but that was something that did not unduly worry Admiral Togo.

Approaching the Russians from the north-east, Togo turned his battle line to starboard and, one after the other, his ships crossed from the starboard to the port side of Rozhestvensky's fleet. It was done ahead of the Russians, at the very limit of accurate gunnery. But having crossed the T – Togo's ships were the horizontal top of the T and Rozhestvensky's the vertical – the Japanese were now sailing in the opposite direction to the Russians.

In order to correct this, Togo implemented another turn; a wide, 180° semi-circle that brought him back onto the same course as Rozhestvensky. It was the speed of the Japanese manoeuvres that took everyone by surprise. It meant that Togo was now facing the weaker part of the Russian fleet and was able to forge ahead or drop back as he saw fit.

By boldly crossing the T, Togo had seized the advantage and set up the very situation that Rozhestvensky had tried to avoid. Yes, there had been risk – which many of the British and other foreign observers on board his ships thought unacceptable – but he had faced it head on and won.

The risk involved in the manoeuvre came from the fact that, while crossing the Russian T, every one of Togo's ships would, in succession, come under fire. Being side on to the enemy they would, undoubtedly, be prime targets and, watching Togo begin the manoeuvre, the Russian sailors on the

Suvorov confidently expected to destroy the Japanese fleet as soon as they came into range.

It was not an unreasonable expectation. If Rozhestvensky could direct his gunfire accurately he could cause serious damage to the exposed Japanese ships as they crossed in front of him. Accurate gunnery, however, had hardly been the strongest Russian attribute.

The advantage to Togo in crossing the T was two-fold. During the crossing – which was done well ahead of the enemy line – only the leading Russian ships would be able to fire and then only with their forrard guns. It meant that well over three-quarters of the Russian fleet would be doing little more than twiddling their thumbs for the first part of the battle. At the same time, the Japanese would be able to bring all their main armament to bear, one after the other, as they crossed the T.

Rozhestvensky saw the danger and ordered his four Borodinos to reform in a single line. Unfortunately, he failed to order speed changes, with the result that some of the vessels had to grossly reduce their speed or swerve to one side – several of the older ships had to stop altogether – and the usual chaos immediately ensued.

The *Suvorov* had fired the first shell, opening up on the *Mikasa* at 13.49 as she crossed in front of the Russian line. The Russian gunnery had been surprisingly good; fifteen shells stuck the Japanese flagship in just five minutes:

> The *Suvorov* fired the first shot at a range of 6400yds ... I watched closely through my glasses. The shots which went over and those which fell short were all close, but the most interesting, the hits, could not be seen ... Our shells on bursting emitted scarcely any smoke, and the fuses were adjusted to burst inside after penetrating the target. A hit could only be detected when something fell – and nothing fell.[3]

At first Togo did not return fire. He wanted to see his turning manoeuvres successfully completed before engaging in combat. Russian gunnery, which had begun so well, now began to fall away as inexperienced gunners tired or became over-excited. By 13.50 Togo had successfully crossed the Russian T. He had completed his about-turn, his ships were in line, and now at last the *Mikasa* began to return fire.

Early Japanese firing was not good, but this was soon rectified and after five minutes their shells were hitting the Russian ships with increasing regularity. The *Mikasa* and the other three Japanese battleships concentrated their fire on the *Suvorov* while the armoured cruisers targeted the *Oslyabya*. With Felkersam's flag still flying from her yards the Japanese thought, rightly enough, that the *Oslyabya* had to be the flagship of Rozhestvensky's second-in-command: all that was missing was Felkersam himself.

The Russian line was still disorganised, with the result that most of the older ships in the 3rd Division took no real part in these early encounters. Even the 2nd Division was limited in its participation with only the *Suvorov*, *Alexander III* and *Borodino* playing a particularly active role in this first stage of the combat.

At 14.15 a shell from the *Mikasa* exploded in the captain's quarters on the *Suvorov* and immediately started a serious fire. For the first time the Russian crews were now encountering the terrible effect of the *shimosa* that the Japanese big-gun vessels were using. The effect on the young, inexperienced sailors who had never experienced modern warfare before was mind-numbing.

Shimosa, a picric acid, was contained within a thin-skinned, newly developed shell casing and was ignited by what became known as the 'Ijuin fuse'. This remarkable Japanese invention caused the shells to explode on impact rather than, like the Russian armour, simply penetrating the steel plating of enemy vessels and exploding below deck. It was not just the terrible effect of the explosive charge that caused panic. When the shells hit they immediately threw out a wall of fire over everything in range.

The Japanese shelling was terrifying and to the watching eyes of the Russians what was hurtling towards them seemed to be carton after carton of liquid fire:

> The shells flew over us. At this range some of the long ones turned a complete somersault and could be seen clearly with the naked eye, curving like so many sticks through the air. They flew over us, making a sort of wail, different to the ordinary roar.[4]

At times it seemed as if the whole side or upper works of any ship that had been struck were on fire. The *shimosa* simply set the paint aflame before ploughing on to cause even more damage. Nobody had ever seen anything like these shells before:

> They burst as soon as they touched anything, the moment they encountered the least impediment in their flight. Hand railings, funnel guys, topping lifts of the boat's derricks, were quite

sufficient to cause a thoroughly effective burst. The steel plates and superstructure on the upper deck were torn to pieces and the splinters caused many casualties. Iron ladders were crumpled up into rings and guns were literally hurled from their mountings.[5]

The *shimosa* did not only cause immense damage when it exploded, it also stank and gave off an unusually fierce heat so that many crewmen felt as if their whole bodies were about to catch fire. Apart from the initial burst of flames and fire, the effect of the shells when they exploded was devastating. Vladimir Semenov, in his account of the battle, was particularly vivid in his descriptions:

> Liquid flame from the explosives seemed to spread over everything. I actually watched a steel plate catch fire from a burst. Of course the steel did not burn but the paint on it did. Such non-combustible materials as hammocks and rows of boxes, drenched with water, flared up in a moment.[6]

By now the *Suvorov* was in serious trouble. The bodies of dead sailors littered the decks and blood lay everywhere in wide, deep pools. Already many of her guns were out of action. In the conning tower splinters of steel had managed to slice their way through the embrasures, killing three sailors outright. Rozhestvensky and Ignatzius were not hurt but the captain urged a change of course to get away from the hail of shells that were constantly striking the ship.

Rozhestvensky refused to change course. He and his ship had always been intended to act as the fleet leaders and regardless of enemy fire he was adamant that the *Suvorov* would continue to stay at the head of the battle line. As the first ship in the column, the flagship was in a suicidal position; the fire of the *Mikasa*, the *Shikishima* and the other two Japanese battleships concentrated on her with devastating accuracy.

Only when it was reported to the admiral that the *Suvorov* had been holed below the waterline and was taking on water did Rozhestvensky bow to the inevitable. Knowing that this was a crucial moment in the action he reluctantly ordered a turn to starboard.

Limping out of the battle line, the flagship was at first followed meekly by the *Alexander*, *Borodino* and *Oryol*. None of their captains realised the *Suvorov* was mortally wounded, and that their task was now to take the fight to the Japanese rather than follow Rozhestvensky.

With her masts gone the *Suvorov* was unable to signal and it took several minutes for Captain Bukhvostov on the *Borodino* to understand what was happening. Then, reluctantly, he changed course and headed back into the fight, leaving the immobile *Suvorov* dead in the water. The other battleships followed his change of course, challenging the Japanese once again.

Shell splinters were now entering the *Suvorov*'s conning tower on a regular basis and six of the men inside the supposedly impregnable enclosure were already dead. Inevitably, Rozhestvensky was hit, but it was not too serious. He sat heavily in a chair as his wound was treated and bandaged with a towel.

Every few minutes more shell splinters smashed into the conning tower and it was not long before the admiral was hit again, this time in the head and legs. Within seconds Captain Vasily Vasilyevich Ignatzius was also struck on the head and collapsed unconscious onto the conning tower floor: 'The skin of his skull opened like an envelope and blood poured from the wound. He was taken below to the doctors. He never returned.'[7]

Surprisingly, Ignatius survived his appalling wound. Bandaged up like an Egyptian mummy, he emerged from the sick bay, giddy and unsteady on his feet but still having the courage and ability to lead a party of sailors in an attempt to extinguish some of the flames. A shell dropped onto the deck next to him and when the smoke cleared Ignatzius and his band of warriors had simply disappeared.

By 14.30 the *Suvorov* was listing to port, her masts gone, her funnels toppled and her steering gear damaged beyond repair. Despite her wounds, she continued to fire at Togo's ships as she lay stopped in the water, unable to move, a perfect target for the Japanese gunners.

As the Russian Fleet ploughed on past the *Suvorov*, now with the *Alexander* as the lead ship, Rozhestvensky left the conning tower and began to wander aimlessly about the decks of his battered flagship. Physically he was not too badly hurt, but emotionally he was crippled and all but destroyed. His plans, his schemes, even his notions of duty to the empire and the czar lay in ruins, shattered like the decks of the ship beneath his feet.

* * *

At first glance it seemed that the carnage was all on one side, but against all the odds admiral Nebogatov, at the rear of the Russian lines, had actually managed to achieve a limited degree of success.

There was no way he could keep up with the ships of the 1st and 2nd Divisions, and the enemy battleships were far beyond the range of his much-despised 3rd Squadron. Instead his ships concentrated their fire on the Japanese cruisers, and fired with considerable accuracy.

A salvo from Nebogatov's flagship *Nicholas I* disabled the steering gear of the Japanese *Asama* and forced her to pull out of the line. Three more of the Japanese vessels were hit and seriously damaged, with several high-ranking officers killed or wounded. It was scant success but it was success, something that the Russians were desperately short of that afternoon.

Arguably, if Rozhestvensky had been able to order his leading ships to come about and swing behind the Japanese battleships, thus joining Nebogatov's 3rd Division to concentrate their fire on the rear of Togo's battle line, he might have achieved a limited but unexpected victory. Instead, he allowed Togo to force him further and further away from Nebogatov's vessels. In effect he became trapped in a situation where the range eventually came down to less than a mile and his ships were no more than sitting ducks.

Meanwhile, Nebogatov's gunners, previously so accurate, were being increasingly hampered by the ships of the 1st and 2nd Divisions. The huge, looming shapes of the Russian battleships, shrouded by smoke, were now almost all the 3rd Division gunners could see and they dared not fire over their colleagues at Togo's fleet.

On the *Suvorov* things degenerated quickly from bad to worse. Hoses that were supposed to put out fires were ripped to shreds while the sailors detailed to deploy them were cut down in their dozens. And from the deck of the flagship it was clear to anyone who cared to look that the Japanese ships were edging closer and closer to the disabled vessel. The situation appeared hopeless. Togo had seized almost total control of the battle:

> I crossed over to the port side, between the forward 12 inch and 6 inch turrets, to have a look at the enemy fleet. It was all there, just the same – no fires, no heeling over, no falling bridges – as if it had been at drill instead of fighting, and as if our guns, which had been thundering incessantly for the last half an hour, had been firing – not shells but the devil alone knew what. It was now 2.20pm.[8]

Clapier de Colongue and Vladimir Semenov finally managed to locate Admiral Rozhestvensky who had found refuge in one of the battered 6-in gun turrets. With Captain Ignatius dead it was more vital than ever that

Rozhestvensky should assume tactical as well as strategic command of the ship. Yet from first glance de Colongue could see that it was an unlikely prospect.

Rozhestvensky had been wounded again, a jagged shell splinter having pierced his leg, and he could not walk. The shell splinter had severed the main nerve in his leg and blood was pouring like a waterfall onto the metal floor of the gun turret. There were jagged wounds to his skull and body and almost as soon as de Colongue and Semenov reached his side he collapsed in a stupor. For the next forty-eight hours he continued to drift in and out of consciousness.

* * *

It was obvious to men like Clapier de Colongue that the *Suvorov* was finished. She had taken a dreadful battering and it could only be a matter of time before she eventually sank. And yet, surprisingly, the fleet flagship was not destined to be the first Russian ironclad to disappear beneath the waves that day.

Since the battle began Togo's armoured cruisers had kept up a relentless fire against the *Oslyabya*. Shell after shell had ploughed into Felkersam's old flagship, setting her on fire and destroying masts and spars as if they were made of paper. Listing sharply to port the *Oslyabya* could finally take no more punishment and, just after 15.00 hours, she turned on her side and began to capsize.

As the ship heeled over, many of the crew from the upper decks scrambled onto her weed-encrusted bottom, some sliding down into the sea, others simply standing on the upturned hull, awaiting their fate. Many of those who leapt for safety smashed into the keel of the ship and were unconscious before they hit the water. Within a few minutes the *Oslyabya* had disappeared, leaving 400 men fighting for their lives in the icy seas.

It is tempting to wax poetic about Admiral Felkersam's coffin sinking slowly to the sea bed along with the *Oslyabya* but over 500 sailors had also gone down with the ship, trapped below decks and unable to escape the rising water level inside. Their deaths were cruel, and far more poignant and tragic than the final disappearance of Felkersam's coffin.

Japanese gunners had continued to fire at the sinking ship until she finally disappeared. She was the first modern armoured warship to be sunk by gunfire alone; a dubious honour that nobody would have wanted to claim. Meanwhile the death and destruction continued.

On the dying *Suvorov* a strange mood of lethargy had settled across the battered decks. It was an acceptance of fate, punctured here and there by almost hysterical good humour. Commander Semenov summed up the emotions:

> A stupor seems to come over men who have never been in action before, when the first shells begin to fall, a stupor which turns easily and instantaneously … into either uncontrollable panic which cannot be allayed, or into unusually high spirits, depending on the man's character.[9]

There was also bravery and courage of the highest order. Men who knew that to remain on board the stricken flagship meant certain death, either from shell fire or by drowning, refused to leave their posts. As gun after gun was put out of action it was a strange sense of duty rather than a desire to fight that kept the sailors standing erect even if they had no weapons to fire, waiting for the end.

The other Russian battleships of the 1st Division were faring no better than the *Suvorov*. At 15.20 the *Alexander III* wheeled out of the column, her decks battered and her hull consumed by fire from the *shimosa*. The *Borodino* steamed past the sinking hulk and took the lead place. From the fate of the *Suvorov* and *Alexander* it was clear that lead ship in the column was a suicidal position that would eventually lead to only one conclusion. Yet the crew of the *Borodino* all knew where their duty lay.

Just after 16.00 hours the fog returned with a vengeance. Now the Japanese and Russian fleets could no longer see each other and the firing, at least at the front of the column, stuttered to a halt. In the eerie silence the distant sound of small guns firing and torpedoes exploding showed that, at the rear of the line, the cruisers and destroyers of Togo's fleet were continuing with the destruction of their targets.

As evening approached four Japanese torpedo boats, now called from their station on the coast, swept in to attack the *Suvorov*. Most of their torpedoes missed their mark, but one struck her in the stern and water poured in through the open wound. Still the battleship fought on. The Japanese sailors looked on with a degree of admiration, marvelling at the ability of the ship and her crew to keep fighting. Eventually the torpedo boats retired to rearm, their crews knowing that after dark they would be back.

It was a temporary respite, one that could be used to save as many of the *Suvorov*'s crew as possible: hundreds of them were already dead; dozens more were determined to fight on; and some were more than happy to take any opportunity to save themselves. Clapier de Colongue was careless about his own safety but he knew that if he was ever going to save the life of the admiral then an attempt to get him off the dying flagship had to be made within the next few minutes.

In the rapidly falling dusk de Cologne spotted Russian torpedo boats quite close to the doomed *Suvorov*. One of them he recognised as the *Buiny* and, using their hands and arms as semaphore poles, he and the admiral's remaining staff requested Captain Kolomeitsky to come alongside and take the wounded Rozhestvensky on board. Without hesitation, Kolomeitsky agreed.

For what seemed like hours the torpedo boat bobbed about just a few hundred yards off the *Suvorov*'s beam. There were no ships' boats left intact on the flagship and so transfer of the admiral to the *Buiny* was going to be a hazardous and difficult operation. The moment had to be right and Kolomeitsky would need every ounce of his skill if it was to be done successfully.

It was not just the flagship's boats that had been destroyed. There were no fenders left to protect the sides of either ship; nothing that could, in their absence, be dragooned into use. The sea was still decidedly 'lumpy' and the tiny torpedo boat rose and fell away again every few moments. The evacuation of Rozhestvensky had to be timed to perfection.

For want of an alternative, Clapier de Cologne was forced to ask crewmen to risk serious injury and form themselves into a human fender. They did it willingly, joining hands and laying themselves across the shattered hull.

As the *Buiny* rose on a large swell the unconscious admiral was simply rolled down the side of the *Suvorov* onto the deck of the torpedo boat. De Cologne and six others leapt after him onto the already crowded *Buiny*. Then the torpedo boat increased speed and pulled away into the gloom. The men on the deck of both ships watched with sadness and understanding.

It was 17.30 and everyone who wanted to leave the doomed flagship had now done so. Those left on board would go down with her.

After the brief pause caused by the fog the two battleship divisions began firing at each other once again. It was now nearly 18.00 and the Japanese shells continued to pound the *Alexander* and *Borodino* at the head of the Russian column.

Observers from foreign nations were commonplace in most of the military and naval campaigns of the nineteenth and early twentieth centuries. From the battles of the American Civil War to the desperate calamities of the British defeats in South Africa, neutral observers were there to report back on things like tactics and weapons.

Being an observer was a duty that almost anyone in the army or navy could have, should he desire it. A good experience was how commanding officers would describe it. Winston Churchill, a young and eager cavalry subaltern who was fed up with playing polo and visiting Indian temples, was desperate to experience war. He volunteered and was plucked out of the security of his regiment and despatched across the world to the Caribbean island of Cuba to observe and report back on the Spanish-Cuban War of 1898. It was an iconic moment in his career: he was noticed, and the rest is history.

One of the British observers in the Russo-Japanese War was Captain, later Admiral Sir William Packenham, who came away with a high opinion of Japanese fighting qualities but a less than complementary view of Russian seamanship. He was also lucky to come away with his life, being narrowly missed by shrapnel and seeing the two sailors standing next alongside him ruthlessly cut down.

The comments of Packenham and other British observers, particularly on the end of the *Borodino*, might not have been very positive but none of them could deny the bravery of the doomed Russian sailors. They are heart-rending and revealing, and Packenham's comments on the end of the *Borodino* are particularly poignant: 'The unexampled lengths to which human bravery and fortitude were carried in defence of this ship were such as reflect undying glory not only on her gallant crew, but on their navy, their country, on humanity.'[10]

The *Borodino*, smoke trailing behind her like winter mist, still had almost an hour to live, though perhaps 'endure' is a better description. The Japanese navy had other work to do and the *Suvorov*, though no longer any sort of threat, needed to be despatched before they moved on to the other targets.

At 19.00 the *Suvorov* was finally blasted apart by torpedoes from the Japanese torpedo boats that had now returned to the fray. She had been like a dead man walking for so long that her eventual demise was, to many, a blessed relief. There were no survivors from the handful of brave men who had remained on board to fight to the end with her last remaining quick-firing gun.

Packenham was generous in his description of the flagship's demise, remarking on her appearance with both funnels gone and just the stump of a mast showing above the waves: 'The extensive conflagration raging amidships showed its reality. Less than half the ship can have been habitable; yet she fought on.'[11]

By some bizarre quirk of fate, Rozhestvensky's nemesis, the ever troublesome *Kamchatka*, was sunk a few minutes later, having strayed too close to the dying flagship. Quite what her captain thought he was doing will never be known as the repair ship was hit by a salvo of shells and immediately blew apart in a gigantic ball of smoke and flame.

Just a few minutes later, at 19.03, the *Alexander III* was also engulfed by a rain of shells. After replacing the *Suvorov* as the new leading ship in the Russian line she was now the perfect target and the Japanese gunners did not miss. Shell after shell smashed into her hull, then the *Alexander* slowly turned on her side, capsized and sank, taking virtually all of her crew with her.

The *Borodino* survived her by a bare forty minutes. Finally, her decks awash and smoke pouring from her shattered hull, she turned turtle, throwing hundreds of men into the sea. Within a few seconds she exploded in a cloud of smoke and fire that shot a thousand feet into the air.

Now only the *Oryol* remained out of Rozhestvensky's four great battleships and she was already badly damaged. If the battle continued much longer it was obvious that she too would disappear under the waves.

The decimation of the Russian capital ships was as complete as it was unexpected. Naval authorities around the world had recorded the statistics of each ship, carefully logging things such as the number of guns, width of armour plating and speed. Collecting such data was important to all maritime powers, but there was also an intense interest in ships and war fleets from the general public.

None of them had expected the Russian ironclads to be so completely demolished. These were not old 'self-sinkers'; they were brand new vessels of immense power. So new, in fact, that few experts even knew what they looked like. There were very few photographs of the *Suvorov* and her sisters for use in books like *Jayne's Fighting Ships* or in the plethora of nautical magazines that were then available. Everyone knew their strengths, however, and they had been smashed to pieces like a child's collection of matchstick models.

By 19.40 it was virtually dark, the blackness of the sea and sky broken only by the glow of burning ships. Admiral Togo signalled an end to the day's hostilities for his battleships. Job now done, he withdrew. It was hardly much of a respite as the Japanese commander quickly switched the main thrust of attack from his big-gun vessels to the tiny but deadly torpedo boats.

As Togo withdrew, the *Oryol*, with dead bodies littering her deck and with many of her guns already destroyed or disabled, moved slowly to the head of the Russian column. Nobody on board expected her to survive for long but no one, not even in their worst nightmares, had ever imagined the horror that was soon to come.

The sea was full of struggling men from the *Borodino*, dozens of them, shouting and appealing for rescue or hurling useless curses at the Japanese ships. There was never any expectation that battleships would stop to pick up survivors, but theory and reality were two different things. As far as the sailors on board the *Oryol* were concerned, common humanity would surely dictate what should happen next.

These were Russian sailors in the water, comrades and friends; men with whom they had hunted in the wilds of Madagascar or drunk with in the wine shops of St Petersburg. Nobody would leave them there to drown. Would they?

It was not deliberate, but to the horror of the shocked and traumatised sailors standing helplessly at the *Oryol*'s rails, it soon became clear that the battleship was not slowing down. Now it was not just a case of being left to drown; their end would come far sooner than that.

Men screamed out warnings or cursed as they thrashed about in the water and watched the *Oryol* bearing down on them. All thoughts of rescue vanished as they struck out to get away from the approaching vessel.

Many of the swimming men were sucked down by the wake of the passing battleship; many more were cut to pieces by the battleship's churning propellers. It was, in many respects, the final tragedy of a doomed and fatal enterprise.

The officers on the bridge of the *Oryol* tried to close their eyes and ears to the sights and sounds that seemed to be coming from all around them. It could not be helped, they tried to convince themselves. This was war. There was still a battle to be fought and, you never knew, maybe even a battle that might yet be won.

Chapter 11

Last Acts

Despite the carnage going on in the battle line ahead of him, Rear Admiral Nebogatov remained intent on doing his duty. So far he and his 3rd Squadron had got away quite lightly with just a dozen enemy shells striking his ships and causing minimal casualties. He had seen the disaster unfold around him but, stuck at the end of the Russian line of battle, he had had little or no opportunity to influence the outcome.

Rozhestvensky had always declared that, in the event of disaster, ships should make their way to Vladivostok independently. There was no contradictory word from the admiral and so this was what Nebogatov knew he had to do.

However, Nebogatov also understood that the advent of darkness would bring with it the howling predators of the night: Togo's torpedo boats. It did not take a genius to work out that they would be a different proposition altogether from the *Mikasa* and her comrades.

In a desperate attempt to throw the tiny killer ships off his track, Nebogatov turned south-west. It was the last direction the Japanese would expect him to take as his ships were now inching away from Vladivostok. It was a gamble, but the situation was desperate and the important thing was the survival of his ships.

By 20.00 hours the night was already black as Satan's cloak and Nebogatov decided that his ruse had worked. It was time, he felt, to risk turning back towards Vladivostok. Slowly, and more than a little unsure, his squadron began to swing round.

And now he began to lose ships. First to go was the *Ushakov*, which had been previously hit in the bow and now found that she was unable to maintain squadron speed. She dropped away and lost touch. She was followed into the darkness by three other vessels that had, out of desperation, attached themselves to Nebogatov's squadron. Their crews were not happy to risk running the gauntlet to Vladivostok with Nebogatov and the remains of the Pacific Fleet and were now willing to take their chances alone.

Despite his ploy, the enemy torpedo boats soon picked up Nebogatov's motley collection of ships, and as the night wore on their attacks began. Togo could call on twenty-one destroyers and thirty-seven torpedo boats, ordering them to attack from all directions of the compass. For three hours the action continued, with several of the Japanese craft colliding with the larger Russian vessels. Then the Japanese lost contact with their opponents in the darkness.[1]

It looked as if Nebogatov had managed to escape, but when one of the Russian ships turned on her searchlights – in an attempt to pick out the attackers who repeatedly danced in and out of sight – the Japanese discovered them again. Within a few hours the old battleship *Navarin* struck a mine and was forced to come to a halt. Almost immediately she was hit by four torpedoes. There were just three survivors.

The attacks continued and the losses mounted. The *Sisoy Veliky* was disabled by a torpedo in her stern and scuttled by her crew the following day. She was followed to her watery grave by the old armoured cruisers *Admiral Nakhimov* and *Vladimir Monomakh*. By contrast, the Japanese lost just three torpedo boats in the night attacks.

There was no denying that, so far at least, Nebogatov had done well. With his old 'self-sinkers' and a motley collection of non-combatant vessels he had certainly achieved as much, if not more, than Admiral Rozhestvensky. He had spent a watchful and terrifying night on the bridge, personally commanding the ship after her captain had been wounded and had refused to return to the bridge.

By dawn on 28 May Nebogatov, on the *Nicholas I*, found himself accompanied by just four other vessels. There were no signs of any other Russian ships and to Nebogatov it seemed that his small and battered unit was the last surviving element of the once mighty 2nd Pacific Fleet. If he could somehow get his ships to Vladivostok, his part in the affair would at least have been successful.

At 05.15 lookouts reported smoke on the horizon. The ships were too far away for anyone to identify but Nebogatov despatched the fast cruiser *Izumrud* to take a closer look. When she came hurrying back it was with the disquieting news that they were Japanese scout vessels. Within the hour they were joined by Togo's battleships, the *Mikasa* in the lead. The way to Vladivostok was barred.

That morning was bright with brittle sunshine and not a trace of fog or mist anywhere: hardly ideal weather conditions for anyone trying to slip past a vigilant enemy. Between the weather conditions and Togo's waiting warships, Admiral Nebogatov knew that the odds were stacked against him.

* * *

On board the torpedo boat *Buiny* Admiral Rozhestvensky lay, drifting in and out of consciousness. There was no surgeon on the torpedo boat, just a sick berth attendant, but a quick examination revealed that all was not well with Rozhestvensky. His skull was fractured and a small sliver of bone had, it was feared, pierced his brain.

The *Buiny* was packed to the gunwales with survivors from the *Oslyabya*, but Rozhestvensky was given the luxury of a tiny cabin to himself. It had proved impossible to staunch the flow of blood from the torn artery in his foot and his situation was thought to be critical.

At times Rozhestvensky was delirious and called out hoarse commands that made little or no sense. To Clapier de Colongue and other members of his staff it was important to save the admiral's life; far more important than any minor damage the *Buiny* might be able to inflict on the enemy. That might mean escape or, less palatably, it might also mean surrender.

In one of his more lucid moments the admiral was able to authorise the sending of two signals: one, the order that surviving vessels should head for Vladivostok; and two, command was to be passed to Admiral Nebogatov. Then he lapsed into a delirious coma once more.

To begin with, the torpedo boat hugged the company of the cruiser *Donskoi*, but the vessels somehow became separated during the night. Soon Lieutenant Kolomeitsev, commander of the *Buiny*, announced that his ship was in trouble. Her engines were on the point of failing and his recommendation was that they should make a landfall, disembark the sick and wounded, and then destroy the boat.

Heated debate between the ship's officers and Rozhestvensky's staff – the former wanting to fight on, the latter intent on saving the admiral's life – was broken by the reappearance of the *Donskoi*. She now had two more torpedo boats sailing with her and the decision was taken to transfer the admiral to one of these, the tiny *Bedovy*.

The cruiser *Donskoi* sent one of her cutters to facilitate the transfer, which was considerably easier and more dignified than the way Rozhestvensky had left the *Suvorov*. With the operation complete, the admiral's new flagship immediately headed north at full speed, and in the company of the other torpedo boat.

At 15.00 hours the two Russian boats were intercepted by a pair of similarly armed and equipped Japanese vessels, the *Sazanami* and the *Kagero*. Desperate to avoid capture, the second Russian boat increased speed and shot away, pursued by the Japanese *Kagero*. With the seriously wounded admiral lying delirious and, for all anyone knew, dying, there was no alternative for the *Bedovy*. She would have to surrender.

When Japanese officers and a boarding party of ratings came aboard their captive vessel they were astounded to find that none other than the famous 'Mad Dog' Rozhestvensky was lying seriously injured down below.

The Japanese captain was persuaded not to move the admiral onto his own ship, which would have been normal practice, and together the two torpedo boats headed for the Japanese naval base of Sasebo. They reached port early in the morning of 29 May and Admiral Rozhestvensky, still drifting in and out of consciousness, found himself a prisoner of the Japanese.

He was too badly wounded to complain at that stage, and the Japanese doctors, with better equipment and medicine than had been available on board the *Bedovy*, immediately set about trying to save his life.

* * *

Admiral Enkvist had not enjoyed a fruitful time with the 2nd Pacific Fleet. It was clear to everyone, Enkvist included, that Rozhestvensky hated him and, bit by bit during the voyage, the admiral had gradually stripped him of his responsibilities. By the time the two fleets came to blows on 27 May Enkvist's command had been reduced to just three cruisers: the *Oleg*, the *Zhemchug* and the *Aurora*.

Apart from Rozhestvensky, the dapper but inefficient Enkvist was also disliked by most officers in the fleet. Even his deputy, Captain Dobrotvorsky – the man who had brought his squadron of new cruisers to Madagascar – treated him with a detached and icy superiority. Despite this, Enkvist relied heavily on Dobrotvorsky and on Evgeny Yegoriev, captain of the *Aurora*. Yegoriev, a skilled and much-respected officer, was the man who had led the transport detachment out of Libau many months before.

Both Dobrotvorsky and Yegoriev were disappointed to find themselves at the rear of the Russian line during the battle and it was not until the *Suvorov* heeled away, mortally wounded, that they took any real part in the action. The *Oleg* was hit several times and the *Zhemchug* all but disabled, but the most grievous disaster occurred on board the *Aurora* when a shell exploded in her conning tower and killed Captain Yegoriev.

Enkvist was disturbed by Yegoriev's death and when he and the rest of his staff witnessed the sinking of the *Borodino*, within a minute of being struck by the first shell, it was obvious that the battle was lost. Enkvist knew that darkness would bring attacks from the torpedo boats that were already blocking the way to Vladivostok.

The three cruisers twisted and turned, heading first one way, then another in a desperate attempt to throw the torpedo boats off the scent. Enkvist was unsure what he was now expected to do. Like the *Zhemchug*, the *Oleg* was badly damaged and had been forced to reduce her speed. Added to that, all three ships were running short on coal.

Suddenly Enkvist decided that he would move his flag to the *Aurora*, the least damaged of the three ships. The reasons for this remain unclear. He had moved his flag several times during the voyage, but now, with the *Oleg* in significant trouble and Yegoriev dead, it was a move that smacked of self-preservation rather than tactical significance.

Even before Enkvist's move there was considerable discussion between the officers and staff on all of the cruisers about what to do and when to do it. Vladivostok, cut off by the enemy, seemed to be out of the question so Enkvist eventually decided they should attempt to reach Shanghai. Dobrotvorsky immediately suggested an alternative: Manila, in the American-owned Philippines. Ever fickle, and possibly even a little afraid of the domineering Dobrotvorsky, Enkvist agreed. His mind was now finally made up; or had been made up for him.

Once he arrived on board the *Aurora* Enkvist set course for Manila, despite protests from his crew that they were deserting the battle, and Admiral Rozhestvensky whose fate was then unknown. But, as the destruction and the wrecks of so many sinking Russian ships began to fade into the distance behind him, Enkvist managed to convince himself that he had done the right thing.

It was a long trip to reach the Philippines, a journey of well over 1000 miles. The Japanese battle fleet might be close behind him or might have sat back, satisfied after their victory. But Enkvist knew that Togo was no fool. Regardless of what the battleships might do he would have cruisers out, searching for him, ready to send the *Aurora* to join the *Suvorov* and the rest of the Russian fleet at the bottom of the ocean.

Slowly, infinitely carefully, they sailed on. The weather now was tropical once more and the constant glare of the sun began to cause problems for the exhausted crew. The heat and humidity were oppressive and certainly not helpful for Enkvist's state of mind. He pondered on his actions, all the time growing more and more despondent. And the further they went the hotter it became.

It was not only the debilitating effect of the heat. The bodies of the dead sailors – including Captain Yegoriev – which had been held for burial when they reached port were now beginning to decompose in the humidity. The smell was dreadful and there was a significant health hazard. Captain Yegoriev and the other victims of the battle were duly buried at sea.

It was early June before Enkvist's battered cruisers eventually reached Manila. They were met by a detachment of American battleships and cruisers and escorted into the harbour. The American vessels made a point of anchoring close to the Russian ships.

Enkvist, by now thoroughly depressed and unsure of his next move, had hoped that he would encounter the Japanese outside Manila and end everything in a blaze of glory. It was not to be. He and his ships would be interned. The admiral went below deck, and in the best traditions of Rozhestvensky himself, shut himself in his cabin and refused to acknowledge the outside world.

* * *

Admiral Nebogatov was a caring and conscientious man. He was also a realist. Late on 27 May he had received the news that Rozhestvensky had passed on command to him and was equally as relieved to find that his decision to head for Vladivostok was a move that had been condoned by the admiral.

However, when the last shadows of night finally disappeared on the morning of 28 May he was able to see that the situation facing him was desperate. His five ships were surrounded by no fewer than twenty-seven Japanese vessels, not counting torpedo boats, and total destruction could only be a matter of minutes away.

After consulting with Captain Smirnov, the unwilling and decidedly unheroic commander of the *Nicholas* – who did finally agree to climb the steps to the conning tower – Nebogatov decided that his only course of action was to surrender. Already Togo's ships had opened fire and the Japanese guns outranged him by at least 1000yds. Surrender was not a universally popular option; several officers on the *Nicholas* protested strongly, adamant that they should go down fighting and that was what Rozhestvensky would have wanted, had he been there.

Nebogatov's word was final, however, and XGE, the international surrender signal, was hoisted. Despite this, Togo and his battleships continued to fire: they did not have the signal in their code books. In desperation, white table cloths were ripped up and hauled to the mastheads. Still the Japanese fire continued. Togo had once had a Chinese warship escape his clutches by using exactly that ploy.

It was not until Nebogatov ordered the Japanese flag to be run up that the firing eventually stopped. With the enemy now closing to short range, the Russians prepared to hand over control of their ships to the Japanese.

The one exception was the cruiser *Izumrud*. Her commander, Captain Ferzen, had noticed that the ring of encircling ships was not quite complete. There was a gap in the eastern corner and Ferzen ordered his ship to head for this opening at full speed. As she powered through Togo's encircling ships there were many, on both sides, who felt this was the right thing to do. Togo ordered his torpedo boats to give chase and the vessels soon disappeared over the horizon.

Admiral Togo and his fleet had not escaped totally unscathed from the battle. The *Mikasa* had been hit by nineteen shells in the first ten minutes of the battle, and by the end of the day thirty separate hits had been recorded on the Japanese flagship. Togo himself had been struck by a piece of shrapnel, but it was a minor injury and did not force him to leave the bridge.

Russian armour-piercing shells had certainly struck home and caused problems for Togo, but to a casual observer there was little outward sign of damage. The odd hole might be seen in the hull or decking of the Japanese ships, but it was nothing when compared to the devastation that had been wreaked on Rozhestvensky's fleet.

Following the decision to capitulate, Nebogatov and his staff were taken to the *Mikasa* by a Japanese torpedo boat to formally surrender to the victorious Togo. After the debacle of the battle in which Rozhestvensky's four main ships had been decimated by over 250 shells, Nebogatov and his officers viewed the enemy vessels with amazement:

> As they passed by Togo's ironclads, the Russians could not believe their eyes; no matter how closely they looked, they could not find a single mark of a Russian shell. It looked like Togo's main force had passed through yesterday's battle unharmed.[2]

The difference lay firstly in the accuracy of the Japanese gunners and then, more significantly, in the *shimosa* fired by the Japanese battle fleet. This had not only caused terrible damage to crew and superstructure, but actually made the stricken Russian vessels look like they had been dragged through the pits of Hell: burned, blackened, and engrained by smoke and dust. In contrast, the Japanese fleet appeared as if they had been engaged in a mere training exercise.

Togo received Nebogatov and his officers quite cordially, even asking them what conditions they wanted. All Nebogatov wanted was for the Japanese to treat his men as well as possible and, in due course, return them to Russia. Such a promise did not lie within Togo's remit but he promised to send a message to the emperor, making that request. The meeting finished with champagne being served to everyone; a civilised ending to a brutal confrontation.

Back on Nebogatov's ships there was a far less cordial atmosphere. The sailors were demoralised and angry at the surrender; as they saw it, one without even the pretext of attempting to put up a fight. The men felt humiliated, their pride and dignity ignored or deliberately destroyed by the desire of the officer class to save their own skins.

The behaviour of the 'officer class' after Nebogatov returned from his meeting with Togo did not make things any easier. Almost as soon as they arrived back on board, as Russian tradition demanded, the bursar on the *Oryol* began distributing the ship's purse among the officers. The ordinary crewmen received nothing, but they noted with growing bitterness exactly where the money was going.

After that the men vented their spleen on Nebogatov. Admiral Rozhestvensky, they said, would never have agreed to give in so meekly, conveniently forgetting that Nebogatov's capitulation had undoubtedly saved their lives: 'He had decided on the shame of surrender, knowing full well he might be shot when he returned to Russia. He said "The lives of the two thousand four hundred men in these ships are more important than mine."'[3]

The men promptly repaid him by breaking into the ship's wine store and proceeding to drink the place dry.

* * *

The first Russian ship to reach friendly waters was the cruiser *Almaz*. She had taken no part in the battle, having left the fleet before the fighting began, but was able to report that the *Suvorov*, *Oslyabya* and *Ural* had been sunk and that Rozhestvensky wounded. She could offer no more information than that.

The *Almaz* was soon followed into Vladivostok by the torpedo boat *Grozny*, which reported simply 'Fate of the Admiral unknown.' A second torpedo boat, the *Bravy*, was next to appear, her crew having painted her funnel white in order to make her inconspicuous against the sea and sky.[4]

No other Russian ships managed to make it to Vladivostok. Heartbreakingly, the cruiser *Izumrud* which had valiantly broken through Togo's ring of steel, rather than meekly surrender along with Nebogatov, almost made it. She managed to evade her pursuers and did actually get as far as Russian territorial waters before running aground in Vladimir Bay. There she was destroyed by explosive charges set by her crew who then continued on foot to the port of Vladivostok.

By the beginning of June it was obvious that most of Rozhestvensky's once mighty armada had been destroyed. Apart from the ships that had reached Vladivostok, those that had managed to escape destruction could (almost) be counted on one hand.

There were one or two isolated sinkings after 28 May. In an act of supreme bravery, ships like the ancient *Admiral Ushakov* refused to surrender and went down with her flags flying. At the end of the battle the cruiser-cum-yacht *Svetlana* found herself isolated and surrounded but would not surrender. She was sunk, pummelled to death by a flotilla of Japanese cruisers, and her captain, having evacuated his wounded men, refused to leave his sinking ship.

The auxiliaries, which had caused Rozhestvensky so much trouble during the voyage, fared little better. The hospital ships *Oryol* and *Kostroma* were both soon in Japanese hands, with Natalia Sivers and the other nurses being held captive for some weeks. They were eventually released, but Natalia decided that Paris was more in keeping with her lifestyle than St Petersburg.

The little tug *Rus* and the *Ural* joined the wilful, bungling *Kamchatka* at the bottom of the Tsushima Strait on 27 May. They had battled their way around the world but their end could almost have been predicted.

One vessel, the transport ship *Anadyr*, managed to make a spectacular escape from the Pacific and from the Japanese guns. She was the ship that had caught her anchor on the telegraph cable in Tangier several months before, an accident that had subsequently cut off the port's communications with Europe for several days, much to the fury of Admiral Rozhestvensky.

After the battle the *Anadyr*'s captain had found Vladivostok out of reach and too well guarded by patrolling Japanese cruisers and had therefore turned south. It was a risky manoeuvre. The route had taken him through Japanese-held seas where the *Anadyr* might have run across patrolling enemy warships at any moment. Hugging the coast, making use of the weather conditions and trusting to luck, the *Anadyr* and her crew held their collective breath and ploughed onwards.

After many weeks, using coal that Rozhestvensky had intended for other vessels, the transport ship managed to reach Madagascar. In light of all that had happened since the Russian fleet had left the island, it must have seemed like a tropical paradise.

Captured Russian vessels were promptly commissioned into the Japanese navy, even if they were old and of little use. They would, if nothing else, make useful targets on which the Japanese battleships could practice their gunnery in the months ahead.

Japanese medical assistance was clearly of a high standard. Admiral Rozhestvensky survived his wounds, had the piece of bone removed from his brain, and made a slow but steady recovery. For several weeks he lay in the Naval Hospital at Sasebo, treated like a visiting dignitary rather than a prisoner. On 3 June he was visited by Admiral Togo.

It was an unexpected visit, hardly the normal type of encounter between a victorious and a defeated commander. The obvious analogy is the Duke of Wellington making a hypothetical visit to see Napoleon after the Battle of Waterloo. Such an event simply would not happen; except that this time it did.

The two opponents formally shook hands, Togo retaining his firm grip for much longer than was necessary. He comforted Rozhestvensky with kind and genuine words:

> Defeat is a common fate of a soldier. There is nothing to be ashamed of in it. The great point is whether we have performed our duty. I can only express my admiration for the courage with which your sailors fought during the recent battle, and my personal admiration for yourself, who carried out your heavy task until you were seriously wounded.[5]

The two men spoke quietly and informally for several minutes. There seemed to be a genuine and mutual degree of respect and admiration in each of them.

A few months after his victory at Tsushima, Togo's flagship *Mikasa* blew up and sank in the harbour at Sasebo. The cause was never discovered but it was quite possibly a terrorist attack from protesters unhappy about what they considered soft or easy peace terms with Russia. The *Mikasa* was later refloated and is still preserved as a museum piece in Japan.

Rozhestvensky heard the news while still in his hospital bed and immediately wrote a letter of condolence to his illustrious adversary. Togo replied with a brief thank you note.

If anything expressed the pointless stupidity of war it was surely the meeting in the Sasebo hospital of the two leaders and the letter of commiseration after the sinking of the *Mikasa*. The fact that two men who had spent months plotting, planning and finally attempting to destroy each other could come together in such a civilised and friendly manner underlines quite poignantly the ridiculous nature of human conflict.

Chapter 12

Aftermath

When the smoke cleared and observers were finally able to take stock of the battle it was immediately apparent that Admiral Togo had won a great victory. The Battle of Tsushima was possibly the most one-sided and yet most significant naval encounter of modern times: a confrontation that changed the balance of world power and laid the foundations for further conflict in the years ahead.

The losses of ships and men on both sides drew a neat line underneath the human suffering and tragedy of the Russo-Japanese War. Those who had witnessed it at first hand could hardly believe the extent of this latest and, as it turned out, final Japanese victory. The Battle of Tsushima ushered in a new phase in naval warfare; new tactics and new weapons that would change the role of warships for ever. The gap between Russian failure and Japanese success was vast and for those who were interested there were significant lessons to be learned.

Admiral Rozhestvensky went into the battle with thirty-eight ships under his command. These included battleships, both new and old, coastal defence vessels, cruisers and destroyers/torpedo boats. At the end of the confrontation he had lost twenty-one of them, sunk by Japanese shells and torpedoes. This figure included six battleships, three of them modern Borodino-class vessels which were supposedly the height of naval construction and power.

In addition to those that were sunk, thirteen ships from Rozhestvensky's command were either captured or interned in neutral ports. By a combination of good seamanship and pure luck, three managed to reach Vladivostok and one escaped back to Madagascar.

By any reckoning those were stunning losses, but the human casualty figures were equally as devastating. A total of 4,380 Russian sailors were killed in the battle; a further 5,917 being captured and imprisoned by the Japanese.[1]

In complete contrast to the sufferings of the Russian fleet, the Japanese seemed to have got away quite lightly. They fought – and they fought brilliantly – and finished the battle not markedly worse off than when they started.

Admiral Togo, who may have been outnumbered in the strength and quantity of battleships in his fleet (just four compared to Rozhestvensky's eight) held a great advantage as far as cruisers, destroyers and torpedo boats were concerned. In total, when adding auxiliary cruisers and supply ships to his command, he had over eighty vessels to deploy.

As far as casualties and ship losses were concerned, Togo lost a miniscule total of just three torpedo boats, all of them during the night-time attacks, in what was effectively the second phase of the battle. Several of his capital ships sustained minor damage and 117 sailors were killed. A further 583 were wounded or injured.[2]

The discrepancy between Russian and Japanese losses was frightening as well as revealing. Ultimately it came down to the accuracy of the Japanese gunfire and to the damage caused by every hit they achieved. The *shimosa* had been devastating, setting fire to the Russian ships each time one of the shells struck home. There were precious few 'duds' in the Japanese armoury, with their explosive charges being four or five times greater than the Russian shells.

After the Battle of Tsushima, the Russo-Japanese War stuttered to a stagnant pause. Czar Nicholas had no option but to rein in his anti-Japanese feelings and, in June 1905, allow US President Teddy Roosevelt to organise and mediate at a peace conference between the two nations.

The Treaty of Portsmouth was signed on 5 September 1905. It formally brought the conflict to an end, with Russia agreeing to withdraw her remaining forces from Manchuria and accepting Japanese control of Korea. That meant that Port Arthur was no longer a Russian domain.

The handing over of Port Arthur, the spark that had ignited the war, was accepted without too much opposition. The Russians no longer had a fleet in the area anyway and, compared to the humiliation of losing the war, the succession of Port Arthur was no more than a mild irritation.

The shift in the balance of power in the east was of near-seismic proportions. It was an event that heralded a new and powerful military force: Imperial Japan. The influence of the dynamic and thrusting Japanese empire was to grow and remain strong for several decades, ushering in a new period of uncertainty and fear in the region. Ultimately, of course, the Japanese empire was revealed as a power based on fragile foundations victory at Tsushima has to bear some of the blame for that.

Arguably, in the words of one historian, victory at Tsushima 'created a legend that was to haunt Japan's leaders for forty years.' It was erroneously believed that bigger and better ships, along with a warlike and aggressive foreign policy, would allow Japan to control the whole Pacific region and enable her navy to comfortably challenge and even defeat the might of Britain and the United States of America.[3] Eventually that belief would lead Japan into an unwinnable war against the USA; one that was unparalleled in its ferocity and appalling conclusion, and with devastating and far-reaching consequences.

In the short term, however, things were very different. For the people of Japan, victory in the Russo-Japanese War was a massive confidence boost. It gave them credibility and recognition that had been sadly lacking: 'Suddenly Japan was recognised by the advanced western countries. There was a sense of exhilaration. We, a small country, had won a war against a big country. It made everyone intensely patriotic.'[4]

Importantly, the defeat of Imperial Russia by an Asian nation was a huge setback for the generally accepted view of white supremacy. It might not have destroyed racism altogether, but it certainly went some way towards exposing it for the fallacy that it was.

The defeat was a severe blow to the Romanov dynasty. The czar and his regime were already unpopular. This further damage to their prestige merely strengthened the revolutionary factions within the country and undoubtedly contributed to its eventual demise in 1917. There was probably no greater aid to Lenin and the forces of Bolshevism than Rozhestvensky's humiliation at the Battle of Tsushima.

Even before they left Libau and Kronstadt, revolutionary factions had been prominent on board most ships in the fleet. The defeat at Tsushima left even more sailors fuming at the inconsistencies and inefficiency of the czar's government. By the end of 1905 most of them were shouting for reform; all were desperate for change. It was no accident that when the November Revolution of 1917 saw the Bolsheviks overthrow Kerensky's post-Imperial government and seize power for themselves the sailors of Kronstadt were at the forefront of the action.

The eventual crushing of the Kronstadt sailors by the new Bolshevik government can be looked on as part of the inevitable 'second revolution' that follows most successful uprisings. Things might easily have gone the other way, with the Bolsheviks destroyed as completely as the Kronstadt sailors eventually were. Even so, the influence of the sailors should never be underestimated. Their influence can be traced to the defeat at Port Arthur and the disaster at Tsushima.

Novikoff-Priboy, who went on to become a prominent writer and member of the Bolshevik movement, was mentored by Engineer Vasilieff.

During the epic voyage of the 2nd Pacific Fleet, Vasilieff had kept him and many other socialist crew members well supplied with communist literature and with advice about how to change Russian society. As he was leaving the captured *Oryol*, the engineer forcibly insisted that things were moving at last. Defeat at Tsushima, he insisted, was not a bad thing and would only galvanise the revolution that much quicker. Pulling Novikoff-Priboy to one side, Vasilieff whispered in his ear: 'Take good care of yourself for important work awaits you. We are on the eve of great happenings. Today a new chapter opens in the history of the Russian people.'[5]

In the wake of the 1905 defeat, revolutionary ideas and programmes suddenly became rampant right across the Russian Empire. The czar and his government had been exposed as inept and rotten at the core. Perhaps it was time for change? It took another twelve years and the advent of another war – a global one this time – but for Imperial Russia the writing was on the wall in 1905.

Prophets of doom and advocates of change in Russia quickly seized on the defeat as a portent of disaster; not for the people but for the ruling regime. *The Times* correspondent in St Petersburg saw it as a huge promise of reform:

> Russia has become a vast object lesson in the evils of government by irresponsible bureaucrats and police officials, thanks to which initiative and enterprise have been systematically eradicated from the nation ... The fearless criticism of the present administration gives an earnest example of the revival of the national energies which will enable Russia to recover from her present distress and to assume her rightful place among the great nations of the world.[6]

The effects of the Russian defeat were not restricted to the Pacific. They also had a huge effect in Europe, where everyone saw that one of the major players on the international stage had been defeated and humiliated by what had previously been thought of as a minor power. It was a situation that required a serious reorganisation of alliances:

> Britain's joint military plans with France were begotten in 1905 when Russia's far-off defeat by the Japanese, revealing her military incompetence, unhinged the equilibrium of Europe ... Every nation became aware that if any of them chose that moment to precipitate a war, France would have to fight without an ally.[7]

Russia, clearly, had become something of the 'poor man of Europe', a position that left France – the only friendly nation the czar had been able to count on in his war with Japan – high and dry as far as alliances were concerned. The coming together of Britain with France, previously traditional enemies, was as inevitable as the increased sabre-rattling of the kaiser. Wilhelm suddenly saw that Russia posed him little threat and believed that, when it finally erupted, a war on two fronts might not be as disastrous as had been previously feared.

The Kaiser's view of European politics and of war was eventually exposed as both fragile and disastrously mistaken. It plunged the world into the most vicious conflict it had ever experienced and saw the end of several ruling dynasties, including Germany's own Hohenzollern regime. All because of a conflict in distant Asia.

* * *

Admiral Togo did not glory in his victory, but in the years after 1905 he became something of a national hero for the Japanese. Applauded everywhere, in Japan and abroad, as 'The Nelson of the Orient', he quickly came to appreciate the comparison with his hero, even going so far as to make the bold statement: 'I am firmly convinced that I am the actual reincarnation of Lord Horatio Nelson.'[8]

He was ennobled as Count Togo and became Chief of the Japanese Imperial General Staff. One of his last public appearances was at an artillery exercise where, by supreme irony, the target was none other than Nebogatov's old flagship the *Nicholas I*. Togo died peacefully in May 1934.

Rozhestvensky, the defeated commander at Tsushima, fared rather differently. In November 1905 he was discharged from hospital, even though his wounds had not completely healed. Soon afterwards he left Kobe on the Russian steamer *Voronezh*, along with 300 angry and bitter repatriated Russian soldiers and sailors.

Veterans of the recent conflict the Russians spent their time on board the *Voronezh* singing revolutionary songs and threatening the admiral and his entourage. As soon as they were well clear of the coast, they declared, Rozhestvensky and every single one of the officer classes on the ship 'would immediately go overboard'. It was no idle threat.

Angry at their disrespect, Rozhestvensky clashed with the soldiers, treating them to a taste of his trademark 'Mad Dog' temper. The officer and aristocratic classes, however, no longer inspired the fear they once had and his outburst did little to pacify the soldiers. So great was their resentment that guards had to be posted outside Rozhestvensky's cabin door to keep him safe from the would-be revolutionaries who were soon storming around the decks looking for him. They were clearly out for his blood.

At Nagasaki, Japanese police had to be put on board to keep things quiet, but rumblings of protest continued. In the end Rozhestvensky and Admiral Viren, last commander of the Port Arthur garrison, had to be transferred to another ship in order to reach Vladivostok safely. Neither man objected, which might say something about Rozhestvensky's state of mind at this time.

The two admirals disembarked at Nagasaki but did not stay long at the port. Here, anti-government and anti-Russian feelings were equally as vicious and dangerous as on board the *Voronezh*. A new ship and a short cruise soon saw the admirals safely in Vladivostok.

On the last day of November, just twelve months since his voyage had begun, Rozhestvensky, left Vladivostok, still in the company of Viren, on the Trans-Siberian Express. The journey was long, cold and arduous and the Siberian countryside they passed through was seething with revolution. Several times the train was halted by revolutionaries who thronged the station platforms or gathered together on the rails in front of the locomotive, but rather than try to lynch the admiral – as he was expecting – the crowds cheered him and wished him well. Rozhestvensky was stunned but also happy at his reception. It was certainly different from his treatment on board the *Voronezh*.

For some reason he had become an acceptable figure of the imperial regime. The majority of the revolutionaries at the station platforms across Siberia were not died-in-the-wool extremists: they were simply men who wanted security for their families. Having gone through the first excesses of revolution they were now more interested in stability than achieving power. Let others hold the power (and Admiral Rozhestvensky, despite his recent defeat, symbolised that power): all they wanted was plenty of food and decent accommodation.

In complete contrast, when Rozhestvensky reached St Petersburg, after twenty days of travel, there was no formal reception and no one to greet him at the station. He had spent his time on the Trans-Siberian railway thinking over what had happened and how he might help to improve things in the empire. He had ideas about reforming the navy and was hopeful that the Admiralty and the czar would listen to his experiences and learn from them.

The empty platform at St Petersburg did not bode well for the future, however. A puzzled and disturbed Rozhestvensky shrugged away the oversight and went home. Two days later he met with the czar in a secret but formal conference and shortly afterwards a formal investigation was launched into the defeat at Tsushima.

Rozhestvensky did not seek scapegoats, but the czar's regime certainly did. Now, rather than being involved in debating the future of the navy, the admiral found himself having to defend his honour and his performance in the war. It should have been no more than he expected. The Russian Empire had a reputation for the way it dealt with defeated military commanders.

Rozhestvensky, as commander-in-chief, and several of his staff officers, including Clapier de Colongue were put on trial. They were accused of having been poor leaders and having initiated the surrender. Admiral Nebogatov and several of the ship commanders of his squadron were likewise accused.

After some debate and much deliberation Rozhestvensky was acquitted, something he resented to the last day of his life. The fault, he often declared, should have been his and his alone. He felt that he should have been allowed to go down in history as the martyr of Tsushima.

The government held a rather different view: scapegoats yes; martyrs no. Admiral Rozhestvensky was too high profile a man to be publicly 'strung up', even metaphorically. Nebogatov, however, who by surrendering without damage to his ships had brought the Russian navy into disrespute, and Clapier de Colongue, who had placed the safety of his admiral above the need to attack the enemy, were certainly far more culpable. Rozhestvensky might have been cleared, but both Nebogatov and de Colongue were found guilty and sentenced to death.

Whatever else might be said about Czar Nicholas, he was not an unduly vindictive man. He reviewed the evidence against both officers – and several others who had been similarly condemned – and commuted the sentences to imprisonment of up to ten years each.

Rozhestvensky lived out his retirement in St Petersburg with his much-abused wife and beloved daughter. It might be speculation but it would be interesting to know his opinion of the czar and the other members of the royal family during those final days of the regime as it slowly crumbling around him. Rozhestvensky, loyal to the end, left no hint of his true feelings.

Foreign newspapers regularly offered him a fortune to tell the story of the Battle of Tsushima but he always refused. He would do nothing that might cast the czar in a poor light, even though he was sure that much of the blame for the disaster could be heaped at his door.

On New Year's Eve 1908 (Russian calendar) Rozhestvensky enjoyed a warm and happy evening with his family. He told jokes, gave many toasts and entertained his grandson Nicolai who had been born while the admiral and his fleet were still heading for Madagascar. Just after midnight Rozhestvensky excused himself from the room. A sudden crash brought everyone hurrying to see what had happened. Admiral Rozhestvensky had died from a massive heart attack.

Like many of the other accused men, Nebogatov was released early from the ten-year prison sentence he had been given. Like Rozhestvensky, he kept a low profile and lived quietly in territory held by the counter revolutionary Whites during the Russian Civil War. He died in 1934 in Communist Russia.

* * *

And what were the exact causes of the defeat? They were many and varied. The obvious one, that the Japanese had fought a better fight was, for many years, taken for granted, although it has been recently suggested by some commentators that this is actually untrue:

> Russia lost the war not because her troops fought badly, but because her military commanders had not prepared effectively. They understood neither the enemy they were fighting nor the territory in which the struggle took place.[9]

That certainly applied to the naval war. Rozhestvensky might have outnumbered Togo as far as battleships were concerned, but he was woefully inadequate in destroyers and torpedo boats; hardly surprising when he had just cruised 18,000 miles around the globe. Battleships and cruisers might have been able to withstand the rigours of such a voyage, but smaller, less structurally sound vessels most certainly could not.

The plan had always been to relieve Port Arthur before venturing out to challenge the Japanese fleet. Small torpedo boats were supposed to come from Port Arthur or from Vladivostok, but the vagaries of war stopped that idea in its tracks, and by the time he heard that Port Arthur had fallen, Rozhestvensky was already in the Indian Ocean.

The motley collection of ancient and obsolete ships that made up the 2nd Pacific Fleet performed a miracle in just getting to the Tsushima Strait, let alone then having to fight a battle against an experienced and capable opponent.

To travel halfway round the world without adequate dockyard and refuelling facilities was a major achievement; one that speaks volumes for the Russian sailors and officers. In particular, it is a tribute to the capabilities of Rozhestvensky. He cajoled, he bullied, he encouraged and he managed his crews with skill and understanding. He performed deeds that were thought to be entirely beyond his capabilities. But at the end of that epic voyage neither the ships nor the crews were in any condition to fight a battle.

Critics back home in St Petersburg had been right about the unwieldy nature of the Borodino-class battleships. As predicted, they were top heavy and difficult to control. The wonder was that they had survived so many serious storms on the voyage, particularly when rounding the Cape of Good Hope. When they finally came under fire and were disabled, their propensity to capsize or turn turtle was evident to all.

The speed of the Japanese ships, particularly during the crossing the T manoeuvre in the early stages of the contest, was a significant advantage. Unencumbered with weed and other detritus that had been collected during the Russian Fleet's 18,000 mile voyage, Togo's ships had an advantage of six or seven knots over Rozhestvensky – maybe even more – and that was a crucial factor.

The time wasted in simply 'hanging about' in Madagascar and Indochina, waiting for Nebogatov's relief fleet to join him, undoubtedly cost Rozhestvensky dearly. While he fumed, fretted and waited, Togo had his ships in dockyard, where they were hauled out of the water, cleaned, refitted and made ready to face the Russians. It gave him a major advantage and Admiral Togo was not the type of man to let something like that slip past.

Togo, of course, had already fought two major fleet actions. He had the ability to learn from his mistakes in those previous combats, just as he had the foresight to train his crews effectively, particularly in the field of gunnery. Regular firing practice, even when the Russians were close at hand, was a natural and accepted state of affairs.

In complete contrast, Rozhestvensky's men seemed to have spent their time cleaning the decks and did not fire their guns between the debacle at Dogger Bank and the moment Togo's ships appeared out of the mist on 27 May. The neglect of intense gunnery practice and lack of experience on their weapons were undoubtedly two of the most significant causes of the Russian defeat.

Japanese gunfire was markedly superior during the battle; it was far more accurate and considerably more effective than the Russians. Hundreds of Japanese shells struck Rozhestvensky's ships, while the Russian warships managed, at best, no more than a couple of dozen hits. Most of those had been fired by the *Suvorov* while Togo was crossing the Russian T.

Together with more accurate range finders, the use of *shimosa* destroyed not only the Russian ships but also their morale. They simply had no answer to what appeared to be shells of liquid fire that burned them and their ships to cinders.

Shimosa was a new weapon to the Russian sailors, most of whom were simple peasants swept up by the draft and sent to crew the vessels of the 2nd Pacific Fleet. For such men, being under fire like this must have been like standing in the middle of Dante's Inferno.

Superior Japanese seamanship was evident at every stage. From the way Togo's cruisers taunted the Russians by appearing and disappearing in and out of the fog, to the way the whole fleet reassembled after having crossed the T and changed the direction of the attack, the Japanese demonstrated a masterclass in how to sail modern ships in battle: 'The enemy had finished turning. His twelve ships were in perfect order at close intervals, steaming parallel to us ... And astern of us the *Alexander* and *Borodino* were already enveloped with smoke.'[10]

Rozhestvensky and his crews had marvelled at the performance of Charles Beresford's cruisers in the Atlantic. Togo's handling of the entire Japanese battle fleet was equally as impressive. He controlled and manoeuvred his capital ships as if they had been destroyers, all the time knowing exactly what he was trying to achieve. It was a performance without parallel.

Arguably, the greatest problem Rozhestvensky faced on the whole of the voyage was in having to sit twiddling his thumbs in Madagascar and Indochina. Weeks were wasted; weeks when the Russian fleet could, and should, have been doing something considerably more purposeful than collecting exotic animals or counting the sharks around the ships' hulls.

Had the fleet been allowed to proceed at once, as Rozhestvensky repeatedly urged, the outcome might have been very different. He would at least have caught Togo on an even footing with his ships as weed-encrusted as the Russians. The battle might then have had a different ending and the history of the twentieth century could well have been very different.

Unfortunately, Rozhestvensky had been forbidden to move until Nebogatov and his 'self-sinkers' joined him. He knew it was a wrong decision, but the orders came from above, and no matter how he might have longed to disobey the czar, ultimately his training – and his indoctrination after years spent serving the Romanovs – meant that he would knuckle down and do as he was told.

When, eventually, he sailed from Nossi-Be without orders he was at the end of his tether, driven to distraction by the ineptitude of the czar's government. While he was, initially, not forthcoming about his location or his destination, he knew that sooner or later he would have to pause in his journey and come clean about his intentions.

Rozhestvensky was fighting a losing battle and had been ever since he was first appointed to command the 2nd Pacific Fleet. An inept and easily manipulated ruler, the czar was too willing to listen to bad advice, particularly if it was sugar-coated and intent on praising him to the hilt.

Nicolai Klado, the discarded intelligence officer, had vowed to avenge the slight of being put ashore at Vigo. He was not just looking for revenge, however; he was also seeking vindication. He had always dreamed of helping to make things happen in the world and, in his articles and his constant whispering in the ear of Czar Nicholas, he was determined not to allow Rozhestvensky 'off the hook'.

The fact that Klado's opinions and ideas could assume such significance – he was actually considered something of a naval genius by those who knew no better – speaks volumes of the gullibility of Czar Nicholas and the whole of the Romanov dynasty. Klado, of course, was duplicitous in the extreme; something that Rozhestvensky had known all along.

Far from sticking to his view that the be-all-and-end-all of the expedition was the quantity, not the quality of the ships sent to oppose Togo, he was later to write a very different summary and explanation of the Russian defeat. By then Rozhestvensky had been consigned to retirement and his own part in the affair conveniently forgotten:

> Only well-trained and instructed crews can make a good navy ...
> All attention was concentrated on the number of our ships. To all this must be added the entire neglect of any instructions for officers in the art of war.[11]

Klado must have had a very thick hide to risk such a volte-face but few people noticed his change of heart. Rozhestvensky might have managed to supress a smile but by then he was probably past caring.

It was perhaps a tragedy that the admiral had no close friends or allies back in St Petersburg who could have countered Klado's poison. He had no one to fight his corner and was therefore a constant victim to the vagaries of the czar's constantly changing opinions.

The 'desk jockeys' of St Petersburg insisted on reinforcing Rozhestvensky with out-of-date and virtually useless ships that condemned his fleet to failure. For that Czar Nicholas and Commander Nikolai Klado, not Rozhestvensky or any of his subordinates, have to take the blame.

* * *

The most notable early artistic commemorations of the Russo-Japanese War came in the field of painting. During the conflict foreign correspondents regularly sent drawings and reports of the various battles to their papers and these sketches were soon being produced as lithographs and postcards. Japanese woodblock prints, always more elegant and artistic than western examples, were also popular for many years.

Several melancholy Russian waltzes, compositions such as *Amur's Waves* and *On the Hills of Manchuria* were popular for a while, their themes and lilting, dreamy chords fitting the mood of disaster that had settled over the Russian Empire. Their popularity was short lived.

The most significant western composer to attempt any form of commemoration was Nikolai Rimsky-Korsakov. His epic *The Golden Cockerel* was clearly an anti-czarist composition and as a result it was banned by the czar's government. It did not receive its first performance until 1909 and by then Rimsky-Korsakov was dead.

Poetic compositions were rare although the Japanese verse *Outside the Fortress at Goldland* by General Maresuke Nogi, who fought in the war, became hugely popular. For many years Japanese children were compelled to learn the poem by heart, reciting it almost every morning.

Further quality poetic responses had to wait for over half a century before Scottish poet Douglas Dunn produced *The Donkey's Ears*. Sub-titled *Politovsky's Letters Home*, the sequence followed the journey of the *Suvorov* from Russia to her watery grave off Tsushima.

In the wake of the Russian defeat quality novels were also few and far between. Numerous 'Boys' Own'-type stories were produced, mainly in

Europe, and aimed at the youth market. Such stories did not attempt any form of assessment of the war but focussed on adventure and derring-do. For a long while that was more or less it.

Then, in 1968, the Japanese writer Ryotaro Shiba published *Clouds above the Hill*. The story of two ambitious brothers who become involved in building up Japanese military might, the book became an instant best seller in Japan although its appeal in other parts of the world was more limited.

In 1912 the war was used as a central theme by the British writer Allen Upward in his book *The International Spy*. It covered only the early part of the Russian voyage, however, culminating in the Dogger Bank Incident. The villain of the story is not the czar or Emperor Maiji, not even Rozhestvensky or Togo, but Kaiser Wilhelm II, whose schemes of world domination would bring Britain and Germany to the edge of war. It was a work like *Riddle of the Sands* and other 'invasion' stories of the time, intended to frighten the British public while still attempting to entertain them.

Apart from Rozhestvensky and Nebogatov, the fate of those who managed to survive the disaster at Tsushima was varied and not always particularly clear. The Revolution of 1917 and its aftermath were times of chaos and unease and many people were, quite literally, lost in this turbulent and unhappy period.

Clapier de Cologne was released early from his ten-year jail sentence, but, cashiered from the navy, he then seems to have disappeared from the pages of history. He came from an aristocratic family and it may well be that he perished during the 1917 Revolution. It remains guesswork, however.

Nikolai Klado fell out of favour with the royal family after publishing an article in *Novoye Vremya* critical of naval leadership and, in particular, of Grand Duke Alexis. Being distanced by the Romanovs did not appear to hurt his career too much, and after a period of so-called disgrace he went on to teach at the Naval Academy, where he finished as Emeritus Professor. He retained his position after the Revolution, probably due to his criticism of the Romanov hierarchy and his consequent acceptance by the Bolsheviks. He died in 1919.

Alexei Novikoff-Priboy was another man who was highly caustic in his views on the Russian naval command and its effectiveness. The first of his critical works on the voyage to the Far East and the Battle of Tsushima was published in 1906 but was immediately banned by the czarist authorities. Novikoff (his real name, without the addition of Priboy) was forced to flee the country and spent a number of years in exile. He met and became friendly with another exile, Maxim Gorky, and returned to Russia in time for the First World War.

Novikoff worked on hospital trains during the war and after the 1917 Revolution went to live in a writers' and artists' commune. He became well known as a writer of fact and fiction, much influenced by Gorky and specialising in sea-faring novels. He died a much-lauded and well-respected Russian writer in April 1944.

Vladimir Semenov was unique in that he was the only man to experience, and write about, the two great sea battles of the war: the Battles of the Yellow Sea and Tsushima. After the publication of his two books he came in for some heavy criticism, admittedly from people who were not actually there, but his accounts remain fascinating due to the intense and highly personal first-hand approach that he adopted. The date of his death is uncertain.

The most significant 'casualty' of the Russo-Japanese War and the Battle of Tsushima was obviously Czar Nicholas II. He struggled on for several years after Tsushima, finding solace in his wife Alexandra and taking advice from the mysterious Gregory Rasputin. When war broke out in 1914, and after several Russian defeats, he decided that his place was at the front, at the head of his armies. Nothing much improved, however; Nicholas was as bad a general as he was a ruler.

Going to the front was a mistake. His absence from St Petersburg left him isolated and out of touch with government. When rebellion and strikes broke out amongst his soldiers and the people of St Petersburg, he did try to return to the capital, but his way was blocked by revolutionaries. Acting on advice from his army commanders he abdicated from his position as czar at the beginning of 1917. After that it was only a matter of time before the Bolshevik government decided on the ultimate punishment for their previous Emperor.

* * *

Possibly one of the most significant results of the Battle of Tsushima did not affect Japan or Russia at all, at least not directly and certainly not immediately.

Acting on the reports of observers at the battle, Admiral Jackie Fisher, Britain's First Sea Lord, immediately set up a Committee on Designs. Its purpose was to look at the possibility of developing a fast new cruiser armed with the same 12-in guns that had been so effective for the Japanese in the Tsushima Straits. Such cruisers, Fisher dictated, should have a speed of over 25 knots. The result was the battlecruiser concept that began with the launch and commissioning of the *Invincible*, *Indomitable* and *Inflexible* in 1908. And that was not all:

> It was clear that battlecruisers would not be enough on their own ... Fisher's Committee studied the most recent naval battles, those of the Yellow Sea and Tsushima. It revealed a new world of technology and tactics.[12]

Wireless telegraphy and the new rangefinders of Barr and Stroud (a Glasgow firm) had enabled Togo to stand off at 6000yds and blast the Russian ships into oblivion. Future battles, Fisher was told, would be fought by big-gun battleships firing at long range. Fisher listened and the dreadnought battleship was born.

HMS *Dreadnought*, the first in a long line of such vessels, was launched in February 1906. In due course she was superseded by the 'super-dreadnoughts' of the Orion-class which carried 13.5- in weapons.

Soon afterwards came the mighty Queen Elizabeth-class battleships with their eight 15-in guns. The British dreadnoughts were quickly followed by a similar range of ships designed and built by every nautically minded nation in the world: Germany in particular.

The race to build bigger and better dreadnoughts than any potential enemy dominated naval policy in the early 1900s. It was, without doubt, one of the causes of the First World War. The big-gun warship had come of age at Tsushima and had set a pattern that would lead them to Jutland and, in the next war, to the creation of massive juggernauts like the *Bismarck* and *Tirpitz*. Such ships were a portent of naval wars to come, until the advent of the aircraft carrier rendered all battleships redundant.

All these developments were triggered by the Battle of Tsushima. It was hardly what Togo and Rozhestvensky had envisaged as they stood on decks of their respective flagships on 27 May 1905, but that was the nature of naval warfare. Significant events invariably had an effect on the development of tactics and ship design, and the Battle of Tsushima was certainly a significant event.

Conclusion

In the early hours of 17 July 1918 Czar Nicholas II, who had so recently abdicated his position as ruler of all Russia, was taken to the cellar of the house in Ekaterinburg where he was being held prisoner by the Ural Soviet Council. There he was confronted by a firing squad and summarily executed. With him were his wife, five children and several servants, none of whom survived.

With White Russian forces – men still loyal to the czar and supported by troops from Britain and America – rapidly approaching Ekaterinburg it was feared that Nicholas and his family might fall into the hands of the counter revolutionaries. The thought of the czar being reinstated, or even held as a political prisoner, was not to be countenanced. Therefore, to many influential Bolsheviks – maybe even as high up as Lenin – the royal family was dispensable.

It was a botched assassination, though perhaps murder would be a better term. It certainly appeared to be a poorly thought through deed carried out almost on the spur of the moment by local Bolsheviks and party officials. Some of them were drunk; others were unhappy and unwilling to end the lives of the czar and his family in this fashion. After all, he had abdicated and was no longer able to influence their future, or for that matter the destiny of the country.

None of the killers were particularly good shots. The less committed or convinced of them, feeling that it was wrong and that the whole business of despatching Nicholas and his family was unlawful, simply fired into the smoke. There had been no trial and no formal condemnation, and they felt that, in the long run, it would only work against the progress of the Revolution.

Regardless of how they felt, the men were poor executioners. Once the firing began, panic and mass hysteria took over. Most of them repeatedly fired blindly and frantically at their victims in a room that was now filled with screams and the smoke of pistol shots. Many of their bullets missed their mark, others merely wounded the helpless and defenceless

Romanovs, and several members of the royal family had to be finished off with bayonets.

When it was over the dead were searched. A rumour soon began to circulate that the four princesses had stitched diamonds and other jewels into their corsets and that, as a consequence, the bullets of the executioners simply bounced off. Like much of the fantasy around the deaths, there is no truth in the story.

Before their bodies grew cold, the corpses of the royal family were then taken and buried in the nearby woods, where they lay undisturbed for nearly one hundred years.

The czar had come a long way since he was attacked by one of his samurai guards in the streets of Otsu, but he never really grew into a man of good judgement. His complex personality – inflexible one minute, indecisive the next – combined with an inability to listen to sound advice, meant that Nicholas, throughout the course of his reign, invariably made the wrong choices.

In the end it was his propensity to go the wrong way that brought him to his dreadful end in the forests of Ekaterinburg. If there is one phrase that could be used to sum up his life and career it has to be 'poor judgement'. It was poor judgement that compelled him to launch Admiral Rozhestvensky and the 2nd Pacific Fleet on a fruitless 18,000-mile journey halfway around the world. Poor judgement and a propensity to listen to advice from men like Nicolai Klado fatally delayed Rozhestvensky from his final confrontation with the Japanese. Poor judgement convinced Nicholas that quantity was better than quality when it came to ships. The list goes on.

The resulting disaster at the Battle of Tsushima was the start of a slippery slope that ended in a smoke-filled cellar in the Urals with the death of Nicholas and his family. And that, really, is the significance of the inevitable failure of Rozhestvensky's enterprise.

Another man – one more capable and more perceptive who really understood what it was to have the power of life and death over millions of his subjects – might have been able to forestall the events of 1917, but a more capable man would not have allowed things to get quite so bad in the first place. A more capable man would not have despatched the 2nd Pacific Fleet into disaster and ignominy in 1904 and thereby begun the slide to disaster.

History, they say, belongs to the victors. In terms of political and naval might, that is certainly true for the Japanese after the Battle of Tsushima. For forty years after Tsushima the power of the Japanese empire grew steadily. Only after the military and naval defeats of the Second World War did the influence of Japan diminish.

History really works off a few known facts, then interpretation and the personal opinions of the historian comes into play. The Battle of Tsushima and the men and women who all played their part in one of the most amazing stories of the twentieth century would surely not have wanted it any other way.

Notes

Introduction
1. Semenov, V., *The Battle of Tsushima*, Dutton & Co, 1906, p.57.

Prelude/Overture
1. Solomon, C., 'Soviet Humour', 1989, p.6.
2. Letter from Chikako Hirano, held by author.

Chapter 1: A Samurai Attack
1. *The Times*, 11 May 1891.
2. Pleshakov, C., *The Czar's Last Armada*, Perseus Press, 2002, p.14.
3. Hough, R., *The Potemkin Mutiny*, Four Square, 1964, p.42.

Chapter 2: War, Terrible War
1. Hough, R., *The Fleet That Had to Die*, New English Library, 1969, p.10.
2. Carradice, P., *Nautical Training Ships*, Amberley, 2009.
3. Pleshakov, C., *The Czar's Last Armada*, Perseus Press, 2002, p.32.
4. Carradice, P., *The Town Built to Build Ships*, Accent, 2006, pp.136–137.
5. Hough, R., *The Fleet That Had to Die*, New English Library, 1969, p.12.
6. Pleshakov, C., *The Czar's Last Armada*, Perseus Press, 2002, pp.34–35.
7. Semenov, V., 'Rasplata', War Times Journal, 1998 (online).

Chapter 3: Rozhestvensky
1. http://en.wikipedia.org/wiki/zinovy_rozhestvensky
2. https://dokdo-takeshima.com/the-russo-Japanese-war-dokodo-ii-html
3. Hough, R., *The Fleet That Had to Die*, New English Library, 1969, p.21.
4. Pleshakov, C., *The Czar's Last Armada*, Perseus Press, 2002, p.68.

5. Massie, R., *Dreadnought*, Pimlico, 1992, p.474.
6. Novikoff-Priboy, A., *Tsushima*, 1936, p.11.
7. Hough, R., *The Fleet That Had to Die*, New English Library, 1969, pp.25–26.
8. Hough, R., *The Potemkin Mutiny*, Four Square, 1964, p.43.

Chapter 4: Early Disaster
1. Dixon, N., *On the Psychology of Military Incompetence*, Pimlico, 1976.
2. Pleshakov, C., *The Czar's Last Armada*, Perseus Press, 2002, p.81 and 91.
3. Regan, G., *The Guinness Book of Great Naval Blunders*, Guinness, 1993, p.5.
4. Hough, R., *The Fleet That Had to Die*, New English Library, 1969, p.44.
5. Captain Whelpton, *Scarborough Evening News*, 24 October 1904.
6. www.scarboroughmaritimeheritage.org.uk
7. Massie, R., *Dreadnought*, Pimlico, 1992, p.596.
8. Klado, N., *The Russian Navy in the Russo-Japanese War*, Blackett Ltd, London, 1906, p.34.
9. *The Times*, 22 October 1904.
10. Tuckman, B., *August 1914*, Papermac, 1980, p.67.

Chapter 5: On Into the Wastes
1. Winton, J. *Hurrah for the Life of a Sailor*, Michael Joseph, 1977, p.38.
2. Novikoff-Priboy, A., *Tsushima*, 1936, p.45.
3. Hough, *The Fleet That Had to Die*, New English Library, 1969, pp.62–63.
4. Pleshakov, C., *The Czar's Last Armada*, Perseus Press, 2002, p.123.
5. Hough, *The Fleet That Had to Die*, New English Library, 1969, p.64.
6. Novikoff-Priboy, A., *Tsushima*, 1936, p.48.
7. Ibid, p.41.
8. Ibid, p.52.
9. Ibid, p.49.
10. Ibid, p.45.

Chapter 6: Felkersam's Fleet
1. Pleshakov, C., *The Czar's Last Armada*, Perseus Press, 2002, p.165.

2. Gilbert, M., *A History of the Twentieth Century Vol. 1*, Harper Collins, 1997, p.105.
3. Pleshakov, C., *The Czar's Last Armada*, Perseus Press, 2002, p.172.
4. Hough, *The Fleet That Had to Die*, New English Library, 1969, p.92.

Chapter 7: A Stagnant Pause

1. Novikoff-Priboy, A., *Tsushima*, 1936, p.89.
2. Ibid.
3. Ibid, pp.83–84.
4. Ibid, p.77.
5. Ibid, p.82.
6. Lynch, M., *Reaction and Revolution*, Hodder, 2005, p.33.
7. Gapon, Father Giorgi, *The Story of My Life*, January 1905.
8. Novikoff-Priboy, A., *Tsushima*, 1936, p.72.
9. Ibid, p.74.
10. Ibid, p.62.

Chapter 8: Togo Waits, Mad Dog Moves

1. http://en.wikiipedia.org/wiki/Battle_of_Tsushima
2. Novikoff-Priboy, A., *Tsushima*, 1936, p.87.
3. Ibid, p.90.
4. Ibid, p.210.
5. Hough, *The Fleet That Had to Die*, New English Library, 1969, p.128.
6. *The Times*, 29 April 1905.

Chapter 9: Towards the Donkey's Ears

1. Dixon, N., *On the Psychology of Military Incompetence*, Pimlico, p.183.
2. Admiral Togo, 'Report on the Battle of Tsushima', 1905.
3. Ibid.

Chapter 10: Battle at Last

1. Ibid.
2. Ibid.
3. Semenov, V., *The Battle of Tsushima*, Dutton & Co, 1906, p.56.
4. Ibid.

5. Ibid, p.64.
6. Ibid.
7. Pleshakov, C., *The Czar's Last Armada*, Perseus Press, 2002, p.272.
8. Semenov, V., *The Battle of Tsushima*, Dutton & Co, 1906, p.77.
9. Ibid, p.59.
10. Pleshakov, C., *The Czar's Last Armada*, Perseus Press, 2002, p.278.
11. Despatch from Admiral Packenham, quoted in Hough, *The Fleet That Had to Die*, New English Library, 1969, p.170.

Chapter 11: Last Acts

1. Admiral Togo, 'Report on the Battle of Tsushima', 1905.
2. Pleshakov, C., *The Czar's Last Armada*, Perseus Press, 2002, p.284.
3. Admiral Togo, 'Report on the Battle of Tsushima', 1905.
4. Pleshakov, C., *The Czar's Last Armada*, Perseus Press, 2002, p.310.
5. Admiral Togo, 'Report on the Battle of Tsushima', 1905.

Chapter 12: Aftermath

1. Ibid.
2. Ibid.
3. Regan, G., *The Guinness Book of Decisive Battles*, Guinness, p.178.
4. Letter from Chikako Hirono (held by author).
5. Novikoff-Priboy, A., *Tsushima*, 1936, p.243.
6. *The Times*, April 1905.
7. Tuckman, B., *August 1914*, Papermac, 1980, p.54.
8. Quoted in 'The Greatest Naval Commander of all Time', article by José Ryes, 2015.
9. Lynch, M., *Reaction and Revolution*, Hodder, 2005, p.32.
10. Semenov, V., 'Rasplata', War Times Journal, 1998 (online), p.70.
11. Klado, N., *The Battle of the Sea of Japan*, Hodder and Stoughton, London, 1906, pp.282–284.
12. Wilson, B., *Empire of the Deep*, Weidenfeld and Nicolson, London, 2014, pp.515–516.

Bibliography

Primary Sources

Klado, N., *The Russian Navy in the Russo-Japanese War*, Blackett Ltd, London, 1906.

Klado, N., *The Battle of the Sea of Japan*, Hodder and Stoughton, London, 1906.

Novikoff-Priboy, A., *Tsushima*, Knopf, New York, 1906, translated version 1936.

Semenov, V., *The Battle of Tsushima*, Dutton & Co, London, 1912.

Semenov, V., 'Rasplata', War Times Journal, 1998 (online).

Admiral Togo, 'Report of the Battle of Tsushima', 1905, unpublished at the time but later published by The Russo-Japanese War Research Society, 2002.

Books

Carey, J.,(Ed), *The Faber Book of Reportage*, Faber, London, 1987.

Carradice, P., *A Town Built to Build Ships*, Accent, Cardiff, 2006.

Carradice, P., *Nautical Training Ships*, Amberley, Stroud, 2006.

Dixon, N., *On the Psychology of Military Incompetence*, Pimlico, London, 1976.

Editors of Krokodil Magazine, 'Soviet Humour', Sidgwick and Jackson, London, 1989.

Gapon, Father Giorgi, 'My Life', 1904, published in *The Faber Book of Reportage*, 1987.

Gilbert, M., *A History of the Twentieth Century, Vol 1*, Harper Collins, London, 1997.

Hough, R., *The Fleet That Had to Die*, New English Library, London, 1969.

Hough, R., *The Potemkin Mutiny*, Four Square, London, 1964.

Lynch, M., *Reaction and Revolution: Russia 1894–1924*, Hodder, London, 2010.

Massie, R., *Dreadnought*, Pimlico, London, 1993.

Pleshakov, C., *The Czar's Last Armada*, Perseus Press, Oxford, 2002.
Regan, G., *The Guinness Book of Decisive Battles*, Guinness, London, 1992.
Regan, G., *The Guinness Book of Naval Blunders*, Guinness, London, 1993.
Tuckman, B., *August 1914*, Papermac, London, 1980.
Wilson, B., *Empire of the Deep*, Weidenfeld and Nicolson, London, 2014.
Winton, J., *Hurrah for the Life of a Sailor*, Michael Joseph, London, 1977.

Newspapers/Magazines

Fosrod, November 2015 (article by José Ryes).
History Today (various, 2014–2015).
Punch Magazine, July–November 1904.
Scarborough Evening News, 24 October 1904.
The Times, October 1904–April 1906.
The Times, 11 May 2016 (reprinting original article).

Interviews/Letters

Letter from Chikako Hirono, September 2018 (Held by Author).

Websites

https://smarthistoryblog.com/2016/07/03/why-did-nicholas-11-hate-Japan
http://wikipedia.org/wiki/Otsu_incident
www.russojapanesewar.com/togo-aa3.html
https://www.navyhistory.orgou/the-battle-of-Tsushima-1905
https://en.wikipedia.org/wiki/Dogger_Bank_Incident
www.scarboroughsmaritimeheritage.org.uk